HEROES

STARS OF HOCKEY'S GOLDEN ERA

Frank Pagnucco

Prentice-Hall Canada Inc., Scarborough, Ontario

To the memory of George Orchard

Canadian Cataloguing in Publication Data

Pagnucco, Frank, 1954-
   Heroes: stars of hockey's golden era
Includes index.
ISBN 0-13-387119-3

1. Hockey players — Biography. 2. National Hockey
League — History. I. Title.

GV848.5.A1P33 1985   796.96'2'0922   C85-099030-0

Prentice-Hall, Inc., Englewood Cliffs, *New Jersey*
Prentice-Hall International, Inc., *London*
Prentice-Hall of Australia, Pty., Ltd., *Sydney*
Prentice-Hall of India Pvt., Ltd., *New Delhi*
Prentice-Hall of Japan, Inc., *Tokyo*
Prentice-Hall of Southeast Asia (Pte.) Ltd., *Singapore*
Editora Prentice-Hall do Brasil Ltda., *Rio de Janeiro*
Prentice-Hall Hispanoamericana, *S.A., Mexico*

ISBN 0-13-387119-3

Production Editor: Mia London
Design: Gail Ferreira Ng-A-Kien
Production: Joanne Matthews
Typesetting: Fleet Typographers
Manufactured in Canada by Webcom Limited

1 2 3 4 5 6 W 90 89 88 87 86 85

Photo Credits

Cover photo by Asher Sadeh. All players' photographs from the Beehive Syrup Collection used by kind permission of the St. Lawrence Starch Co. Team photographs: p. 2 Boston Bruins; p. 58 Chicago Black Hawks; p. 102 Detroit Red Wings, photo by John Maiolo; p. 160 Montreal Canadiens, used by permission of Canapress Photo Service; p. 222 New York Rangers, photo by John Maiolo; p. 276 Toronto Maple Leafs, used by permission of The Globe & Mail, Toronto. All photographs are from the personal collection of Michael Sabadash.

Credits

p. 11 courtesy of The Windsor Star; p. 75 reprinted with permission — The Toronto Star Syndicate; p. 296 courtesy of Syl Amos.

The publisher of this book has made every reasonable effort to trace the ownership of excerpts and visuals and to make full acknowledgement for their use. If any errors or omissions have occurred, they will be corrected in future editions, providing written notification has been received by the publisher.

Contents

Introduction

This book is about men, very special men who were part of what many consider hockey's golden era. In the prime of their athletic lives, they were part of the most exclusive group in sport — 120 individuals who made up the best hockey league in the world. They survived a Darwinian struggle in the amateur and minor pro leagues to make the NHL. And the struggle didn't let up once they were part of the six-team circuit. They were certain to lose the battle eventually in the face of aging and the continual challenge of younger talent. Tight-fisted control of the league by the owners ensured that the competition would remain. Just one bad game on a player's part might spell his return to the limbo of the minor leagues.

Each player was competitive and, together, their collective will to win was strong. Clubs faced each other fourteen times, seven games at home and seven on the road. Given the strong survival instincts that prevailed, this familiarity inevitably bred a spirited contempt. Players and fans still wax eloquent about the intense rivalries that existed between teams. Games were close checking affairs, stressing the defensive side more than it is today.

The players and their rivalries made professional hockey the most popular spectator sport in Canada. The autumn of 1952 saw the inaugural telecast of *Hockey Night in Canada*. Professional hockey on Saturday night radio had been a ritual in many homes for many years. And Saturday night's heroes were now visible, easily identifiable, their feats made real by television. So deep was the audience's identification with the athletes and the sport that *Hockey Night in Canada* became part of our national culture. Television had ushered in a golden era of hockey.

For whatever length of time he spent in the league, and no matter what team he played for, an NHL player earned the scrutiny of a nation. He was known only for his efforts on the ice or those off the ice that related to the game. Once retired, in most cases he melted into the faceless reality of the everyday world and moved away from public view.

What has happened to these men after their hockey careers ended is the subject of this book. We are often curious about someone who happened to be in the public eye, whether as an athlete, politician, soldier, or entertainer. This curiosity is especially strong with these men who formed such an important cultural and athletic touchstone for so many.

For the sake of length (several hundred played in the league for varying lengths of time between 1952 and 1968) it was decided to look at the men who had played at least 210 games (three seasons) in the 15-year span between the advent of televised hockey and expansion. This book is not an exercise in investigative journalism. It is not an effort to dig up and dwell upon the personal problems of these ex-athletes. Consider it a means of reacquainting yourself with the heroes of another time and learning about their views on the past and the present.

As background and as a way of avoiding a festival of cliches in the text, it may do the reader well to know that nearly every player professes a love for the sport, and because of that love, wanted to prolong his career as long as he could and stay in the game in some capacity after retirement. Most agree that getting to the NHL was tough but staying there was even tougher. With rare exceptions their most memorable moment was the first time they stepped on the ice in the NHL. Almost all agree that just being in the six-team league was an honour and a privilege. If they had it all to do over again, hardships not withstanding, only a few would change the course of their careers.

Acknowledgements

Special thanks go to a host of individuals who made this work possible: Paul Rimstead who suggested the concept and the place to start; Gerry Toppazzini who provided many insights and leads to ex-players, as did Dollard St. Laurent; the staff at Prentice-Hall Canada who, through their knowledge and professionalism, made the life of a rookie writer so much easier; and to some very special friends for their advice and support, Phil Smith, Sr., Karen Stagg, Wally Stukaylo, and Lauri Welsh.

Action in the Boston Gardens: Montreal's Bobby Rousseau (15) beats Boston Bruins' goalie Ed Johnston as a disappointed Gilles Marotte (10) looks on.

BOSTON BRUINS

The six-team era for the Boston Bruins was one of moderate success and im-moderate failure. Throughout the 1950s, the team, though not blessed with superstars, featured a solid journeyman lineup. With players such as Flem-ing Mackell, Bill Quackenbush, Fern Flaman and Real Chevrefils, it finished out of the play-offs only once in that decade. On three occasions, 1953, 1957 and 1958, it was a championship finalist, losing each time to the Montreal Canadiens. In 1953 the Bruins executed a monumental upset over the greatly talented and prohibitively favoured Red Wings in the semi-finals, beating them in six games.

However, the 1960s were a different story. The Bruins could not manage to replace the talent that had carried the club over the previous decade. The team found itself in a nosedive that resulted in almost exclusive possession of the league's cellar until a youth movement began in 1966. Bobby Orr, of course, was the focal point of the rebuilding process. The transition from also-ran to contender was completed when Milt Schmidt or-chestrated a trade that brought Phil Esposito, Fred Stanfield, and Ken Hodge from Chicago. In 1970 and 1972 the Bruins won the Stanley Cup, regaining the glory that had been theirs in 1939 and 1941 when they were led by Milt Schmidt, Woody Dumart and Bobby Bauer, the high-flying Kraut Line.

Soon after the Bruins became the first American team in the NHL in 1924 they established a tradition of excellence. In large part, their success was due to the playing abilities of fiery defenceman Eddie Shore and the organizational talents of coach and general manager Art Ross. The arrival of Orr rekindled that tradition and today the Bruins are perennial con-tenders for Stanley Cup honours.

Bob Armstrong

Boston Bruins

(b. 1931, Toronto, Ont.)
Games played 542
Goals 13
Assists 86
Total points 99
Penalties in Minutes 671

Bob Armstrong

Bob Armstrong was a playing coach with Hull-Ottawa of the Eastern Professional Hockey League in 1962 when he and Don Cherry had a run-in, an incident anecdoted in Cherry's auto-biography, *Grapes*. "He forgot to mention," Armstrong remarks, correcting the record for posterity, "that he broke his stick over my head and I was concussed."

Throughout his decade-long career with the Boston Bruins, Armstrong was considered a solid performer in the club's defensive corps. The ex-Bruin rates his talents a little more severely. "I had to work like hell. I wasn't a very good skater. I couldn't go around my grandmother," he admits. "I tried never, ever to let anybody go inside . . . ever." The threat of scoring is minimized that way, he adds.

While Armstrong was playing in the NHL, he finished his education part time. After 12 seasons he completed the course requirements for an arts degree from the University of Western Ontario. In 1963, he was traded to Toronto and while attending the Leafs' training camp in Peterborough, Ontario heard of a teaching position at a private school, Lakefield College. He got the job and has been there ever since.

In addition to teaching history and economics, Armstrong has been coach of the hockey team which plays in a provincial league of private schools. His son, Ian, is a member of the Peterborough Petes of the Ontario Hockey League and was recently drafted by the Boston Bruins.

Conjuring up the memories of his campaigns in the NHL, Armstrong comments wistfully, "They went by too quickly. It seems like it was a minute of an hour of my life."

Leo Boivin

Boston Bruins

(b. 1932, Prescott, Ont.)
Games played 1150
Goals 72
Assists 250
Total points 332
Penalties in Minutes 1192

Leo Boivin left the game in 1970, having spent 18 seasons in the league. He turned to scouting which he still does for the Hartford Whalers. Travelling across the continent, he eyeballs the talent available in the various junior and collegiate leagues. "I go to a game nearly every night. I'm pretty well always on the go," he reports from his home in Prescott, Ontario. "Come the end of March you're a little weary. You've covered a few miles and seen a few games. I have a car I bought two years ago. I figure we put in over 90,000 kilometres."

What appeals to Boivin most about the job is "the idea of watching the kids play, watching them improve, seeing how they play in the National League." The reduction of the draft age to 17 has not made a scout's work any easier. "With this 17-year-old draft we have today, it's pretty hard to tell unless he's an outstanding hockey player. The real good ones are no problem but they're few and far between."

It's the others with more marginal talent, the ones drafted after the top five, that make life interesting for a scout. "Like anything else, it's a gamble. A kid can play well this winter and next winter he's horseshit," philosophizes Boivin.

Boivin came into the NHL via the Toronto Maple Leafs in 1951. After three seasons, the stocky defenceman was traded to Boston where he spent most of his career. "We had a good club," he says in hindsight. "We had a fairly big club, a good skating club. I don't suppose there was a lot of talent on it but there was a lot of work and hustle." He remembers the Bruins losing play-off duels to the Canadiens in four consecutive years. "For about four years we never changed a hockey player. All of a sudden we changed and we went right to the bottom."

Boivin took his hitting and checking style to Detroit, Pittsburgh and Minnesota until he retired and turned to scouting, a good way to stay in the game. Other than a couple of brief coaching stints with the St. Louis Blues and the Ottawa 67's of the Ontario Major Junior Hockey League, he has preferred to stick to what he knows best, scouting.

John Bucyk

Boston Bruins

(b. 1935, Edmonton, Alta.)
Games played 1540
Goals 556
Assists 813
Total points 1369
Penalties in Minutes 497

Johnny Bucyk

A native of Edmonton, Alberta, John Bucyk joined Detroit in 1955 where he played infrequently for two seasons. He was traded to Boston in 1957 where he found his niche and a home. He lasted a total of 21 NHL seasons, an all-time longevity record for Bruins' players. In that time he collected more assists, 794, and goals, 545, than any Boston player before or since.

Bucyk arrived in Boston to find himself reunited with his linemates from the Bruins' Western Hockey League affiliate in Edmonton, Bronco Horvath and Vic Stasiuk. Dubbed the Uke Line because of their Ukrainian ancestry (though Horvath is Yugoslavian), the unit proved to be among the most effective in the league. Bucyk's role was to dig the puck out of the corner and send it to the trigger man, Horvath.

Bucyk's career took him through Boston's lean years in the early 1960s before the arrival of Bobby Orr. He concedes that they were discouraging times though he was "just more excited and thrilled" about playing. Those lean years were forgotten when, as team captain, he skated victoriously around the rink hoisting the Stanley Cup aloft on two separate occasions, 1970 and 1972.

Bucyk retired in 1978. "I didn't even want to then," he chortles. "I think it was time for a change. I was getting a little slower. They were starting to bring kids up. I had a job offer with a little bit of security, so I took it." Today he acts as an administrative assistant in the Bruins' organization doing a lot of public relations work as well as other things. He also acts as a colour commentator on the Bruins' radio broadcasts.

Hockey is still his life. He travels with the team and continues to be involved with the game, albeit in a different capacity. He skates with the Bruins' old-timers whenever they get together for charity events.

Charlie Burns

Boston Bruins

(b. 1936, Detroit, Michigan)
Games played 749
Goals 106
Assists 198
Total points 304
Penalties in Minutes 252

Charlie Burns

When Charlie Burns suffered a double fracture of the skull during a minor hockey practice, it not only almost killed him, it should have ended any of his aspirations of playing big-time hockey. Surgery was required to remove a blood clot in his brain and the procedure brought him to the brink of death. He was given the last rites.

Some people, including those in Detroit who owned his contract, felt that Burns' prospects in hockey were gone. Jack Adams, the general manager, wrote him a letter suggesting that it might be best for him to get out of hockey. But he continued to play after his recovery and was with the Whitby Dunlops when they represented Canada at the world championships and won the gold medal. "I was pretty young then and I would have appreciated it more now," he notes about the experience. His effective play in the tournament earned him the most valuable player award.

Detroit invited Burns to training camp in 1958 and he made the lineup. "It was like a dream come true in those days," he remembers. After one season with the Red Wings he was claimed by Boston in a draft. During his five seasons with the Bruins, he became primarily a defensive specialist who killed penalties.

But Burns' head injury came back to haunt him in Boston. He suffered a seizure which, he feels, prompted a change in management's attitude towards him. "At the time you don't understand it," he comments, "but if you look back at it, you probably would have done the same thing yourself." He found himself playing in San Francisco for a Bruins' farm team. Expansion gave him new life and in 1968, Burns found himself back in the NHL, first with Oakland, then Pittsburgh, and finally Minnesota. He acted first as a player-coach with the North Stars and then, after his retirement in 1973, as a coach and assistant manager.

Burns got caught up in "a financial crunch" and became "just another body". He found himself on the lowest rungs of the organizational ladder, coaching a club in Sioux City, Iowa. "It just got to the point where you had to face some reality," he says. "It was time to get into something else. I didn't feel like hanging around rock bottom. That's all it was." He and his family moved to Connecticut where he is now a foreman in a shop at United Technology, a firm that manufactures helicopters. For a couple of years he forced hockey out of his mind, never watching a game or following the sport at all. Recently, he started to watch games again as well as playing with the Hartford Whalers' old-timers in their charity matches.

Real Chevrefils

Boston Bruins

(b. 1932, Timmins, Ont.)
Games played 387
Goals 104
Assists 97
Total points 201
Penalties in Minutes 185

Real Chevrefils

Hap Emms, longtime coach and general manager in junior hockey, once called Real Chevrefils the best hockey player he ever coached. Indeed, it was "Chevy" who, with his deft puckhandling and quick skating, led Emms' Barrie Flyers to a Memorial Cup in 1951. He turned professional that autumn. Playing brilliantly for the Bruins' farm team in Hershey, he was called up to the parent club mid-way through the season.

Chevrefils garnered 25 points in the 33 games he played in his rookie season and showed the potential he had for stardom in the National Hockey League. His totals improved the next year with 33 points in 69 games. A broken leg ruined the 1953-54 season for him but he came back in 1954-55 to notch a respectable 18 goals and 22 assists. Linemate Leo Labine called him "a finesse hockey player who had the strength and the ability and didn't give up the puck."

Even as he was living the dream of every young Canadian boy, Chevy was sowing the seeds of his own slow destruction. Booze had become his burden.

"When I played for Barrie, I never drank one drop, honest to God," he once told a reporter. "But when I went to Hershey all the guys used to go out drinking after practice, so I started going along. I was so lonely it wasn't even funny. I didn't know what to do with myself. A beer here, a beer there and I just kept going — and that's it, that's it." A souring marriage that eventually led to separation and divorce made things worse.

Chevrefils was traded to Detroit in 1955-56. Unable to control the fast-living skater, Red Wings' general manager Jack Adams eventually traded him back to the Bruins. Chevy, briefly in control of his life, posted his best-ever showing of 48 points in 1956-57 with the Bruins with 31 goals and 17 assists and a nomination to the second all-star squad. He never played that way again. Two years later he was out of the NHL and bouncing around various professional and semi-professional leagues.

Chevrefils ended his hockey career with the senior A Windsor Bulldogs in 1964 at 33 years of age. He had no prospects for the future. For the next 12 years he lived on welfare. Suffering from cirrhosis of the liver and Korsakoff's syndrome, he qualified for a disability pension and spent his days and nights watching television, drinking beer and playing pool.

Chevrefils always maintained that he was happy in this existence. "Peace of mind, that's all I've ever asked the Lord for and that's what I've got," he said. He died in 1982.

David Creighton

Boston Bruins

Dave Creighton

(b. 1930, Port Arthur, Ont.)
Games played 615
Goals 140
Assists 174
Total points 314
Penalties in Minutes 223

Dave Creighton has taken a hockey player's second love, golf, and parlayed it into a substantial enterprise. The ex-centre who played with Boston, Chicago, Toronto and New York from 1948 to 1959 recently moved to Tampa, Florida where he oversees the Northdale Golf Club. He owns two others, one in Florida and another in Welland, Ontario.

Perhaps Creighton's best efforts in the NHL were first in Boston where he had three consecutive 20-goal seasons in the early 1950s and later in New York when he once again reached that significant scoring plateau with the Rangers. In New York, he teamed up with Camille Henry.

His last NHL games were played with Toronto. For another ten years he continued skating in the minor leagues in places like Buffalo, Rochester, Hershey and Providence, first as a player and then as a playing coach. His climb into the managerial ranks ended when he and the parent club New York did not agree on player personnel policy.

"I had planned ahead," Creighton says. "I was looking at doing something in the golf end. I got involved with Eddie Shack and two lawyers and we built a golf course." He eventually sold out and nine years ago bought a course in Fonthill, outside of Welland. Five years ago he acquired the Tampa course and one in Orlando.

To learn the sport and the trade of golf first in the off-season and

13

then after his hockey career ended, Creighton admits he worked hard to get where he is today. Behind the man with a hand in three golf courses lie countless "13, 14, 15-hour days in the pro shop" where he learned the basics.

Creighton's son, Adam, is a strapping 6'5" centre who was a member of Canada's world champion junior hockey team in 1984. He was the Buffalo Sabres' third-round draft pick in 1983. "He's a much better hockey player than I ever was," laughs his old man.

Lorne Ferguson

Boston Bruins

(b. 1930, Palmerston, Ont.)
Games played 422
Goals 82
Assists 80
Total points 162
Penalties in Minutes 193

Lorne Ferguson

Lorne Ferguson says he enjoyed his stay in the pros and would do it all over again in the NHL but the second time around, he would make one or two changes. The swift-skating left winger played for Boston, Detroit and Chicago between 1950 and 1959.

"First of all I'd get an agent," Ferguson comments, pointing to a creature who did not exist in the pre-expansion era. "They used to have us wait outside. Five guys lined up for a job. If you asked for $500 more than the other guy, he got the job."

Second, Ferguson would hope for slightly improved sports medicine. In a game during the 1957-58 season he separated a shoulder and fractured a collar bone. "I sat out a couple of shifts. I came back and scored a goal. I thought it was only a bruise and I was treated for a bruise." When he asked to have it examined Jack Adams thought his player was "jaking it". "Immediately after I was better I was traded to Chicago. It was very discouraging," he elaborates. "It didn't heal properly. To this day it still bothers me. It's very painful. Sometimes it flames up. I think it shortened my career by four or five years. But I figure I had a good career. I enjoyed every minute of it." When he quit playing, Ferguson says, it was of his own volition. "I think, if anything, my attitude when I finished hockey was that I wanted to go to work." He moved to Kingston, Ontario and became a sales representative for a brewery. "I was a high school dropout. I consider myself very fortunate to end up with a good job and make a career out of it."

Ferguson's children have also accomplished themselves in the realm of sport. One son, Bob, played for the Oshawa Generals and was drafted by Winnipeg of the NHL. He now coaches junior hockey in Iowa. His daughter Kim was a hockey player for McMaster and Queen's Universities. His youngest, Tim, plays for the Cornwall Royals of the OHL and he is expected to be drafted this spring.

Fernie Flaman

Boston Bruins

(b. 1927, Dysart, Sask.)
Games played 910
Goals 34
Assists 174
Total points 208
Penalties in Minutes 1370

The "Bean Pot Bowl", a popular university tournament in Boston, packs them into the Garden. Last year's event [1984] was a very important one for Fern Flaman, coach of the Northeastern University Huskies. His team won and its members dedicated the victory to his son Terry who was suffering from and later died of cancer. Flaman says that emotional moment was the greatest in his career.

Flaman, a hard-hitting, all-star defenceman, had his share of great moments throughout a career that spanned 15 seasons with Boston and Toronto. With Boston, he participated in one of the greatest upsets in the realm of sport when the underdog Bruins upset the powerful Detroit Red Wings in six games in the Stanley Cup semi-finals in 1950. With Toronto, he was on the ice when the late Bill Barilko scored his dramatic goal to win the Stanley Cup in 1951.

Flaman retired from hockey in 1961 and turned to coaching in the minor leagues in Providence, Fort Worth and Los Angeles. He was then hired at Northeastern as an assistant and for the last 15 years has been the head coach of the Varsity hockey team. In addition to a pair of Bean Pot victories, his club wound up the third best hockey club in the U.S. in 1982.

Assessing the difference between coaching in the university ranks and the professional ranks, Flaman says college coaches are able to spend more time teaching basic hockey skills to the players.

There are more practices and fewer games so more time is provided to teach skills. Coupling an education with hockey is ideal for a young athlete, he adds. For the number of people aspiring to the pro ranks, "few are chosen" so an education is a valuable commodity to acquire along the way. The ultimate satisfaction to him as a university coach, he states, is that his charges "develop into good citizens".

Cal Gardner

Boston Bruins

(b. 1924, Transcona, Man.)
Games played 696
Goals 154
Assists 238
Total points 392
Penalties in Minutes 517

Cal Gardner

As a youngster in Transcona, Manitoba, Cal Gardner heard Foster Hewitt's voice describing the fortunes of the Toronto Maple Leafs over the radio. He found himself sharing the dream of every Canadian boy—to play hockey in the NHL. He realized his desire in 1945-46 when he was called up from the Eastern Hockey League by the New York Rangers. The big centre lasted 11 seasons, spending time with the Rangers, Toronto, Chicago and Boston.

A self-described "rugged hockey player" Gardner has known his share of on-ice combat. Late in the 1947 season, he precipitated what has been described as the biggest, longest brawl in hockey history. The last place Rangers were playing the league-leading Canadiens in Madison Square Gardens. Kenny Reardon of the Canadiens was accidentally clipped by Gardner's stick as he was checked, resulting in a bad cut that needed stitches. On his way to the infirmary Reardon exchanged insults with players and spectators from the opposing team. He started to tussle with a fan. The entire Canadiens' team leapt off the bench and skated across the ice into the corridor to rescue him. The Rangers followed. A pitched battle broke out in the corridor and on the ice. Vast quantities of blood were spilled in the resulting fight.

When Gardner left the NHL he spent four years as a play-coach in Boston's farm system. "That, possibly, was the wrong thing to do," he reflects. "If you were a defenceman it wasn't too bad. If you're a forward it's pretty tough to tell a guy he made a mistake because he saw you make the same mistake on the ice. You've got to be one or the other, either a player or a coach, and you've got to be behind the bench to know what you're doing."

"I could have stayed in hockey after that and been a coach but my kids were going to school and I thought, 'It's about time, let's hang 'em up. I've been in hockey long enough. Let's go home.' The wife [Mary] was getting tired of travelling, too."

During the following 20 years, Gardner was in the transport business and then got involved in radio broadcasts of Boston Bruins' hockey games. Later he moved to CKFH in Toronto where he did Maple Leafs' games for 11 years. He currently is an accounts manager and promotions man with CHEW, a country and western station in Ajax, not far from his Toronto home.

Gardner's sons followed in their father's footsteps. Dave spent seven years in the NHL and is now a playing coach in Switzerland. Paul is in the Pittsburgh Penguins' organization.

Ted Green

Boston Bruins

(b. 1940, Eriksdale, Man.)
Games played 620
Goals 48
Assists 206
Total points 254
Penalties in Minutes 1029

"I played 20 years as a pro and I had a lot of success with a lot of successful teams. I've been an all-star. I've played 12 years in the National League. I was there when there were six teams. And today, 15 years after that injury, people come up to me and say, 'You're Ted Green? How's your head?' That's all they seem to remember of a long career. So I find it really hilarious sometimes," says Ted Green, excusing his laughter after being asked about the stick swinging incident that nearly killed him in an exhibition game in 1968.

Today he jokes about the injury. He claims it helps his golf game because the weight of the steel plate in his head forces him to keep his head down. "But the bad part is I can't play in the rain because I'm a human lightning rod."

The stick swinging duel with the late Wayne Maki of St. Louis resulted in serious head injuries for Green. Three major operations were necessary to save his life. The left side of his body was paralyzed and it seemed obvious that he would never play again. He made a miraculous comeback, the story of courage and determination he detailed in his book *High Stick.* After a year's absence from hockey he returned to help the Bruins win a Stanley Cup in 1972. He savoured the victory not only because of his superb battle against tremendous odds to return to hockey but also because he had suffered with the club through the tough years.

He joined the Bruins in 1961 and grew into a tough, scrappy, competent defenceman. For five seasons his teammates and he found themselves at the bottom of the league, until Orr, Esposito and company came along to change the Bruins' fortunes.

The aftermath of the fight in which he was involved as well as others, Green says, resulted in the game being cleaned up quite a bit, though not as much as he would like to see. "The rules are a little stronger because the public will not accept some of the stuff that happened. Once the law courts want to get involved, they naturally have to cut down a bit." He adds that the Green/Maki affair illustrated that the league was at fault for its lax system of rules although NHL president Clarence Campbell chastised the two players for their behavior. "In the days when I played, anything was allowed, anything happened. The league did not step in on anything at all and then blamed the player for it," he says. "In the case of Ted Green and Wayne Maki, the National League never got any blame for that. Clarence Campbell dumped all over Wayne Maki and myself in that particular situation. 'We're not assuming any responsibility for allowing these things in the past many, many times.' And then, finally, because somebody gets hurt, they dump on the two guys that are involved. That's totally wrong. Wayne Maki suffered more than I did."

"They forced me out of the hospital to a meeting, not because they were concerned about me or Wayne Maki. Clarence Campbell forced me out of a hospital bed in Ottawa. I wasn't really equipped to go anywhere because I was still dragging a leg and I had a paralyzed left arm and my speech was like Donald Duck's. I had to go to a National League kangaroo court with Clarence Campbell and Wayne Maki and his lawyers and my lawyers, not because of us but to whitewash and clean up the National Hockey League's image. They were more worried about that [the image] because they were getting a lot of bad publicity. I made the mistake of saying that the National League should take some of the responsibility. Clarence never asked me how I felt or how I was or how my career was going because my career at that point was pretty well finished; he couldn't care less. All he said to me was, 'Did you say this in the paper?' " Green says his career was pretty well destroyed because of that incident; he was never the same afterwards.

Green jumped to the World Hockey Association and the Hartford Whalers in 1972. Later he moved to the Winnipeg Jets. He found the WHA, particularly the Jets, refreshing. He was exposed for the first time to international hockey and a new style of play. Tournaments, training camps and exhibition games with European teams both here and there "were very interesting, seeing hockey on a world-wide basis other than in Canada and the United States." The experience illustrated to Green that "we've become very parochial in our thinking [about hockey]." It made him feel like a kid again, he says.

Green notes that Edmonton coach Glen Sather has said that he has fashioned his very successful club after the Winnipeg Jets of the WHA. Green is an assistant coach for Edmonton. "The foundation of our team here is finesse, playmaking and conditioning, exactly what we had in Winnipeg from 1975 to 78. Those are the reasons I really enjoyed playing the game and I probably extended my career because of them. Other than that I would have been finished years before."

Green retired from playing in 1979 and joined his brother in the hotel business in Manitoba. "I was glad to get out," he notes. "At the end my injuries were bothering me so much I could barely walk. I had six knee operations and three operations on my head, nine major operations in all." Rather reluctantly he started coaching senior hockey. "Because of the business, I got involved with some senior hockey clubs. I got involved in coaching not because I wanted to. I felt sort of coerced into it. Much to my surprise I really enjoyed that aspect of the game." After two years of success at senior, he wondered what it would be like at the pro level. A few phone calls later he was part of the Edmonton Oilers' coaching staff.

Although happy with the situation in Edmonton, he knows that becoming a head coach with the Oilers is a remote possibility. Glen Sather is still leading the team and assistant John Muckler is the heir apparent. "I feel I'm a qualified person," he comments about becoming a head coach. "I have the experience and I feel I have the knowledge. I know I have the experience as an assistant coach behind some good coaching in the organization and I have a lot of experience as a player I can draw on. I don't feel intimidated at all by getting involved as a head coach. I realize it's one step closer to getting fired, but it's a challenge I'd like to have one day."

The more sophisticated coaching evident recently makes Green wish he had been born with his talent a few years later so that he could have started professionally around 1975. "It has nothing to do with the money aspect." Better conditioning techniques, fitness evaluations, interesting practices, video tapes for both players and coaches to study, all encourage a player to realize his fullest potential. Old attitudes have been superceded by new ones. "In my day you were embarrassed and forced to play with injuries. I played no matter what in most games. Unless you came in on crutches with a band-aid on your head and a cast on your leg, they wouldn't believe you," he recalls. Today, management would rather not take a chance on someone injuring himself further. "Today, if a player misses a game [due to an injury] we feel it's to our benefit as well as the player's."

Near tragedy became triumph for Green. Since that fateful day he has acquired something of a golden touch in hockey. He has been part of championships wherever he has gone — Boston, Hartford, Winnipeg, senior hockey and, most recently, the Edmonton Oilers.

Sugar Jim Henry

Boston Bruins

(b. 1920, Winnipeg, Man.)
Games played 404
Minutes 24,240
Goals Against 1166
Shutouts 28
Average 2.88

Sugar Jim Henry

The image is unforgettable. The forward, still bleeding from a gash inflicted on his forehead by an opposing stick; the goalie, eyes blackened from a nose fractured the previous night, blood oozing from a cut received in that game. Two worn and wasted warriors congratulating one another after the decisive battle, hands clasped and bodies bent forward in mutual homage and respect.

This photograph, captured after the Stanley Cup final in 1951, is a statement about the men who played then and the game they played. The subjects are the great Rocket Richard who had dashed Boston's hopes with his heroics in that series, and Sugar Jim Henry, one of the best goaltenders of the 1940s and 1950s.

Was there an element of insanity in a goaltender who ignored obvious pain and subjected himself to more injury? Henry, who played ten seasons with New York, Chicago and Boston and lasted much longer than the average goaltender of his era, replies, "I always used to say, you didn't have to be [crazy], but it helped."

On another occasion, Henry, who operated a fishing lodge in Kenora with his goaltending partner in New York, Chuck Rayner, severely burnt his hands in a gasoline fire. After he was released from the hospital he went to training camp where he had to wear "little white gloves under his hockey mitts" to prevent lesions caused by leather rubbing against the tender, healing flesh. "For the first month I couldn't lace up my own skates," he says in his folksy fashion. "I had to get the trainer to do them up 'cause when you pull on them I got blood blisters on my fingers." Why would a human being continue playing under those circumstances? The answer is simple and almost cliche among the hockey fraternity: "I just liked it a lot."

A deflected puck in a game against Montreal shattered Henry's eyesocket and led him to retire in 1955. He played briefly in the minors and in the senior ranks, still operating his lodge but, after 21 years of operation, Henry sold his interest in the tourist business. He then worked in the service department of a Toyota dealership and today has joined the ranks of Canada's retired in Winnipeg.

Despite the multiple wounds his visage has suffered, Henry preferred the maskless approach of his day. "I don't see why they wear them . . . You lose sight of the puck too much . . . No way you can see as well with them as you can without them. It gets me as to why they wear the damn things. I think it would be better if they took them and threw them in the garbage can and played without them. I think it would do most of them some good."

Bronco Horvath

Boston Bruins

(b. 1930, Port Colborne, Ont.)
Games played 434
Goals 141
Assists 185
Total points 326
Penalties in Minutes 319

Rudy Horvath

His style certainly changed when Bronco Horvath received $100 for signing a contract in the early 1950s. "I was a kid. I needed the money," he recalls. "I had to buy a new suit. I wore a shark skin then. I always went first class with the 16 inch cuff and 22 inch knee. I had the big hat. Warren Godfrey taught me that!"

However it was not for his sartorial splendour that Horvath became known in the NHL but rather for his play on the Uke Line with Vic Stasiuk and Johnny Bucyk in Boston. In the 1959-60 season, Horvath, a native of Port Colborne, Ontario, led the league with 39 goals. "If Chief hadn't got injured," he says, referring to Bucyk by his nickname, "I'd have shattered 50 goals or more." Commenting on the offensive nature of today's game he adds, "I'd love to be able to play hockey today with Bucyk and Stasiuk on the wings. I'd score over a 100 goals a year with the 80 game schedule. It'd be a snap with those two guys. They'd get the puck out to me and I'd just shoot it."

Horvath's nine NHL seasons were divided among New York, Montreal, Boston, Chicago, Toronto and Minnesota. 1960, the year he finished second to Bobby Hull in the NHL points derby, he was nominated as an all-star.

After Toronto claimed him on waivers in 1963, Horvath spent most of the rest of his career skating for the Maple Leaf AHL affiliate in Rochester. He was loaned to Minnesota briefly in the 1967-68 season. "I wanted to stay in Minnesota," he says. "I wanted to buy my contract and they [Punch Imlach and Joe Crozier] wouldn't sell it to me. I made a good dollar in the minors, as much if not more than some guy in the NHL. But that's not right. I wanted to be in the big leagues. But I learned every time I was in the minors. It was hard to come back. They control you. They tell you what you can do and what you can't do. No matter how good you are, they're going to stick you."

Horvath retired in 1970 from Rochester and joined Minnesota as a scout. "I could have played for many years like Gordie Howe," he maintains. "It was just a conflict between management and myself. I just couldn't get along with management." Later he coached in the Ontario Junior A Hockey League for London and in Cape Cod for a semi-pro organization. For the last six or seven years he has been operating a successful cleaning service in Cape Cod. "I wasn't looking ahead," he explains about his retirement. "I thought I could play hockey for 50 years. I went from day to day. I thought I was going to be a millionaire or something in hockey. When I quit hockey, I was going to be in coaching. Let's face it, it's a dream. Dreams don't work out that way. You've got to work at it; you've got to put your mind to it seven days a week."

Eddie Johnston

Boston Bruins

(b. 1935, Montreal, Que.)
Games played 592
Minutes 34,209
Goals Against 1855
Shutouts 32
Average 3.25

No one understood the significance of being a member of the exclusive circle of athletes who belonged to the six-team NHL better than goaltenders. "I felt very privileged because at that time there were only six goalkeepers in the National Hockey League," explains former Bruins' goalie Eddie Johnston. When he came to Boston in 1962 he joined an elite group — Jacques Plante, Terry Sawchuk, Johnny Bower, Gump Worsley and Glenn Hall.

Johnston joined a Boston team perennially mired at the bottom of the NHL heap. He remembers that the Bruins and the Rangers always fought it out for last place honours in the early 1960s. Shortly after Christmas each season, after it became almost certain that neither team would make the play-offs, the games they played took on a new significance. "We used to call it the Eastern Seaboard Championship," he laughs. The two Stanley Cups the Bruins won in 1970 and 1972, he feels, "sure made up for all the hard work of the guys and me who played there in the lean years."

In 1963-64 Johnston played the entire 70-game schedule, one of the last goaltenders to do so. Johnston was also one of the last goaltenders in the NHL to adopt the face mask. Only after a serious injury did he decide to wear one. During the warm-ups before a game in Detroit in 1965, he was struck in the side of the head by one of Bobby Orr's shots. He was hospitalized for eight weeks and doctors worried about possible brain damage. "I had no idea where I was for five or six weeks," he says. "A fellow named Higgins designed a mask for me. He was a plumber at the time. The mask became so famous he got out of the plumbing business and made a lot of money."

Johnston says the Stanley Cup wins with the Bruins "revived" him and gave him the desire to keep playing. In 1973 the Bruins traded him to Toronto. Before retiring in 1978, he also guarded the twine for St. Louis and Chicago. He was 42 when he decided to quit and he still had offers to play another season with a couple of clubs. "I just had enough of it," he states.

Johnston turned to coaching as his new career. Since he was used to helping out his own coaches over the years, he was no stranger to the job. Goaltending and coaching demand similar qualities, he says. "They always used to say that the number on our back was our IQ," he kids. "But it's a responsible job. You're the last means of defence. Goaltenders have got to be thinking a little ahead of time. They've got to read plays. Concentration is the number one thing with a goalkeeper." Coaching, he adds, "is extreme concentration. You have to be well aware of what's going on, the line changes, the guys coming out of the penalty box, the system the other team's playing. You've got to be a step ahead of everybody. Once again, you're total concentration. Like goalkeeping, you have to have it."

Coaching the Black Hawks in 1979-80, Johnston guided them to a 34-37-19 record and a berth in the quarter finals, a marked improvement over the previous season. "In Chicago they told me I had a lifetime job after going from 70 to 90 points," he recalls. "Unfortunately, just before the draft, there was a controversy. I don't really know what happened to this day but they decided to let me go." The following season he went to Pittsburgh as a coach. After three seasons he became the Penguins' general manager. He is now trying to turn the fortunes of that franchise around. After nabbing three first-round draft choices in 1984 he feels he is on his way to molding a contender whose style, he says, will be a cross between Boston and Montreal.

Forbes Kennedy

Boston Bruins

(b. 1935, Dorchester, N.B.)
Games played 603
Goals 70
Assists 108
Total points 178
Penalties in Minutes 988

Forbes Kennedy fondly recalls the fun times that he associates with his ten seasons in the NHL, even if some of them saw him become the victim of a locker room practical joke.

Kennedy says that once his teammates in Boston discovered his great fear of mice, they would unleash wind-up or rubber versions of the rodent on the unsuspecting centreman whenever the chance arose. The state of agitation this trick induced was great enough to force him to bolt from the locker room and refuse to return. One ex-Bruin remembers players having to make an agreement to stop perpetrating the trick because of the disruption it caused. "They had me going for awhile," Kennedy laughs.

Raised on Prince Edward Island, Kennedy moved to Barrie, Ontario to play junior hockey. In 1956 he joined the NHL with Chicago. He was later traded to Detroit and Boston and moved to Philadelphia in the 1967 expansion draft. His last NHL campaign, 1968-69, was divided between Philadelphia and Toronto. Checking and penalty killing, he says, were his main roles over the years. The scrappy forward could handle himself in the rough going despite his 5'8", 185-pound frame.

Kennedy's last NHL game was played as a Leaf on April 2, 1969 against the Boston Bruins. He ended it all with a big bang. After a memorable melee he was assessed four minors, two majors, one ten-minute misconduct and one game misconduct. The total earned him a share of the Stanley Cup record for most penalty minutes in one play-off game in a season in which he led the league in penalty minutes. "I got by," he says rather modestly when describing his pugilistic abilities.

After a couple of knee operations led Kennedy to retire, he turned to coaching in the minor leagues. Over the last six years he has been at the helm of a junior team in Charlottetown, Prince Edward Island where he now lives. He continues to employ a traditional style of coaching: "I try to coach like the old days. You have to have respect; you've got to show them who's the boss."

Joseph Klukay

Boston Bruins

(b. 1922, Sault Ste. Marie, Ont.)
Games played 566
Goals 109
Assists 127
Total points 236
Penalties in Minutes 189

Joe Klukay

Joe Klukay joined Toronto in 1946. He was one of six new faces installed in the lineup by Conn Smythe who was fed up with the Maple Leafs' lacklustre showing the previous season. He and Nick Metz were paired to kill penalties and one of the most effective specialty teams in league history was born.

"We just concocted a system for us," explains Klukay, who was dubbed the Duke of Paducah for some unknown reason by a Toronto scribe. "It had to be the easiest, the most effective way to go about killing a penalty. You had one guy going in and we'd try to contain them in their own end. It worked for ten years so we couldn't knock it."

In his time with the Leafs, Klukay shared in four Stanley Cups. Then, in 1952, he became a victim of a new youth movement and was traded to Boston where he says he spent two of the most enjoyable seasons of his career. No longer having to play Toronto's "regimented" style, he was allowed to freewheel a little bit more.

Klukay found himself once again in Toronto two years later in an exchange for Leo Boivin. He wondered why, after being culled for the sake of youth, Toronto wanted him back now that he was two years older, and "over the hill" according to the standards of the day. "The 'Old Man' [Conn Smythe] just wanted me back."

Klukay was used sparingly by Toronto and was eventually dispatched to their AHL affiliate in Pittsburgh. At the time, he says, there was "sort of a promise" of a coaching position "or something" for him there the following season. "Unfortunately they folded up there the year after," he remembers.

Then Klukay was contacted by George Gee about playing hockey for a senior team in Windsor. "They had a job lined up for me which was something I was looking for," he adds. "I said, 'What the hell, it's never too late to learn a trade.' That's where I am today." He is in the tool and die business for the automotive trade. "Learning a trade and playing hockey, I had two jobs going here for a few years."

Klukay, now living in Detroit, participates in the game with the Red Wing old-timers. "If it wasn't for that I'd only see them [other ex-pros] at funerals and weddings. This way we're almost in constant contact with each other."

Leo Labine

Boston Bruins

(b. 1931, Haileybury, Ont.)
Games played 643
Goals 128
Assists 193
Total points 321
Penalties in Minutes 730

Leo Labine

"I was lucky to get out of the game alive," remarks Leo Labine, a veteran of 642 games with the Boston Bruins and Detroit Red Wings between 1951 and 1962. "I was a little aggressive sometimes." The loquacious Labine developed a reputation as a tough bodychecker and a better-than-average needler. In one game he almost annihilated the great Rocket Richard with a thunderous check. Though dazed, the Canadiens' forward only seemed to play better. "He went on to score the winning goal that night," moans Labine.

Now living in North Bay, Ontario, Labine says that his only disappointment in hockey was never playing on a Stanley Cup winning team. "I just wish we had had better hockey players. We didn't have any snipers," he says, referring to the Boston Bruins. "I've made a lot of Frenchmen famous by losing to them. Those Canadiens always had superior bench strength."

The contracts signed by players in the six-team NHL were worth a mere fraction of the mega-buck deals signed by athletes today but Labine contends he was happy with what he was paid. The ones who got cheated in those days, he maintains, were the superstars since they were only slightly better compensated than the average player. They were certainly worth more, he adds.

Labine spent five seasons in the Western Hockey League after his tour in the NHL. He returned home to North Bay and got a job as a sales representative for Carling O'Keefe. Ten years later he lost his job in the corporate shuffle that followed Rothmans' purchase of that brewery. Since then he has been a salesperson for Husband Transport. He and his wife, Rosemary, have four children; one is a teacher, one is a secretary and two are university students.

Fleming Mackell

Boston Bruins

(*b. 1929, Montreal, Que.*)
Games played 665
Goals 149
Assists 220
Total points 369
Penalties in Minutes 562

Fleming Mackell

At one time Fleming Mackell, a forward who played with Toronto and Boston from 1948 to 1960, ranked as one of three fastest skaters in the NHL. The centreman was an important part of the Bruins' attack in the 1950s as an all-around player. He played a regular shift, killed penalties and was on the power play. Though he had savoured a Stanley Cup victory with the Leafs earlier in his career, the one time all-star and his Boston teammates could never turn the trick in the finals. "We were a good team in Boston," he says, "not a lot of stars, but a good spirit on the team. The guys played together."

Standing 5'8" and weighing 175 pounds during his playing days, Mackell recalls the game in the six-team era as being perilous for smaller men. "There was a lot of intimidation if you weren't big," he explains. "If you weren't a rough, tough player, you could never show that you didn't like the rough stuff or they would run you out of the league. I don't know," he adds with a laugh, "guys tell me that when I played the game I was chippy, too."

Mackell's NHL career ended when he and Bruins' management failed to see eye-to-eye. "The Bruins and I had kind of a falling-out. They thought they had better younger players to bring in. They sold my contract to Quebec," he remembers. "I went to the Quebec Aces as a playing coach. That was a big mistake. It didn't work out at all." He decided not to return for a second season, instead opting to work for Dow Brewery in Montreal in the promotions field. For the last 16 years he has been in the automobile business where he is now assistant manager of Avenue Pontiac Buick. He has done well in the car trade. "I guess that desire to win helped because the desire to win a sale is the same thing. I've done alright."

"The Bruins themselves didn't do very much after I left either. They went downhill pretty fast. They could never beat anybody. When I was with them we never missed the play-offs except the year I had a bad knee," he comments.

If he were given another whirl at his career, Mackell says he might "look after myself a little better" and pay more attention to the individual side of the game. "I could have been a little more intense, maybe a little more cooperative . . . I wasn't cooperative with management, when you look at it now from a different perspective."

Reflecting further, Mackell remarks, "Whether we realize it or not, indirectly you took it [the game] home [to your family] with you. Everything was winning or losing. You look back, it wasn't as important as we thought."

Pit Martin

Boston Bruins

(b. 1943, Noranda, Que.)
Games played 1101
Goals 324
Assists 485
Total points 809
Penalties in Minutes 614

Pit Martin, best remembered for his playmaking abilities at centre over 12 NHL seasons, has noticed that the average career span has shortened somewhat in recent years. "They keep bringing on the young talent. A guy really has a lot more trouble making a long career of it now."

Addressing the problem of retired athletes should be a concern of the players' association, Martin, a former member of that organization, suggests. "They've done a lot for hockey but they could do a helluva lot more. They should stop being so selfish and start looking at the guys who are out of hockey as well as the guys who are in it."

Retirement comes too quickly for many. "The guys who are playing hockey right now don't think about it. I know I didn't think about it when I was playing. All of a sudden it was there," Martin comments. He says he did nothing for a couple of years and then bought a bar-restaurant business in Windsor, Ontario.

Martin's establishment was "a very popular place" but a human rights controversy erupted over the ejection of a black man from the premises. Though no discrimination was proven, bad feelings "snowballed" in the ensuing publicity and Martin decided to sell out. "People come in, they don't behave themselves, you throw them out. If they happen to be black they say you threw me out because I'm black. You didn't throw me out because I was a jerk, you threw me out because I was black."

"Now I'm retired again," Martin says. He is looking at buying into another enterprise in the near future. He and his family live in St. Clair Beach, near Windsor. The Noranda native played in the NHL with Detroit, Boston and Chicago. His efforts in the Windy City made his name as a quality player in hockey.

Don McKenney
Boston Bruins

(b. 1934, Smith Falls, Ont.)
Games played 798
Goals 237
Assists 345
Total points 582
Penalties in Minutes 211

Don McKenney

According to Don McKenney, most players, if they had their druthers, would like to remain in the game after retirement. "After 20-25 years [of playing the game from the minor level up] you're afraid to go into anything else," the Smith Falls, Ontario native comments. He calls himself one of the lucky ones — circumstances permitted him to stay in hockey. For the last nine years he has been coaching at Northeastern University in Boston.

McKenney is an assistant to his former teammate Fern Flaman. The job, he adds, involves doing "a little bit of everything." In addition to helping with practices and games, he spends about six weeks on the road recruiting talent in and around Detroit, Windsor, Ottawa and Boston. Flaman describes McKenney's role at Northeastern as vital to the success of the hockey program at the university.

In 1954 McKenney joined the Bruins where he developed into a smooth-skating forward. A combination of ability and orderly conduct on the ice earned him the Lady Byng Trophy in 1960. Two years later he was traded to the Rangers and the next season he was part of the famous transaction that brought him and Andy Bathgate to Toronto in exchange for four Leafs. The play of the two new Maple Leafs was credited with helping Toronto earn a third consecutive Stanley Cup.

Retirement for McKenney came in 1969 after stops in Detroit and St. Louis. He and Doug Mohns operated hockey schools in Massachusetts, possibly the first in the state. He coached in a New England hockey league before accepting the position at Northeastern.

John McKenzie

Boston Bruins

(b. 1937, High River, Alta.)
Games played 691
Goals 206
Assists 268
Total points 474
Penalties in Minutes 917

"The 'third man in' [rule] killed my career," jokes John "Pie" McKenzie, one of the peskiest needlers ever to play in the NHL. He took impish delight in making opponents' blood boil to throw off their game. "I never fought that much," he concedes, something confirmed by the fact he has no false teeth. "I just got things going and let the big boys take over."

A native of High River, Alberta, McKenzie developed in the Black Hawk chain. "Those were the days when if you were old enough to walk and they saw you, they put you on the list," he says. A small (5'7") right winger, he came up to Chicago in 1958. He bounced between Detroit, Boston, and back to Chicago with stops in the minors before landing in Boston in 1966. There he became a popular component of the Boston attack. "Thank God for the Bruins," he salutes.

At one time McKenzie worked in rodeos during the off-season. He had been calf-roping since he was a youngster. The Bruins called a halt to his cowboy ways. "After I scored 31 goals they made me stop," he laughs.

McKenzie left Boston in 1972 after two Stanley Cups for the WHA and a playing coach position with Philadelphia. He stayed in that league until 1979 when he retired. The last team he played for was New England. "I played 21 years and it got to be a lot of hard work after a while. I hated to practise and I was 42 years old. I was old. I knew I was finished. You couldn't fool yourself and just keep going on."

Withdrawing from a lifetime in athletics was not easy, McKenzie says. "It took me two to three years to get back to reality and establish myself again. That's the hard thing to do. It's tough. All of a sudden you're out of the league. There you are and you have to start all over again."

McKenzie found a job as a sales representative for a lumber company service contractors in the Boston area and has been successful at it. Says one of his former Boston teammates, "The guy who hired him remembered Johnny McKenzie as a feisty little bastard who swore and everything else on the ice. He probably figured, 'Hell, we'll never be able to refine this guy.' He got the shock of his life. McKenzie's done just a fantastic job for the guy."

One of McKenzie's most recent endeavours was to get involved with some other former athletes in the opening of a new bank in Boston, Olympic International. Now a grandfather of four, McKenzie still finds time to lace on the skates with some other Bruins' old-timers, a great way, he says, to get together with some of the old guys and swap stories.

Doug Mohns

Boston Bruins

(b. 1933, Capreol, Ont.)
Games played 1390
Goals 248
Assists 462
Total points 710
Penalties in Minutes 1250

Doug Mohns can sum up the ethic that got him into the NHL in 1953 and kept him there for 22 years. "I just couldn't see myself failing. I had an opportunity to be successful at something. I wanted to prove to myself and others that I could do it. I've always maintained that it's important to do the best at what you're doing." He applied his ideas to his life after hockey, particularly his business of operating private hospitals.

Mohns was a quick-footed player who was used mainly on defence but occasionally doubled as a forward. In fact, when he first came to Boston in 1953, he had never played defence before. His ability to skate backwards and his good balance earned him a spot on the blueline. The ex-forward never complained. "I never said much of anything in those days," he says. "I did what they told me to do. I was happy to be around."

Mohns played the two positions equally well. Later, in the 1960s, he joined Chicago and re-ignited the Scooter Line with Stan Mikita and Ken Wharram. Playing two positions, he thinks, adversely affected his chances of earning all-star recognition. "I think if I could have concentrated on one position, I might have been an all-star." He went on to play in Minnesota, Atlanta and Washington before retiring in 1975. Not bad for a fellow who thought he would be lucky to make it into the NHL after playing junior hockey.

At 41 years of age, Mohns was prepared to give up the rigours of the game. "I had skated many, many miles," he states. "I had a good life and a good career. I was looking ahead, not back." His long career in hockey gave Mohns an opportunity to prepare for retirement. He took courses at schools and universities as part of the preparation. He began working and was successful in the construction field. Later, he got involved in the private hospital field with Buddy Larue, former Bruins' trainer who became a real estate millionaire and owner of the Boston Red Sox. Mohns is currently part owner and vice-president of human resources of this expanding firm.

Still living in the Boston area, Mohns is a founder of the Bruins' old-timers organization which continues to play games for charity. More recently he and his wife have become involved with an organization aimed at the prevention of child abuse.

Murray Oliver

Boston Bruins

(b. 1937, Hamilton, Ont.)
Games played 1127
Goals 274
Assists 454
Total points 728
Penalties in Minutes 319

Murray Oliver

The first and only time Murray Oliver used an agent's services in 16 NHL seasons, he became involved in a contract dispute that forced him out of hockey as a player. General managers had only agreed to bargain with agents a few years earlier. So, in 1975, Oliver hired an agent to negotiate with then Minnesota North Stars' manager, Jack Gordon. "I was going to hold out for two years and they didn't want to give me a two-year contract and finally they said to hell with it. So only a week before training camp started, I found myself out in the street looking for a job."

Oliver was not so much peeved with his agent as he was with North Stars' coach Ted Harris. "I was disappointed mostly in Teddy Harris the coach because he didn't go to bat for me. I was one of the older guys and I got along well with the younger players. This is evident by the fact that I can be an assistant coach now," he elaborates. "I get along well with the players and help them and teach them some things. I think I would have been an asset to Teddy Harris."

Lou Nanne, then a North Star, had some connections with a hockey stick company and arranged a job interview for Oliver. He landed a sales representative position. "I was out of the hockey game business one day and I was in the hockey stick business the next," he says. "The transition from playing to not playing was quick and I was out in the business world."

"I dug into selling sticks and the business part of it with the same enthusiasm I had played hockey. Actually it turned out very well because I got a lot of good experience," he comments about his sudden jump from athletics to private life. He only slightly regrets that his career ended prematurely. "As it turns out, it's the best thing that ever happened to me because I got out in the business world. I got a lot of good experience selling and meeting people and learned how to sell and how to handle people. That experience has paid off for me in the business I'm in now."

The quick transition, Oliver says, fostered an appreciation within him. "You just appreciate what you really have here. The real world is tough. I don't think any of these guys who play now or when I was playing realize it. They think they can play forever, that the game's going to go on forever. Then, all of a sudden, one day it's over and you're not prepared for it. I was fortunate enough to get a job right away. It was something I liked and it was related to the hockey business."

Oliver sold sticks for three years until Lou Nanne became general manager of the North Stars and invited him to join the club as an assistant coach. He filled in as head coach for part of the 1982-83 season although he was told when Nanne hired him that the head coaching job would never be his full time. "You'll never coach this team because I don't want to fire you. Coaches are hired to be fired," he said.

During his career, Oliver was a good all-round forward who proved to be an excellent penalty killer as well as a very capable playmaker. Originally with Detroit, he was traded to Boston in 1960 during his sophomore year as a pro. As hapless as the Bruins were in the early 1960s, he always proved to be one of the brighter lights on Boston squads and often put himself in the NHL's top ten in scoring. He spent three seasons in Toronto before going to Minnesota in 1971.

John Peirson

Boston Bruins

(b. 1925, Winnipeg, Man.)
Games played 545
Goals 153
Assists 173
Total points 326
Penalties in Minutes 315

Johnny Peirson

Much of John Peirson's hockey career, both as a player and a broadcaster, has been a matter of chance. The coincidental nature of some of the developments has prompted him to declare, "My career has been one of complete accidents."

Peirson was a student at McGill University in Montreal when he was offered a tryout with the Hershey Bears, the Boston farm team in the AHL. "I gave it an opportunity for a year or two," he remembers. "The money that was there was not very substantial but I could save some money and if I didn't get too far I could always quit and go back to school." He made the Bears and in 1947, due to a gambling scandal in the NHL that displaced a number of players, he got a chance to play with Boston. For ten seasons he was a mainstay with the Bruins.

"I think the older you get the better you were," the former right winger laughs. He describes himself as having been an "above average, not great" player. "I would say I was above average because I was a better-balanced player, a forward that knew how to backcheck. I had some defensive skills as well as being able to find the net sometimes." He scored 20 or more goals in four seasons. Personal marks were not his main worry, he says. Rather he was concerned with team-oriented efforts. Though the Bruins never won a Stanley Cup during his time with the club, the squad was always very respectable. "Boston was never a powerhouse but we had some representative teams. Nobody blew us out of the building. There are some very sad teams today that would've been even sadder in our day."

In 1958, after his "legs sort of disappeared," Peirson retired. To stay in hockey another year or two would have meant uprooting his family and moving to some minor league city. Instead he chose to join his father-in-law's furniture manufacturing firm. He remained in that industry and today acts as an independent sales representative for three American furniture manufacturers.

Peirson is well known in Boston for his role as a colour commentator on Bruins' television broadcasts during the last 16 years. Again an accidental encounter led him to television. While attending a game at Madison Square Gardens, he had a chance meeting with his former coach in Boston, Lynn Patrick. Patrick offered him an opportunity to do some radio work for the Bruins. Peirson accepted and found himself back in the game as a broadcaster.

The only change Peirson might make in his career, other than being part of a Stanley Cup winner in Boston, would be to develop his physical strength more. "The only thing I wish I had done was to work more diligently on my upper body strength because I would've been a better player. I lost a lot of battles and wasn't able to do what I would like to have done from the point of view of strength."

Bill Quackenbush

Boston Bruins

(b. 1922, Toronto, Ont.)
Games played 774
Goals 62
Assists 222
Total points 284
Penalties in Minutes 95

Bill Quackenbush

After seven seasons with Detroit, in 1949 defenceman Bill Quackenbush was traded to the Boston Bruins. Looking back, the Hall of Famer, five time all-star and winner of the Lady Byng Trophy in 1949 thinks the decision was based on style. "I wasn't a body checker. I was a poke checker. I had to play a certain style. I found that if I did a lot of body checking, I got tired very easily. I was on the ice an awful lot because I didn't get penalties." He once played 137 consecutive games without getting one penalty, a remarkable achievement when one considers the nature of the sport.

Quackenbush played until 1956 when, at 34 years of age, he retired. "It didn't seem that they were interested in having me stay around," he explains, so he left to raise his family. Two years later, he was told by Boston general manager Lynn Patrick that the club felt it had let him retire too soon.

Quackenbush became a manufacturer's representative for a building products firm. Over the next seven years, he earned an associate degree in engineering at night school. A partner and he were operating their own business when he decided to return to hockey. He applied for and won the coach's job at Princeton University. Still at the university, he is no longer the hockey squad coach but he is in charge of men's golf and the women's ice hockey team.

Living in Princeton, New Jersey, Quackenbush is seriously contemplating retirement and an eventual move to a warmer climate.

Lawrence Regan

Boston Bruins

(b. 1930, North Bay, Ont.)
Games played 280
Goals 41
Assists 95
Total points 136
Penalties in Minutes 71

Larry Regan

Larry Regan gained a considerable amount of business experience after he retired from the game in 1966. First a coach and administrator in hockey, he now applies that experience to his job as managing director of the Canadian Old-Timers' Hockey Association.

Regan found himself mired in the minors after he turned professional with the Maple Leaf organization. It was not until 1956 when Boston acquired him that he got an opportunity to play in the NHL. When he did, his stickhandling and playmaking abilities earned him a nomination as the league's rookie of the year. At 27 years of age, he became one of the oldest recipients of the honour, a fact that is acknowledged in the board game Trivial Pursuit. "They have it that I'm the oldest, but I think I'm right in thinking that Jimmy McFadden was older," he says.

After five seasons with Boston and Toronto, Regan retired and accepted a playing coach position in the AHL. "From then on, I never believed in player-coaching, I assure you," he states, explaining the lesson he learned. "I guess I was typical of people coming out of hockey with no coaching experience which is so important. As a player you don't realize all that there is involved in coaching."

Regan's intention was to get involved in the business side of hockey. He spent three years helping the Austrian government develop a hockey team capable of playing in the 1964 Olympics. When the NHL expanded in 1967 Regan found himself in the employ of Jack Kent Cooke and the Los Angeles Kings, first as a director of player personnel and then as general manager and coach. He was involved not only with the Kings but also with other Cooke enterprises. They gave him an education he could not even dream of buying. He says, "I learned more about business from him than the average guy with a Ph.D."

In 1974, feeling that it was his "turn to get out" because the challenge had dissipated, Regan left Los Angeles. He spent a season coaching a junior hockey club in Montreal thinking he might wish to purchase it the following season. He decided not to. A series of back operations and a bout with a serious blood disease put him out of commission for three years. By then, he says, he was financially healthy due to some property investments.

Regan later participated in a federal government study of amateur hockey in Canada which eventually offered recommendations on how to improve it. Now with the COHA, Regan is in the process of spreading the old-timer network across Canada, establishing sponsorships by corporations and organizing the recreational tournaments that are burgeoning in popularity among older hockey enthusiasts.

Edward Sandford

Boston Bruins

(b. 1928, New Toronto, Ont.)
Games played 502
Goals 106
Assists 145
Total points 251
Penalties in Minutes 355

Ed Sandford did something unusual for a hockey player before
he turned professional with the
Boston Bruins in 1948; he finished high school. He decided before
his tryout that he would either
make the NHL or return to
school. He played nine seasons,
mostly with the Bruins, and never
did return to continue his educa-
tion, something he has second thoughts about today.

"If I did it over again," Sandford speculates, "I would have
graduated from a college or university and then turned pro. I know,
looking back, 19 was awfully young to turn pro. You're not big
enough. You haven't matured. You're not strong enough. You
haven't got the poise. That league is a quick league. You're playing
against 24, 25, 26-year-olds, the Bentleys, the Richards, the Lachs,
the great players, and the young guys breaking in really had to work
like the dickens to keep up with them."

Sandford feels one of the injustices of the sport in his era was
how it took advantage of young players. "I saw a lot of kids go down
to training camp at 16, 17, leave school, didn't make the team and
didn't come back to school. I think hockey really damaged them permanently. But that's the way the game was, that's the way the rules
were. The boys had to realize that and protect themselves which they
didn't do because they were so fascinated by the fact they were being
scouted by a pro team." It is understandable why he advocates that

young players take the collegiate route when he addresses such groups in the Boston area where he now makes his home.

Trades took Sandford from Boston after eight seasons to Detroit and then to Chicago. As a forward, he says he was better defensively than offensively, something that might have been different if he had been "one or two steps faster". At the 1957 Chicago training camp, the Black Hawks intended to demote him to the minor leagues. "I wasn't going to go down to the minors. I was either going to play in the NHL or go back to work," he recalls. Back to work he went and since then he has been a stock broker.

Long before the end, Sandford had foreseen the day it would come and he prepared himself accordingly. "To me hockey was just an interim," he maintains. "I told everybody else to do the same, look for another career because this wouldn't last long. Not many guys did." Interested in finance and investment, he met people while in Boston who introduced him to various brokerage firms, one of which he worked for in the summers. He learned the bookkeeping and accounting skills he needed for that business so that when he left the game, he was ready to assume the job full time.

Nose habitually buried in the *Wall Street Journal* and *The New York Times* during his playing days, Sandford remembers advising his teammates to invest their earnings in "good, sound securities". "I don't think many of them listened," he surmises. "The temptation to buy cars and take vacations was too much and life was always going to be great for them. They were never going to get old. They were going to play hockey the rest of their lives." More than one of his clubmates admit that they wished they had listened to him.

Living in the Boston area with his family, Sandford is still involved with the Boston old-timers who play several games for charity every year. For the past 16 years he has kept his hand in pro hockey by acting as a minor official tabulating scores, judging goals or noting penalty minutes in the Boston Garden.

Vic Stasiuk

Boston Bruins

(b. 1929, Lethbridge, Alta.)
Games played 745
Goals 183
Assists 254
Total points 437
Penalties in Minutes 669

Vic Stasiuk can sit back and sur-
vey his 600-acre spread in Lethbridge, Alberta, happy knowing
that his involvement in NHL
hockey made it all possible. Over
the years he has harvested "the
sweetest, sweet corn in southern
Alberta" off the land. In the very
near future, it will make him a
millionaire.

A journeyman winger with Detroit, Chicago and Boston from
1949 to 1963, Stasiuk turned to coaching, first in the minor leagues,
then in the NHL and later, after limited success in the big league,
back to the minor and amateur ranks. While coaching the
Philadelphia Flyers in the early 1970s, an opportunity arose to buy a
big piece of land at a good price in his native Lethbridge but the local
bank would not loan him the money he needed.

"I needed to borrow a fraction of the purchase price because I
had the rest in cash in my house," Stasiuk recalls, pausing occasionally
to find the right words to express his thoughts. "And I couldn't get it
through the local banks for whatever reasons. I was a hockey bum. I
never charged anything so I never had a credit rating. So Bud Poile,
my friend, said to talk to Bill [Putnam], the former banker, the president of the Flyers."

"He called a friend in New York who called a guy in Toronto.
He called the Toronto-Dominion in Lethbridge and he phoned my
lawyer. The lawyer went across the street and exercised the option
the day before it expired."

Stasiuk moved onto the 600 acres with its two and a half mile river frontage directly across from Lethbridge. He coached in the winter and farmed in the summer. His intention was to eventually build a golf course on the land. Over the years he has supplied the area with all of its sweet corn. He compares the satisfaction he gains from growing, distributing and receiving praise for the quality of his produce to something all hockey players can understand. "Well," he drawls, "you get satisfaction just like scoring a goal. I don't know which is nicer."

Since he bought the land, the city has expanded around his property, making it a rural oasis prime for development. "They plunked the university right beside us," Stasiuk observes, tracing the genesis of a land price explosion. The bureaucratic wrangling associated with subdividing and developing land has "taken longer than we all liked" but he is now ready to move.

Stasiuk plans to subdivide the land for housing, develop a golf course, "the most beautiful in all of Western Canada" and possibly a ski hill. "We'll take in about $30 million but it's going to cost us $15 to $20 million. It's a lot of work, eh?"

The millionaire-to-be reflects on his fortune and ponders one of the ironies in life. From the time he purchased the land, his commitment to the sport he loved lessened. "If I was to make an excuse for not being a successful coach, it would be that I stopped giving it the 110, 120 per cent. Once you do that, you don't have success."

Gerry Toppazzini

Boston Bruins

(b. 1931, Copper Cliff, Ont.)
Games played 783
Goals 163
Assists 244
Total points 407
Penalties in Minutes 436

Jerry Toppazzini

One patron of the Beef 'n' Bird, a bar-restaurant in Sudbury, Ontario, jokes that the topic of great hockey players has been discussed thousands of times and Gerry Toppazzini's name has never come up. Toppazzini, proprietor of the hotel, laughs, and acknowledges the fate of all journeyman athletes — relative obscurity. He insists, however, that while people remember the superstars, it is the average athletes who make up the greatest part of any team in any sport.

Toppazzini toiled for 12 seasons in the National Hockey League, playing either defence or forward. In 783 regular season games, most of them with the Boston Bruins, he had 163 goals and 244 assists. He once held a record for the most short-handed goals in a season and another for the most goals scored in a semi-final series.

Toppazzini broke into the NHL in 1952-1953. He had just graduated from the Barrie Flyers junior hockey club that had won the Memorial Cup the previous season. He says his first contract was for $6,500 and he loved it. He was being paid to do something he wanted to do. The largest contract he signed as a professional was for $12,800.

After retiring as a player he thought he might like to try coaching. "I didn't have very much success," he confesses. Stints in Port Huron and Springfield proved disastrous as coaching experiences. He spent a year and a half behind the bench of the Sudbury Wolves of the Ontario Major Junior A Hockey League and was voted coach of the year during his first season. For what he calls "various reasons" he was dismissed partway through his second season with the Wolves.

Aware that hockey as a career would end, Toppazzini held down different jobs when he returned to Sudbury each summer. "I always had something going for me. I always had a livelihood." He made investments and became involved in a number of businesses. The hotel he has operated in recent years is a fairly successful enterprise in which his wife of 30 years, Dolly, and their three sons and one daughter are involved.

"Topper", as he is known to his friends, says he has no regrets about his long involvement in hockey. His only connection to sports these days is sitting as president of the Northern Football Conference, a senior amateur football league in Ontario.

Ed Westfall

Boston Bruins

(b. 1940, Belleville, Ont.)
Games played 1227
Goals 231
Assists 394
Total points 625
Penalties in Minutes 544

Though he spent 18 seasons in the NHL, a veritable lifetime by some people's estimate, Ed Westfall, the defensive specialist with the Boston Bruins and New York Islanders, now sees his time as a beginning, not an end.

"Hockey to me was a great start in life. It's a great beginning to get yourself started in your life. To me, it offered everything. People don't take advantage of some of the things around them when they're hockey players. I really feel bad for a lot of the players that haven't taken advantage of the opportunities as they came along. They were too busy doing the hockey thing and they didn't let their minds kind of wander and kind of dream a little bit beyond hockey," Westfall says.

"They got stuck in a trench there. They get off the beaten track and they get their heads buried in the sand. They don't realize they can take hockey and use it as a beginning for a tremendously fulfilling life," Westfall adds. "It is not life in itself. It doesn't have enough to offer to be your whole life."

Westfall retired from the Islanders in 1979 to a new life that hockey had helped create. He stayed in the game in public relations and marketing for the Islanders. That job got him into television broadcasting which he still does in Canada and the United States. As well, he got involved with a successful firm that buys and sells semiconductors, called Semi-Specialists Inc. He also became associated with a travel firm specializing in handling corporate travel for many of the firms on Long Island. More recently he became a beer distributor with Budweiser. "So I've got lots to keep me busy," he says.

Westfall, a native of Oshawa, Ontario, came to the Bruins in 1961. Originally a defenceman, he eventually converted into a checking forward who established a reputation for being able to cover the offensive threats of the day. "I was known as the Lamont Cranston [of hockey]," he laughs. "The shadow!" It was a job he did through the lean years in Boston until they became a power and won two Stanley Cups.

Claimed by the Islanders in the 1972 draft, Westfall continued his checking duties with the expansion club as well as providing the club with solid leadership. "They broke all the negative records that we set with the Bruins in 1961," he comments. "It was like starting over again. The only advantage I had was that I had been through it all before."

In 1979, with the Islanders poised to make a grab at the Stanley Cup, Westfall ended his career. "I could've gone on and played, I guess, according to the people I worked for," he offers. "But I just didn't feel like playing anymore. I knew the team was very close to winning a Stanley Cup. I suppose it would've been nice to be on that team when it did win the Stanley Cup and to see two teams go from adversity to Stanley Cup champions in one career would have been really something."

But the time to leave had arrived. Westfall describes the process, "I think what happens is you grow out of the game. Your ideas and ideals change as you get older. Things that were so vital to you, your thinking on the game and the way it's played, change. And the camaraderie. I think more than anything was that I'd be in the dressing room after the game was over and I'd look around. I was 36 and 37 and 38 years old and, outside of playing the game and loving it, I really didn't have anything in common with the other players. You kind of grow. Your life should be continuously growing and I just kind of grew away from it. Playing just didn't seem to make that much difference to me anymore."

Tom Williams

Boston Bruins

(b. 1940, Duluth, Minn.)
Games played 663
Goals 161
Assists 269
Total points 430
Penalties in Minutes 177

Tom Williams

When Tom Williams broke into the NHL with Boston in 1962 he could claim he was the only American, the only one out of 200,000,000 people, to be part of the six-team league. For years the Duluth native was the original hockey trivia question.

The problem Williams had in adjusting to professional hockey was not associated with any disdain from his Canadian counterparts, but rather from the style of hockey he had learned. "The biggest problem was that in American checking rules," he recalls, "you could only body check in your own defensive zone. So a guy like me liked to freewheel and play with the puck. Then I'd come out of my zone not expecting to get hit until I got up to the other blue line." Needless to say, he made an easy "head down" target for the opposition. He suffered three concussions while playing his first professional season with Kingston in the Eastern Professional Hockey League.

Before joining the Bruins, Williams had been a member of the American Olympic hockey team that won a gold medal in the 1960 Games at Squaw Valley. When he was in grade 12 he attended Detroit's training camp but the Red Wings lost interest when his father demanded a large cash payment for education in case his son didn't make it in hockey.

For three seasons, Williams played on a line with John Bucyk and Murray Oliver. When one year each scored 20 goals or more, they were among the first lines to accomplish this feat. More of a free-skating player, he always found the bump and grind of the professional game difficult to contend with and learn. "I wasn't programmed by the Canadian style of play," he says. "I couldn't hit anybody else, let alone protect myself."

Traded to Minnesota in 1969, Williams later went on to California, New England (WHA) and Washington. Plagued by back problems and feeling like he wasn't contributing to the team, he retired in 1976. "I escaped with my sanity and my health and I'm very grateful for the experience," he comments. "I have no illusions or bitterness. I'm glad I had the chance. How many guys get a chance to say they did something they loved for 16 years?" He draws an analogy about the arrival of an inevitable end: "It's like a love affair with a girlfriend. It's passionate, it's hot and cold, it's highs and lows. When it's over and you've got to part company, it's over."

The change meant having to adapt to a new world outside of the limelight. "When you're a hockey player, when you're an athlete or anybody in the public eye in general, when people give you positive attention and a little adulation is heaped on you, when you're made a special person, you sometimes get a little distorted in your thinking. You might tend to get an inflated ego. I know sometimes I thought I was a little better than I probably was. As a result it's hard to keep things in perspective, think sensibly and use good common sense."

Seven years ago, after a brief coaching stint in the junior B ranks of New England, he joined a pipes and plastics firm as a sales representative. "I had to learn in a hurry that now I'm on the other side of the fence," Williams says. He found that he had to cater to the professionals associated with this field and discovered that he had to start at the bottom and work his way up. "It was the best thing that ever happened to me. I had to eat some humble pie," he adds. He has excelled in this endeavour and is currently a territorial manager for the firm. Now living in the Boston area, he plays old-timers' hockey twice a week just to stay in shape.

Toronto Maple Leafs goalie Bruce Gamble (30) dives for the net hoping to intercept Stan Mikita's (A) attempt to centre the puck for Chicago Black Hawks teammate Doug Mohns. Toronto's Allan Stanley is at left. Chicago won 3-2.

CAGO BLACK HAWKS

In 1961 the Chicago Black Hawks won the Stanley Cup, a feat which would have been considered impossible only a few short years before for a team from the Windy City. Throughout most of the previous decade, the Black Hawks had been the perennial cellar dweller of the NHL. From 1947 to 1957 the team finished last every season, except for 1952-53, when they grabbed fourth spot.

During those dark days, Chicago had its fair share of offensive talent — Bill Mosienko, Harry Watson, and Ed Litzenberger. The problems lay in the club's inability to keep the opposition off the scoreboard. In the late 1950s, the club was doing so poorly and attracting so few fans that the franchise was in danger of folding. League governors came up with a kind of "Marshall Plan" for Chicago whereby the other teams contributed talent to help bolster the Black Hawks. The problems evident in Chicago made it an unwelcome destination for players, some of whom referred to it as the "Siberia of the NHL". In fact those who participated in the attempt to establish a players' association, like Ted Lindsay, Tod Sloan and Jim Thomson, were punished by being dealt to Chicago.

Tommy Ivan, formerly of the Red Wings, was hired to manage the team in 1954. He implemented a farm system to develop the young talent needed to bring the team out of the doldrums. It produced Pierre Pilote and Elmer Vasko, both of whom anchored a solid defence in front of a goaltender acquired from Detroit, Glenn Hall. Then came Bobby Hull and Stan Mikita, two of the greatest offensive threats in NHL history. Others such as Ken Wharram and Red Hay came up through the farm system. The established players and the new talent combined under the guidance of coach Rudy Pilous to become champions in 1961.

From that time on, the Black Hawks remained contenders. They never again slipped into the ignominy they once knew, making the play-offs each season and going to the finals twice. Chicago remained a strong club after expansion. Stanley Cup finalists two times in the early 1970s, the club has not repeated that accomplishment since.

Earl Balfour
Chicago Black Hawks

(b. 1933, Toronto, Ont.)
Games played 288
Goals 30
Assists 22
Total points 52
Penalties in Minutes 78

Earl Balfour

A product of the Maple Leafs' organization in Toronto, Earl Balfour found himself bouncing between the parent club and its farm league affiliates in Pittsburgh and Rochester until he was traded to Chicago in 1958. He was used primarily as a penalty killer with the Black Hawks. "I just killed penalties," he remarks. "It was Rudy Pilous' idea. He sort of kept a couple of guys just to do that and it worked."

Balfour was fortunate enough to be part of Chicago's Stanley Cup squad in 1961. He wasn't originally enthused about being shifted to the Windy City or leaving Toronto, his native city. The steady improvement of the team made the transition much smoother. "It made it a lot easier to play for a good team," he adds, commenting on his good fortune. "The best thing that can happen to anybody who plays pro sports is to get with a good team. You're in a happier frame of mind, the season goes faster, everything goes better if you're with a winning team. When you're losing it's no fun. When you're winning it's fun."

Balfour was traded to the Bruins during the season following the Hawks' championship drive and found himself back in the minors. He played one more season and decided the situation was too difficult for his family which was growing by leaps and bounds. The children numbered nine in the Balfour household. "That was my scoring championship," he quips. "I was the highest-scoring Protestant in the league. That's what they used to tell me, anyway."

Balfour retired and since then has been involved in "more or less sales jobs". Today, he is a sales representative for St. Helene's Seafood in the Toronto area.

Murray Balfour
Chicago Black Hawks

(b. 1936, Victoria, B.C.)
Games played 306
Goals 67
Assists 90
Total points 157
Penalties in Minutes 391

If the death of an individual at the peak of his career, still in his youth, can be considered tragic, then the story of Murray Balfour is the ultimate tragedy.

Born in Victoria, Balfour moved to Regina at the age of ten. It was then he began playing hockey in the minor leagues of that city. From that early age, he dreamt and practised diligently to realize his goal, to play in the NHL.

Balfour left the Regina Pats junior organization to play with a Hull-Ottawa team sponsored by Montreal and coached by Sam Pollock. He graduated to the parent club in 1956 but was unable to crack the star-filled squad. As a result he plied his skills with farm teams.

A break came in 1959 when Chicago purchased his contract. He won a place on the Black Hawk roster with his aggressive play. His ability to dig and control the corners made him a valuable asset to the club in general and to his linemates Red Hay and Bobby Hull on what was dubbed the "Million Dollar Line".

"He enjoyed the rough going," Hay recalls. "He was very aggressive, strong and not afraid to fight, but not mean. He often played with injuries which would keep a normal player on the sidelines. Murray was a kind, honest, clean-living athlete, a non-smoker and non-drinker. Because of his size and toughness he did have a lot of fun. He enjoyed life and had a lot of good friends." He had a love for young people and children's Christmas and birthday parties were special to him. Balfour played a significant role in the Black Hawks' 1961 Stanley Cup victory when he scored five goals and had five assists in 11 play-off games, including the winning marker in the third overtime period of the third game in the finals. Chicago won the game 2-1.

Balfour was traded to Boston in 1964. That season, while recovering from a broken arm with the Bruins' Hershey farm team, he was diagnosed as having lung cancer. The killer disease spread quickly and Balfour died in 1965 at the age of 30.

His teammate and friend since childhood, Hay says about Balfour, "I remember the happy times we had together during our career, the wins more than the losses and the closeness of a good pal. All his teammates remember him in the same light and continue to bring up his name during hockey discussions of the old days."

Hank Ciesla

Chicago Black Hawks

(b. 1934, St. Catharines, Ont.)
Games played 269
Goals 26
Assists 51
Total points 77
Penalties in Minutes 87

Hank Ciesla

Hank Ciesla spent four seasons in the NHL from 1955 to 1959, the first two with Chicago and the final two with New York. A native of St. Catharines, Ontario, he played minor hockey in that town and eventually played junior with the St. Catharines Teepees. Not only did he help his club to a Memorial Cup, but he also garnered awards as the top scorer and the most outstanding on the junior circuit.

More of a skater than the hitter Chicago hoped he could become, Ciesla was traded to New York. Before starting his third season with them, fed up with the antics of coach Phil Watson, he chose to quit. He sat out until Toronto picked him up and put him into their Rochester farm club. Just when the Leafs were about to bring him up, he got hurt. They brought up Pat Hannigan instead and Ciesla missed his last opportunity to return to the NHL.

Ciesla continued in the minors as a player-coach with Cleveland. Eventually he quit and returned to St. Catharines where he and a partner operated a Massey-Ferguson dealership. His widow Jessie Ciesla figures it was his deteriorating health that led him to quit hockey. "It wasn't too long after that that he did take sick. His nerves seemed to give out. From there, after that, he ended up with stomach cancer." Hank Ciesla died in April, 1976 at the age of 39. He is survived by his wife and a daughter.

Phil Esposito

Chicago Black Hawks

(b. 1942, Sault Ste. Marie, Ont.)
Games played 1282
Goals 717
Assists 873
Total points 1590
Penalties in Minutes 910

The expression "wearing many hats" is often applied to all the different interests and activities someone pursues. In this case, Phil Esposito can be considered the Madhatter of Manhattan because of all the enterprises in which he is now involved.

Esposito's inventory of undertakings begins with the television work the former star centre does with the Madison Square Garden Network. He works for and has an interest in a Canadian company, Dynacharge, that sells rechargeable batteries. He also does public relations work for an apparel firm for which he has started to design his own line of "active wear".

One of Esposito's most recent businesses concerns the marketing of "astro-ice", a polymer-based surface that replicates the texture of ice to the point where one can skate on it. Optimistic and confident, the most prolific goal-scoring centre in hockey declares the surface as good as, if not better than, the standard artificial ice of indoor rinks. Citing the product's relatively inexpensive cost and its easy maintenance, he is convinced it will one day become as dominant in rinks as astro-turf is on football and baseball fields. "It will revolutionize ice-skating in the world," states the man who was once so disgusted with the quality of the ice in one NHL arena that he suggested the people in charge of the plant wouldn't know how to make ice cubes. "Mark my words. I may not do it now, I may not do it tomorrow, but astro-turf didn't either." Espo is laying down the surface in the basement of his new home in New York to privately tutor skating, stickhandling and shooting.

The accomplishments of Esposito in his 18-season career in the NHL are well known. He began with Chicago in 1963 and later became part of a pair of blockbuster deals that sent him first to Boston and then to the New York Rangers. In the end, he had scored 717 goals, 1,590 points, won the Hart Trophy twice and the Art Ross Trophy five times. The leadership he provided for Team Canada in 1972 made him a hero of that series. His name festoons the NHL record book. The Great Gretzky sets new marks of achievement with each passing game, but Esposito accepts that "records are made to be broken" and finds solace in the knowledge that he was the first to establish those levels of excellence.

Adroitly applying the popularity and marketability he earned through his successful career, Esposito has time to dabble in a very worthwhile "hobby". The Phil Esposito Foundation is an organization that assists former professional athletes by offering financial assistance, counselling and drug and alcohol rehabilitation programs. Hundreds of ex-athletes not as fortunate as himself have been helped by it. "It's my way of giving something back to the game," he says.

Reggie Fleming

Chicago Black Hawks

(b. 1936, Montreal, Que.)
Games played 749
Goals 108
Assists 132
Total points 240
Penalties in Minutes 1468

Reg Fleming

"Requiem for Reggie" was the title of an article about a rambunctious ex-NHLer in the throes of retirement, pathetically attempting to come to terms with the inevitable end of his athletic career. Powerfully written by Earl McRae, the article became part of a compendium of stories about a number of athletes. The Reggie in this story was one of the toughest scrappers the game of hockey has ever known, Reggie Fleming.

Today, eight years after that book was published, Fleming regrets having ever taken part in that interview. A paragon of a sports era that commanded loyalty to one's benefactors, he feels wronged and is leary about becoming the subject of another article.

Sounding more hurt than angry, Fleming complains, "Instead of writing about what the guys are doing today businesswise and how they're getting along in this world, here he's writing about me playing hockey, fighting, about me driving him to the thing [an industrial league hockey game which Fleming says he played only to stay in shape] at 70 miles an hour."

"I mean what gave Mr. McRae the right to make a judgement on someone he doesn't even know who put himself out for him and tried to make it easy for him," Fleming continues. "If you're going to write something bad make sure you try and write something good about the person. There's got to be something good about me. Ask Mr.

McRae if he could come back to Chicago and look me up again and look me straight in the eye."

Though Fleming, a left winger with Montreal, Chicago, Boston and New York in the six-team era, did not like being portrayed as an aging athlete who did not know when to quit, he does admit leaving a sport one has pursued since childhood is no easy feat for a man in his thirties. "It is difficult to get away from it," he concedes. "I find that most hockey players today have difficulty accepting that they are through playing and finding decent jobs. It's not easy going to a nine to five job where before you only worked for an hour and a half. I don't think a lot of us are prepared for things like that."

"I could accept it," Fleming maintains. "I could always find a job and work. But I was never going to make the kind of money I did when I was playing hockey because of the education that I got. That doesn't mean that hockey was all my life. It's not the same. It's a different system that we've got to get accustomed to."

Following his final fling with the professional game, a tryout with the Quebec Nordiques (WHA) at their 1974 training camp, Fleming, like so many other players, hoped to hold on to his niche in the hockey world by scouting or even coaching at some minor league level. Instead he found himself on the outside looking in. "Nobody wanted me and all that. So I said, 'that's it.' The writing is on the wall; you've got to quit." He explains, "Nobody came and offered me a scouting job or a coaching job." Why does he think he fell out of the hockey fraternity? He guesses, "Maybe because I jumped to the World Hockey league . . . who knows?"

After retirement Fleming acted as sales representative for a brewery in Chicago. He did that, he elaborates, until he could find something he really wanted to do. Opportunity knocked five years ago. "When I was selling Stroh's beer a gentleman approached me and asked me if I liked to make some extra money, which I did, selling these ad specialties," he remembers. "Then I decided to go out on my own." Today his firm, R.F. Industries, deals in promotional items such as pens, T-shirts, baseball caps and jackets.

He is, as he puts it, doing well enough to keep bread and butter on the table. Generally speaking he says, "I'm healthy. I might be a little overweight, but that comes from not exercising." His community project is sitting on a fund-raising committee concerned with the welfare of wards of the courts.

He comments on his policeman's role in the NHL, "One thing I learned was that you play. You play hard. You play to win. Nobody likes losers. Nobody remembers losers." Fleming is still recognized on Michigan Avenue by older Black Hawk fans. What do they remember best? "They all remember the fights," he laughs. "Nobody remembers the goals I scored."

Lee Fogolin (Sr.)

Chicago Black Hawks

(b. 1926, Fort William, Ont.)
Games played 427
Goals 10
Assists 48
Total points 58
Penalties in Minutes 575

Lee Fogolin

How does a former hockey player who has his name etched on Lord Stanley's trophy react watching his son striving for the honour? "In all my years of hockey I never worked myself into such a frenzy," says Lee Fogolin Senior, father of the Edmonton Oiler defenceman and an ex-rearguard who was part of Detroit's championship effort in 1950. "I wanted to see him win a Stanley Cup. The ultimate thing of your career is winning the Stanley Cup and getting your name on it."

Fogolin began a seven-year tenure in the NHL with the Red Wings in 1948. Later he was traded to Chicago. He was known as a steady, stay-at-home defenceman with a passion for body checking. One of his crunches gave then-rookie Dean Prentice a rude welcoming to the league and a spot on the sidelines for a month. "He passed the puck and made the fatal mistake of admiring the beautiful pass he made," he recalls. "I was right inside our blueline. I took one step. I used to hit with the shoulder . . . and I can still remember . . . I was scared really. I caught him with my shoulder in the breastbone and down he went. I said, 'Omigod. I think I killed him.' "

In those days, Fogolin says, an offensive-minded defenceman was usually paired with a defensive-oriented rearguard. "They always teamed a hitting defenceman with a rushing defenceman," he explains. A mobile, high-scoring sort in amateur hockey, in one of his first games as a Red Wing, he raced the length of the ice for a shot on net. With the pride of accomplishment still welling up inside the novice pro, Jack Adams took him aside and said, "Listen, kid, I got enough fancy pants on this team. I need guys who'll stay back there and hit 'em." He got the message.

Fogolin broke his elbow twice early in the 1957 season, injuries that led to the end of his career. He decided to return to his hometown of Thunder Bay, Ontario after a season in the minor leagues as a playing coach. There he got involved in the automobile and service station business. His recent retirement lasted all of three months. "I went nuts," he declares. Lately he has been working as a coordinator with a steel firm.

The only very slight regret that the elder Fogolin expresses about his involvement with the game was that he didn't continue coaching in the minors and wait for a job with one of the major league clubs. "I loved it very much. I loved hockey. I was a student of the game. I like people. I felt I could communicate and put my ideas across about hockey."

Glenn Hall

Chicago Black Hawks

(b. 1931, Humbolt, Sask.)
Games played 906
Minutes 53,484
Goals against 2239
Shutouts 84
Average 2.51

A long, distinctive career as a goaltender for the Chicago Black Hawks earned Glenn Hall accolades, awards and a badge of distinction: the nickname Mr. Goalie. Now the name is a sign of a time for him. If someone calls out just "Hey, Goo!" from behind, "I can pretty well tell if he's from the old school," he jokes.

Hall had graduated to the Red Wings in 1955 after playing for their sponsored teams in his native Saskatchewan and on minor league clubs in Indianapolis and Edmonton. His performance was impressive. He led the league with 12 shutouts and earned the Calder Trophy as the NHL's top rookie that year. After his second season when he led the league with 38 victories, he was traded to Chicago by Jack Adams. "Adams said he let me go to Chicago as a favour to Chicago. It wasn't. He just didn't think I could play in the league," Hall says about the man he considers "one of the really stupid people in hockey."

Hall went to Chicago and became an important part of their rebuilding process that culminated in a Stanley Cup in 1961. He won or shared the Vezina Trophy three times, was selected an all-star 11 times, won the Conn Smythe Trophy in 1967-68 and was inducted into the Hall of Fame in 1975. The man who introduced the "butterfly" style of goaltending once played 552 consecutive games in the nets, almost eight consecutive seasons.

"It might have been a little much," Hall says about a workload that seems incredible in light of today's game. He remains, however, a strong proponent of the one goalie system. If a goalie is playing well he should be kept in. If not, take him out, he states. "I believe it should be this way. If I don't play well, then I shouldn't play. As for being taken out of the lineup for a stupid thing like a rest, give me more practice time," he laughs.

Hall went to St. Louis in 1967 and played four seasons there before leaving hockey. "When I was 35 years old, I said to myself, 'The game's only meant to be played one way and that's played well,' and it became more and more difficult to play well," he explains.

People tend to remember a player's idiosyncrasies long after retirement and Hall's unforgettable habit was throwing up before games because of nerves. "I think I did something better," he says jokingly. "When I got sick there weren't any peas and carrots in it. I just took a glass of water, walked in, threw it up in the bathroom and said, 'Let's go!' I didn't feel right if I didn't get sick." In his opinion you won't get a good game out of someone who is relaxed before the battle. "Give me a hyper goalie anytime!"

Other factors besides ability were behind Hall inhabiting the most tension-filled position in athletics for so long. "The money was there and I couldn't do anything else," he explains. "I would look for a job and they'd say they were looking for full time. They'd say, 'Come back when you retire and we're looking for full time.' So I came back after I retired and said I was prepared to work full time and they said, 'Oh, we're looking for part time now.' You realized they weren't really interested in you. You realized you were limited because all you knew was how to stop the puck." Once he was offered work as a Jiffy truck driver. "I didn't want to become the best Jiffy truck driver in the country." He went back to being the best goalie in the country.

The transition from active player to retirement was an easy one, Hall feels. "Most players find the first year very difficult. Most goalkeepers don't." He lives on a farm on which he used to grow wheat and raise cattle but now rents out. Although semi-retired, he occasionally acts as a scout for Calgary. He also travels to Calgary several times in a season to help coach the goaltenders. That association with the sport and its young adherents is something he relishes. "You can bullshit them a little bit and they enjoy it," he jokes. "They really don't know how to act, they're so damn young. When we were young, the older guys told us what to do and we carried their bags, but now it's such a hectic pace, the kids don't know what's expected of them. I really like kids. You hear so many bad things about kids. But, boy, in my opinion, these kids in Calgary are quality. Maybe these kids are an exception in the league but I don't think they are."

Red Hay

Chicago Black Hawks

(b. 1935, Saskatoon, Sask.)
Games played 506
Goals 113
Assists 273
Total points 386
Penalties in Minutes 244

Bill Hay

As a senior vice-president with Bow Valley Resource Services Ltd., Bill "Red" Hay is responsible for the operation of land rigs in North America and Indonesia, and semi-submersible drilling rigs and six supply vessels working off-shore in eastern Canada. He can often be found jetting to these places and others throughout the world as part of his work.

In 1959 Hay stepped into the league in the livery of the Chicago Black Hawks, one of the first to make the transition from university hockey into the NHL. "I played two years junior hockey with the Regina Pats and after strong persuasion from my father, Charles Hay [a builder in the NHL Hall of Fame] and my junior coach, Murray Armstrong, I decided to go to college," he recalls.

After two years at the University of Saskatchewan, Hay attended Colorado College in Colorado Springs, Colorado for three years. He graduated from that school with a Bachelor of Science in geology. The university education, he adds, was more than a degree in the bank if a professional hockey career did not work out. "I don't consider an education as something to fall back on; it is an instrument which gives one the opportunity to learn as he moves along in a job, the same as skills possessed by an athlete."

After graduating, Hay attended the Canadiens' training camp where the novelty of a player armed with a stick and a degree hadn't gone unnoticed. "A college graduate was new to the league and they looked at me differently in the beginning," he says. He was dispatched to the Calgary Stampeders of the WHL and at season's end the Black Hawks purchased his contract from the Canadiens for $25,000.

Hay sufficiently impressed critics in his rookie season of play to earn the Calder Trophy. He went on to spend eight productive seasons with the Black Hawks. The centreman was flanked by Murray Balfour and Bobby Hull, a trio that Rudy Pilous dubbed the "Million Dollar Line". "The line worked well because it consisted of Murray Balfour, a strong player who worked the corners, a playmaker and a goal scorer [Bobby Hull], all of whom got along well together and were unselfish." The line contributed significantly to the Black Hawks' drive for a Stanley Cup in 1961.

When the NHL expanded, Hay decided to retire at the age of 32. "I knew I'd end up playing as long as I could. I had a job with a good, young, growing company and wanted to raise my family in Calgary." Many felt his departure was premature and St. Louis attempted to lure him back. "I never considered playing with St. Louis as I had given Chicago my word that I was retiring and told them to leave me unprotected in the draft."

The transition out of hockey was a difficult one, Hay explains, "especially when you knew you could still play and most of the people in the centre expect you to return to hockey." Realizing a long time before he retired that hockey would be seasonal and temporary, he had spent his summers working for Esso Resources in the exploration research department. Through this work, he gained experience for the job he acquired following retirement.

Hay still enjoys an association with the game through Hockey Canada, Canada's Olympic team, the Olympic Saddledome (the arena in which hockey games will be played during the 1988 Olympics in Calgary), and committees he sits on with the NHL.

Bobby Hull

Chicago Black Hawks

(b. 1939, Point Anne, Ont.)
Games played 1063
Goals 610
Assists 560
Total points 1170
Penalties in Minutes 640

Million. Golden Jet. The hardest shot. The fastest skater. The strongest player. The life of Bobby Hull as a hockey player has always been couched in terms of the superlative.

The native of Point Anne, Ontario donned a Black Hawks' uniform for the first time in 1957 and in very short order was performing feats that dazzled the fans and catapulted him into the company of superstars: the effortless swift swoop up-ice, the charge for the net holding puck and stick in one hand and fending off defenders with the other, the quick, accurate wrist shot, that booming, deadly and legendary slapshot. With all his verve, dash and awesome power on the ice, he earned the nickname the "Golden Jet".

Million was first used in association with Hull's name when he, Red Hay and Murray Balfour formed a high-scoring unit that Rudy Pilous called the Million Dollar Line. Pilous claimed he would not accept even that enormous sum of money for them. Over a decade later, Hull signed a million dollar contract with the Winnipeg Jets of the newly-formed WHA. It gave him instant security and the WHA instant credibility for having grabbed one of the game's top drawing cards.

Hull's accomplishments and awards are numerous. He was the first player to break the 50-goal barrier. He reached or surpassed that magic level five times. He still holds the record for the most consecutive 30 or more goal seasons — 13. The silverware that has visited his trophy case includes the Hart Trophy (1965, 1966), the Art Ross Trophy (1960, 1962, 1966) and the Lady Byng (1966). He was on one Stanley Cup winner with Chicago in 1961.

Hull retired from hockey in 1980 after playing a few final games with the Hartford Whalers. In a recent interview published in *The Toronto Star*, he said he wasn't sorry to leave the game. "I'm involved in the cattle business and spend a great deal of time with polled Herefords from the East Coast to the West Coast and in both the United States and Canada," he said. "I'm also involved in the promotional end of agriculture with a company which, among other things, makes flytags for cattle that prevent faceflies and hornflies."

Hull has offered his opinions on hockey over the years. He has been particularly vocal about violence in hockey. In 1984 he moved back to Chicago from his home in Demorestville, Ontario. After his return, he commented on the quality of play in pro hockey today. "With ticket prices what they are today, our fans should be royally entertained. But I'm afraid they're not. Today's hockey players are bigger and stronger than ever; they skate faster and shoot harder than ever. But I'm afraid they only do it when they feel like it."

The Black Hawks honoured their former great left winger recently by retiring his number nine jersey in a ceremony. It was then he expressed probably his only regret concerning hockey. He said the biggest mistake he ever made was leaving Chicago for the WHA.

Ed Litzenberger

Chicago Black Hawks

(b. 1932, Neudorf, Sask.)
Games played 618
Goals 178
Assists 238
Total points 416
Penalties in Minutes 283

Ed Litzenberger had a choice when it came to hockey. "I was supposed to be an engineer. I went down to the University of Denver in Colorado and registered," the rangy, ex-forward recalls. "Then I went to the Montreal training camp and they offered me a contract and I kind of forsook my college degree."

"It was a matter of growing up," Litzenberger says, explaining the decision to stay in professional hockey. "When you're a big fish in a little pond and all of a sudden you're a little fish and there's an awful lot of big fish, you become confused. I found out in a week that I had grown up and that I was not only good but better than most of the guys." Litzenberger certainly never looked out of place playing with Beliveau, Geoffrion, Richard and company.

In 1955 he was told he had been traded to the then lowly Chicago Black Hawks as part of the league's "Help the Hawks Plan". Only the night before, he had scored the winning goal for the Habs in an important game. "I cried real tears," he comments. "You become a little bit of an instrument but I look back with affection. It [hockey] gave me a chance to learn what it [life] was all about." He played with distinction in Chicago and was a factor in the club's resurgence and drive to the Stanley Cup in 1961.

Litzenberger was later traded to Detroit and Toronto where he shared in another Stanley Cup, the fourth of his career. The Maple Leafs sent him to Rochester in 1964 where he contributed to two more championship efforts before retiring to become a stock broker. "I thought it was time to quit," he says, citing a desire to see his kids grow up. He had made a promise to himself to retire before he was injured and wanted to leave the game before he was ushered out of it by someone else.

Litzenberger lives with his family in Toronto where he and his brother have a company they are just beginning. Because of a hand problem, he no longer plays old-timers' hockey though he continues to get together with his former teammates. He is still recognized by hockey fans, he says. "I think probably the one thing that delights me more than anything is that they never really knew me as anything except a gentleman."

Al MacNeil
Chicago Black Hawks

(b. 1935, Sydney, N.S.)
Games played 524
Goals 17
Assists 75
Total points 92
Penalties in Minutes 617

Al MacNeil retired as an active player from the Pittsburgh Penguins in 1968. A journeyman defender "who was more defensive-minded and did a lot of work around the corners," he quit 11 years after his first taste of professional hockey. "My back was a little bit of a problem to me and I wasn't enjoying it as much as I liked," he explains. "I figured maybe it was about time I cut bait and did something that I always had a leaning towards — coaching."

MacNeil was brought into the Maple Leaf system as a junior. He joined Toronto in 1955 and spent most of the next five seasons playing in the minors. Montreal acquired him in a trade in 1960 and two years later he went to Chicago where he established himself as a regular. In 1966 the Rangers obtained him in a draft. The following season, his last, was spent with the Penguins.

The coaching game for MacNeil began, as it does for most, in the minor leagues. He eventually joined the Montreal organization in Houston with a club that became the Montreal Voyageurs. That position led to an assistant coaching job with the Montreal Canadiens. Partway through the 1970-71 season, he took over as head coach from Claude Ruel. Though his club won the Stanley Cup, he was openly criticized by veteran centre Henri Richard. "There was a lot of turmoil connected with it," he says of the situation at the time. "You look back on it now and you would have liked to go a little bit farther with it, but at the time it looked like it was going to be basically a dead-end street. It wasn't for Al MacNeil."

MacNeil remained in Montreal's organization as the coach and general manager of its AHL farm team, the Nova Scotia Voyageurs, a homecoming for the Sydney, Nova Scotia native.

After six seasons with the Voyageurs MacNeil came back to the Canadiens as the director of player personnel and stayed for two years. When the club's ownership changed he moved to the Atlanta Flames as the coach. Except for his third and final year behind the Atlanta/Calgary bench, 1981-82, MacNeil posted a winning record as a coach. Today he is the assistant manager for the Flames. Some of his duties in his administrative capacity include taking care of players' contracts and monitoring the progress of younger players in the organization.

The decision to remain in hockey was easy for him to make. He explains, "I stuck in hockey because it's what I did best. Hockey was something I knew all my life and I felt I could contribute and make some kind of personal impact."

Chico Maki

Chicago Black Hawks

(b. 1939, Sault Ste. Marie, Ont.)
Games played 841
Goals 143
Assists 292
Total points 435
Penalties in Minutes 345

Chico Maki

"How do you find something to replace it?" Chico Maki wonders about professional hockey. He spent 13 seasons as a forward with the Chicago Black Hawks. Every game, regular season or play-off, he felt the adrenalin start flowing in response to the unrelenting pressure to perform, to win. "I loved the pressure," he says. "Nothing has ever given me that kind of pressure off the ice."

Maki spent many of those years on Bobby Hull's right flank acting more or less as a "trailer". A better-than-average scorer in junior hockey, he found himself in the Golden Jet's slipstream in the professional game. "He's always ahead of you so let him unload the cannon and let him shoot," he comments. When Hull's supersonic head of steam took him too deeply into enemy territory, Maki would hurry back to cover.

Maki hung up the blades in 1975. He had, he remembers, seen too many players hang on for too long, playing ineffectively and being booed whenever they stepped on the ice. He could leave at that point with dignity and not, as he puts it, "suck the kettle dry". The travelling was becoming a grind, the kids were growing, it was time to "call it a day".

In about 1962, Maki started farming around Tillsonburg, Ontario in the off-season. At one point he worked 300 acres, growing cash crops and raising livestock. After retiring from hockey, he came back to the farm. It kept him busy enough not to have to worry about hockey withdrawal. He sold that operation a couple of years ago and bought a motel. With its two bars, restaurant and rooms, it proved too much to handle. "We decided we'd better get out," he states. Since then he has been "looking around for something else, something where you can make a nice, easy living. You want to find something you really like to do."

Frank Martin
Chicago Black Hawks

(b. 1933, Cayuga, Ont.)
Games played 282
Goals 11
Assists 46
Total points 57
Penalties in Minutes 122

Frank Martin played in the National Hockey League from 1952 to 1957 with Boston and Chicago. A versatile junior hockey player in his native St. Catharines, Ontario, he played defence as well as forward. After he was brought into the NHL by the Bruins, he became a defenceman.

Martin had the unusual choice of attempting a career in pro hockey or in pro baseball when he was invited to attend the Brooklyn Dodgers' training camp at Vero Beach, Florida. He assessed the two possibilities and decided that the chances of a Canadian breaking into baseball's major leagues were tiny compared to his chances in professional hockey.

Martin played extremely well until halfway through his first full season with the Bruins. Then, "things went kind of a little flat for me." He was traded to Chicago the following season, a decision both he and management agreed on. "If I had've stayed there [Boston], as I got a little more seniority, who knows what could've happened?" he speculates. Perhaps, Martin feels, he might have developed into a better player.

Martin put in three seasons with the Black Hawks. Finally "things started to really fall apart" in terms of his playing. "I really couldn't put my finger on what was going on," he says. He was sent down to the minors. "I knew when I went there, I wouldn't be coming back." He played in Buffalo and Quebec until 1965 when he decided to retire from the game. "I had come to the point where I was ready to call it a day," he states.

Martin had picked up carpentry as a trade while he was playing and after retirement got into the home improvement business. He was later hired by the City of St. Catharines as a maintenance man and has been there for the last 13 years.

If he had it all to do over again, Martin admits that he would take better advantage of the career possibilities the sport offered. "I treated it pretty lightly," he says of his time in the NHL. "I was pretty frivolous about it." He might have taken a greater interest in pursuing an education because in hindsight, "it would have made a big difference" in terms of post-hockey employment. He points to some of his former junior teammates who put in over 30 years with the local firm that sponsored their club. Some have good-paying jobs while others have accepted early-retirement incentives. Though the professional hockey experience was a good one, he wonders how things would have turned out if he had taken a job over the hockey route.

Martin, now 52, spends his leisure time golfing, fishing and puttering around the garden. It is in middle age, he notes, that one experiences the final legacy of a hockey career. The various bruises, abrasions and broken bones suffered in countless games are beginning to crop up now, he adds, lightly complaining about the stiffness, aches and pains that have become a daily experience.

Ab McDonald
Chicago Black Hawks

(b. 1936, Winnipeg, Man.)
Games played 762
Goals 182
Assists 248
Total points 430
Penalties in Minutes 200

Ab McDonald never did fill the void created on Montreal's left wing by the departure of Bert Olmstead as was the expectation when he arrived on the scene in 1957. While the fans who booed him in the Forum never thought the tall, lean lad from Winnipeg would add up to much, McDonald went on to Chicago where three years later he became part of the original Scooter Line, one of the game's most prolific combinations.

McDonald finally retired from hockey in 1974 after stints in Montreal, Chicago, Boston, Detroit, Pittsburgh, St. Louis and Winnipeg of the World Hockey Association. Since then he has been operating a rent-all business in his hometown. Over the last five or six years he has also been acting as a part-time scout for St. Louis.

Few injuries and his joy when playing are the factors to which McDonald attributes his lengthy career. When the extensive travelling of the modern game made his experiences less enjoyable, he retired. During his time in the NHL he shared in three consecutive Stanley Cup victories from 1957-58 to 1960-61, the first two with the Canadiens and the third with the Black Hawks.

A photograph on the wall of Winnipeg Stadium immortalizes McDonald and his contribution to the game. It shows him taking the first face-off for the fledgling Winnipeg Jets, then of the WHA. He also notched the first regular-season goal for that franchise.

John McIntyre

Chicago Black Hawks

(b. 1930, Brussells, Ont.)
Games played 499
Goals 109
Assists 102
Total points 211
Penalties in Minutes 173

Jack McIntyre

Once, when he was playing with the Detroit Red Wings, Jack McIntyre and his family were featured on page one of *The Detroit Free Press*. "It was the first Christmas I spent with my family in nine years," says McIntyre, explaining how one of the vagaries of the lives of professional hockey players came to light.

Kicking over the good old days, McIntyre recalls another time when he was part of a multi-player trade between Detroit and Chicago. One of the difficulties associated with getting traded was finding adequate housing for a growing family. Fortunately, he recalls, one of the in-coming players was Lorne Ferguson and they addressed their housing needs by swapping houses.

McIntyre spent ten years in the NHL and saw service with Boston, Chicago and Detroit. A defensive-minded left winger, he now thinks he could have been even more of a defensive player. He scored an important goal in the 1953 semi-finals to help the underdog Bruins upset the heavily favoured Red Wings in six games. In 1960 his NHL career ended and he played in the minor leagues for another four seasons. For a time it looked as though he might join the coaching and managerial ranks of the game in Indianapolis. When that opportunity failed to materialize, he decided to "pack it in".

McIntyre returned to his native Listowel in southern Ontario where he operated a laundromat. He played and coached senior hockey in Guelph. Later he coached the London Knights of the Ontario Major Junior A League, followed by a period as coach and general manager of Johnstown of the International Hockey League. Though he says he enjoyed the experience he felt that "it was too much" and he returned home to run a hockey school which he did for eight years.

Since that time McIntyre has sold cars for East Town Chev-Olds in London, Ontario. He has established himself as one of the top GM salespeople over the last four or five years.

Stan Mikita

Chicago Black Hawks

(b. 1940, Skolce, Czechoslovakia)
Games played 1394
Goals 541
Assists 926
Total points 1467
Penalties in Minutes 1270

Stan Mikita

"Not bad for a poor little D.P.," joked Chicago Black Hawk Stan Mikita when he accepted the Hart, Art Ross and Lady Byng Trophies in 1967, a feat never before accomplished. He was referring to his immigration to Canada from his native Czechoslovakia at the age of eight. "The little D.P." went on to become one of the best centres in NHL history.

"That's all part of the game," he comments about awards. "When you look back on things like that, when you see your name on some of those things, you say to yourself, maybe you did accomplish a few things. At the time I never thought of trophies too much. I thought it was part of the job and if you were a little better than somebody else one year then you were rewarded by it."

Mikita swept the three trophies again the following season. On two other occasions he won the Art Ross Trophy for leading the league in scoring. He wishes however that he could have shared in more than one Stanley Cup. The Black Hawks won in 1961 and came close a number of times in the 1960s and 1970s only to lose in the finals.

Mikita played his minor hockey in St. Catharines, Ontario and moved up to the Black Hawks to stay in 1959. "The first time I stepped on the ice I faced off against Beliveau," he remembers. "That was kind of a scary experience." Who won the draw? "I did." he says. "When you win, you don't forget."

Reflecting on what made him such an effective player, he comments, "I was never overwhelmed with my ability. I thought I had to work quite a bit at it. If you ask a guy how many things he can do, today a guy'll tell you he can do 40 things perfectly. I always thought I could do two things well—I could pass the puck and I could take the face-off. I thought I was better than anybody else in that respect. Maybe I wasn't but I thought that to myself. I had that much confidence in it. I was decent or good or better than somebody else in two things."

Mikita retired in 1980 when "the mind and the body were still saying, 'Yeah, you could go a little further,' but the legs were saying 'We can't really carry you as much as we used to.' " It also took a hell of a lot longer to come back from injuries, he adds. He left hockey and immediately began a new career as a golf pro at the Kemper Lakes golf course near Chicago. Working a golf pro's long hours didn't give him much of a chance to think about anything, not even missing hockey.

Mikita shared in the birth of a unique hockey school in Chicago that is now in its twelfth year. "A friend of mine [Irv Tiahnykbik] has a son who is hearing impaired. The kid liked to skate and play hockey so we used to bring him down to the stadium with us and I used to skate with him after our practices. The kid wanted to be a goalie so Glenn Hall also worked with him. The kid finally got on some teams as he got older and being involved in sports and especially hockey really changed his personality. [Hearing impaired people] as kids get withdrawn and they're very shy individuals. This kind of brought him out of his shell, hockey did." If playing hockey did this for one child, it could do the same for millions of other hearing impaired children throughout the country.

Mikita and Tiahnykbik collaborated to start a hockey school for hearing impaired children. Last year over 70 youngsters attended the week-long session. In terms of both the enjoyment he and fellow instructors derive from their participation and the improvement in the kids' lives, the school, he says, has been extremely successful. "All you need is a little smile from the kid and that's where the reward is," the eight time all-star remarks.

Ron Murphy

Chicago Black Hawks

(b. 1933, Hamilton, Ont.)
Games played 889
Goals 205
Assists 274
Total points 479
Penalties in Minutes 460

Ron Murphy

"I never had it so good as I have it right now," declares Ron Murphy, former NHL forward. "It's the way life should be." He does pretty well what he likes to do when he wants to do it, fishing, hunting, holidaying in Las Vegas and the Caribbean. "You couldn't have it much better," he laughs. "I intend to keep doing it as long as I can."

Murphy retired from hockey in 1970. Acute shoulder problems gave him little choice in the matter. "I was only playing about 60 per cent. It was time to pack it in ," he explains. "I wasn't helping them [Boston] and I wasn't helping myself. The doctor said if you get hurt again we can't fix it. We've cut the tendons as short as we can get them. The tendons kept breaking off my shoulders." Warned that he could be damaged for life if he persisted in playing he replied, "You don't have to tell me twice."

So ended an 18-season NHL career for the man from Mount Hope, Ontario. He had joined the Rangers in 1952, coming from their junior affiliate, the Memorial Cup champion Guelph Biltmores. Until then, he had had no intention of turning professional. "They came to me one day and asked me if I wanted to play professional. I said 'Why not?',", he relates. In five seasons with the Rangers, he played with a number of different linemates. "The Rangers were in kind of a confusion right then," he recalls. "They shifted things around trying to get a club together. They weren't too well organized and we never had a really good hockey club, which showed in the standings."

Murphy found himself at odds with Ranger management in 1956 when New York wanted to dispatch him to the minors after an injury. "I got fed up with them," he says. "I said, 'Well, if you want to talk to me, I'll be at home.' " He walked. "I was cheesed off at the whole outfit." Later, during that summer, the Rangers called to inform him that he had been traded to Chicago, a team which had been faring even more poorly than New York. A combination of young talent developed in Chicago's system and experienced players shoved off to the Black Hawks for their involvement in the formation of a players' association turned that club into a Stanley Cup champion in 1961, he observes. Three of his seasons in Chicago were spent in combination with Tod Sloan and Eric Nesterenko. He describes them as a checking unit with "a fair amount of potential for scoring."

Trades took him to Detroit and Boston before retirement. After hockey, he returned to Mount Hope where he operated a cattle and cash crop farm. With some partners he constructed townhouses in Hagarsville, Ontario. Eventually he rented the farm, moved to Hagarsville and bought a hotel there that he named, quite appropriately, Murph's Place. "Yeah," he drawls, "I got a little bit going here. It's kind of interesting." The hotel, he says, is a good business. Having hired a manager, he has the time to spend his summers salmon fishing in Lake Erie and travelling in the winters.

Murphy tried his hand at coaching junior hockey in Kitchener for a season and a half. "It wasn't what I wanted to do," he says about his last involvement with hockey.

Eric Nesterenko
Chicago Black Hawks

(b. 1933, Flin Flon, Man.)
Games played 1219
Goals 250
Assists 324
Total points 574
Penalties in Minutes 1273

In 1984 Eric Nesterenko's name appeared in Canadian newspapers, not in the sports pages as was common during the 20 seasons he played in the NHL, but in the entertainment section. That summer the former right winger with Toronto and Chicago worked as a technical advisor and bit player in a hockey movie called *Youngblood* being filmed in Toronto.

Skiing, not the silver screen, is Nesterenko's main interest these days. His involvement in the film arose from a chance meeting with the people making the film. He met them in Vail, Colorado where he now lives and works as a ski instructor. In fact they were students of his who made the offer after learning of his hockey background. It was, as he puts it, "something to do," a new challenge for a man with a slightly different outlook on life than his ex-NHL peers.

Nesterenko has been teaching skiing for the last six years. "It's a good life," he comments. "I don't make a lot of money but it's fun and it keeps me fit." He retired from the Black Hawks in 1972 after 16 seasons with the team. He moved to Switzerland where he coached hockey. Hockey, he admits, was a means of letting him stay in Europe. He would probably be there still if his wife had not insisted they return to North America. For part of one season, 1973-74, he came out of retirement to play for Los Angeles of the WHA. "That was a mistake," he asserts. "I did it for the money mainly. I realized I didn't want to play anymore."

"It was a good life for 20 years," Nesterenko maintains. "It was better than being a bank clerk. I had a good time and when it was over, it was over." The sport provided some unique advantages, he adds. "To me it was a passport to the world. When I was single I travelled the world. It gave me money and time and a sense of the world." It has also afforded him the opportunity to meet and talk with people from all walks of life. One of the people he met was Studs Terkel who, after interviewing him in a bar, used the interview in a chapter of his book *Working*.

At one time, Nesterenko assumed he would be attending the University of Michigan on a scholarship rather than joining the NHL. In fact, he was planning to take the money the Maple Leafs had been paying him "under the table" as a junior to go to university, because he "never figured he would turn pro with the Leafs." He did and he stayed for two decades. Looking back now, he thinks he should have gone to university and then become the first graduate to play in the NHL.

During his stay in Toronto while working on *Youngblood*, he participated in the Original Six Hockey Series, a tournament for ex-NHL players. "I don't mind playing no-check, adult recreational hockey, but the old-timers' thing, there's a sadness to it," Nesterenko states. "I think it's ridiculous to live in the past. I think a lot of it involves that, as far as I'm concerned. It's not for me. There's nothing wrong with it. Ironically, I enjoyed seeing the guys again. It's of another era and it's over."

Nesterenko offers this view of his life now: "I'm having a good time. My health is good. Every now and then something comes up like *Youngblood* and sort of brings me back to the game. But I don't live for that." There are other things that occupy him now. "I don't know if you've ever spent a winter in Colorado but . . ."

Pierre Pilote

Chicago Black Hawks

(b. 1931, Kenogami, Que.)
Games played 890
Goals 80
Assists 418
Total points 498
Penalties in Minutes 1251

Pierre Pilote

When Pierre Pilote played in the NHL he was mainly concerned with patrolling the blueline. Over 13 seasons, 12 of them with the Chicago Black Hawks and one with the Toronto Maple Leafs, he established himself as one of the league's premier defencemen. His record speaks for itself. He contributed 80 goals and 418 assists in 890 regular-season games. He was awarded the James Norris Trophy as the NHL's best defenceman three times from 1963 to 1965 as well as being named to the first all-star team five times and the second all-star squad three times. Pilote was the captain of the Black Hawks when they won the Stanley Cup in 1961 and in 1975 he joined the sport's immortals in the Hockey Hall of Fame.

"I didn't think I did too bad," he modestly acknowledges. "I wish I was better but I guess that's what drives you." It's hard to imagine how the versatile rearguard could have been any better.

Now it is the uncertainties of the business world that preoccupy Pilote. During his final season he invested in a small luggage firm which has since blossomed into International Travelwear Products in Scarborough. "We used to have 70 people. Now we're down to 20," he laments. "Last year we made money; two years ago we pretty near blew our brains out. Now we're back on track."

The path of business is strewn with a multitude of obstructions, one can gather from Pilote's conversation about his business. "It's getting very hard to manufacture in Canada, especially anything to do with labour-intensive products. It's best to import them," he claims. Citing the cost of labour and materials and property and business taxes, he complains that they all "make it very hard to do business."

Interestingly enough, Pilote says he never made long term plans for what he would do after he retired from hockey. "Players don't have a definite plan about what they're going to do after they retire because if you start thinking of that, then you don't dedicate yourself to hockey. It absorbs your mind. You more or less have to have a complete dedication to hockey."

As well as the luggage business Pilote owns a farm near Milton, Ontario where he raises purebred Aberdeen-Angus cattle. He calls farming "an exciting, rewarding, relaxing" pastime that "keeps you in shape".

Al Rollins
Chicago Black Hawks

(b. 1926, Vanguard, Sask.)
Games played 430
Minutes 25,717
Goals against 1196
Shutouts 28
Average 2.79

Al Rollins' entry into the NHL was associated with a famous publicity stunt perpetrated by Leaf magnate Conn Smythe. The arrival of Rollins, Smythe suggested, was meant to put pressure on Turk Broda, Toronto's chunky, regular goalie, to lose the weight his boss saw as detrimental to his play. The circumstances, however, were much more serious, Rollins points out.

Toronto acquired Rollins from Cleveland of the AHL in 1949 to bolster a goaltending situation that had deteriorated almost instantly that season. "Toronto at the time had Turk Broda. They had Baz Bastien who was probably the best goaltender in the minors. Howie Harvey [brother of Canadiens' defenceman Doug Harvey] out of St. Mike's was probably the best amateur goalkeeper of the day. They were set forever," he reports. "The first day of training camp they lose Baz Bastien [who lost an eye]. Howie Harvey was probably the first player who retired because of a skin disease — 'guck' they call it." Left with just one netminder, the Maple Leafs were forced to bring in the only available goalie, Rollins.

Serving a period of apprenticeship was the rule in the six-team era rather then the exception. "They brought me in and I spent all year just practising and travelling and watching the visiting goalkeepers," he remembers. "I always sat behind the visitors' net and watched the other goalies and, with coach Hap Day, I had to go over every goal with him, visitor and home team, what the goalie did wrong. That first year I played two games. It was a learning process. I appreciated it. If you were to do it today to a rookie, he'd be insulted."

Rollins, backstopping a great defensive club, won the Vezina Trophy in 1951. When the late Bill Barilko scored his famous overtime goal to clinch the Cup for Toronto, he was in net. In 1952 he was part of a deal that saw him go to Chicago, then one of the weak sisters in the NHL.

In Chicago Rollins had his work cut out for him. The lack of organization was evident when only 18 or 19 players attended training camp. One training camp there was only one goaltender for scrimmages. The trainer suited up to fill in at the other end. "I can remember one game in Chicago where I had more breakaways in one period than I had in three years with Toronto," he laughs. That first season he played 70 games, averaging 38 shots a game. His effort was noticed and earned him second spot behind Gordie Howe in the Hart Trophy nominations. The following year he won the league's prize for being the most valuable player.

In 1957, Rollins was sent to Chicago's farm club in Calgary when he and general manager Tommy Ivan "didn't see eye to eye". Except for a brief appearance with the Rangers in 1959, Chicago marked the end of his NHL career. He could have remained with the Rangers, he says, and he might have if the Rangers had been a great club. But at 37 years of age he was not willing to face another onslaught of rubber of the sort he had faced in previous seasons in Chicago. Three years later, when he helped Drumheller win the Allan Cup, he says "I was a better goalkeeper at 40 years than I was when I won the Vezina Trophy."

After retirement Rollins coached the University of Calgary hockey team for five years. Later he coached in Spokane, Salt Lake City, Houston, Tulsa, and Phoenix and enjoyed a good measure of success including leading Spokane to an Allan Cup in 1970. It was the first U.S.-based club ever to do so.

Rollins doubts he will ever work in the NHL. "I'm from the old era. Now it's all college-type guys. Most of them don't even know I played. I've talked to guys in the National League who don't even know I played the game, which kind of hurts, when you've reached every pinnacle of the game you can reach. The guys who are so-called experts in the game don't even know you played the game. Maybe that's why they're not successful. They don't know the history of the game — but it's changed drastically."

Today Rollins is coach and general manager of the Spokane Chiefs of the International Hockey League. He is also part owner of the Golden Steer Restaurant in that city. Given the lucrative contracts players receive these days, he wishes he had been born 30 years later with the same talent. Then again, he adds, he remembers Turk Broda telling him how lucky he was to be making $8,000. Before the war Broda had to settle for $3,500.

Fred Stanfield

Chicago Black Hawks

(b. 1944, Toronto, Ont.)
Games played 914
Goals 211
Assists 405
Total points 616
Penalties in Minutes 134

Fred Stanfield's 14-year career in the NHL began in 1964 when he broke in with Chicago and stretched well into the post-expansion era. To him, the dilution of the league's talent and competitiveness was noticeable almost immediately.

"It was a tough, tough grind," Stanfield recalled, still looking a bit too young to be a regular fixture at old-timer gatherings. "Billy Reay was the coach and he coached us the way hockey was then. It was a finesse game and all back checking. If you didn't back check and do your job, you were sitting on the bench, especially for the younger players."

Stanfield copped a share of the headlines in 1967 when he was part of the blockbuster trade that saw Chicago send him, Phil Esposito and Ken Hodge to Boston for Gilles Marotte, Jack Norris and Pit Martin. While a Bruin, he shared in a pair of Stanley Cup victories centring linemates Johnny McKenzie and John Bucyk.

"I was very appreciated in Boston," Stanfield says. "I enjoyed it there. The fans loved me. In Boston we felt like a family on and off the ice."

Following stints in Minnesota and Buffalo, the soft-spoken Stanfield found himself in Hershey of the AHL. As his professional career wound down, he adopted a philosophical point of view. "I felt that I had accomplished what I wanted to do in my career and I figured that if this was going to be my last year, instead of sitting at home and just taking the money, I'll go down there and show them I can still play hockey."

The old legs still had some zip. Stanfield not only led the team but found himself coaching it at season's end. Later he coached the Niagara Falls Flyers in the Ontario Major Junior Hockey League. "So I had a little taste of coaching," he continues, "which was good for me, especially now in my business where you have to handle people."

Today Stanfield is involved in an office furniture enterprise outside of Buffalo. "It wasn't that I opened the door and it was right there," he comments about his entry into the business. "I was involved with so many business people outside of my hockey career." Adjusting to a new life outside the game, he says, was no problem.

The only thing Stanfield would change in his long association with professional hockey is the direction, or the lack of it, provided for players in the past on financial matters. "You needed a little more guidance when we were playing. But I was fortunate. I put a little money away every year out of my contract and I'm thankful right now."

"They were not so much agents then. There were more lawyers around. But then they'd kind of take a little more than they should and things like that and take advantage of uneducated hockey players back then . . . but we all learn down the road."

Pat Stapleton
Chicago Black Hawks

(b. 1940, Sarnia, Ont.)
Games played 635
Goals 43
Assists 294
Total points 337
Penalties in Minutes 353

Pat Stapleton

A man who professes a disdain for job titles, Pat Stapleton says he carries a "roofing card" to describe his role with a new hockey development enterprise called Fundamentals In Action (FIA). "It covers everything. Get what I mean?" he quips. "You do what you have to do to make the business work, sweep the floors, shine the windows, deliver the clinics or talk to the sponsors. I can do it all."

In 1980, two seasons after Stapleton retired from professional hockey, he was asked to visit minor hockey associations in New Brunswick "so they could have a look at a National Hockey League player." While there he agreed to conduct a number of clinics. A six-day visit turned into 14 as he moved from one community to another demonstrating drills. "The New Brunswick minor hockey council asked if I could put the drills down on paper that I was doing with these kids. I said it could possibly be done. So, the long and short of it was the birth of this little project we call Fundamentals in Action.

"The main mission of the whole program is to help minor hockey establish continuity in skill development," Stapleton explains from the FIA office in Strathroy, Ontario. "It relates strictly to the fundamentals of the game." Born in the Maritimes, FIA has now spread across the nation. Ten former pro players including Stapleton conduct the clinics. Next year they will be visiting 570 minor hockey associations twice. Part of the program, he adds, involves instructors returning to an association to reinforce the program.

Stapleton has arranged for two major sponsors, Pepsi-Cola and Canadian Tire Corporation, to underwrite the costs associated with the program. The program includes a drill series and reinforces a participant's desire to continue practising hockey basics through chances to win gifts donated by various other sponsors. Asked if he has a 12-month operation he replies with a chuckle, "It's becoming a 15-month-a-year operation. It's my main occupation now. It's becoming so challenging to help kids."

Stapleton's other occupation is farming with which he has been involved since 1964. He owns a 500-acre corn, soybean and wheat farm near London, Ontario, run by two of his sons now that he is occupied with FIA.

Originally the property of the Black Hawks, he was drafted by Boston in 1961. He broke into the NHL with the Bruins in the 1961-62 season. After playing part of the next season with Boston, he was sent to the minor leagues. There he stayed until June 8, 1965 when he was traded to Toronto. Twenty-four hours later he was drafted from the Maple Leafs by Chicago. It was at that point that he began developing into a top flight NHL defenceman.

Stapleton jumped to the World Hockey Association's Chicago Cougars in 1973. Later, when the franchise was near collapse, he invested in it and became one of the very few people in professional hockey history to have the multiple role of player, coach, manager and owner. "Two or three of us got together and said we'll see if we can keep this thing going," he recalls. "I was interested in seeing that a lot of guys there who had little kids in school could continue the rest of the year."

Stapleton admits the venture was a losing one. "Anytime you're willing to put your dollars on the line, you either do well or you lose your dollars. I was willing to put my dollars where they counted and sure, I did lose money. But what you lose in actual dollars you gain in experience," he states philosophically.

Stapleton decided to leave hockey in 1978 because of age and his desire to do other things. Now he has returned to it. "I'm probably more deeply involved now than I was when I played the game but from a different aspect and a different angle of it."

Elmer Vasko

Chicago Black Hawks

(b. 1935, Duparquet, Que.)
Games played 786
Goals 34
Assists 166
Total points 200
Penalties in Minutes 719

From the time Elmer Vasko joined the Black Hawks in the mid-1950s, the leather-lunged fans of Chicago Stadium loved to urge the 6'3", 210-pound defenceman on with the resounding holler, "Moose!", the moniker hung on him during his junior hockey days in Quebec. To fans he meets in Chicago where he now lives, he is still the Moose.

Vasko joined the Hawks during the club's darkest days, when it was a monument to futility and the franchise was in very serious trouble. It is with little affection that he remembers those dismal early days. "Nobody likes to lose. It was a lot of hard work. It was always a lot of hard work in the National League, but when you're down at the bottom of the pile, it just makes it that much tougher."

Vasko, patrolling the blueline in tandem with Pierre Pilote, contributed to the Black Hawks' rise from chumps to champs. By 1961 he and his teammates had brought the Stanley Cup home to Chicago. Twice he was voted an all-star in the league.

In 1966 Vasko retired from Chicago. His departure was short-lived and the following season he joined the Minnesota North Stars. Back problems and subsequent surgery forced him to retire for good in 1971. "I wasn't ready to quit," he admits.

For a time after retirement, he acted as a sales representative/consultant for Northland Hockey Sticks, a job that entailed promoting the company's products in the NHL and the various minor leagues. He worked later at several jobs until seven years ago when he invested in a fast food enterprise, the Dogpatch Restaurant, located in a suburban Chicago shopping mall. "Between the wife [Claudette] and me, we split up the day," he says. "We both enjoy it."

Vasko's only regret about his hockey career is that he could not carry on another few years to reap the wage windfalls brought on by the birth of the World Hockey Association. "I missed the big salaries," he adds wistfully. "I missed out on all the big stuff. Who knows? I might have had a few more fast food places."

Ken Wharram

Chicago Black Hawks

(b. 1933, Ferris, Ont.)
Games played 766
Goals 252
Assists 281
Total points 533
Penalties in Minutes 222

Ken Wharram

Ken Wharram skipped between Chicago and its farm clubs for several years before earning a spot with the Black Hawks in 1958. He went practically unnoticed until 1960 when he was teamed with Ab McDonald and Stan Mikita to form the Scooter Line. McDonald was the digger, and Mikita, the playmaker, but it was Wharram, with his fast skating who provided the real scoot.

In addition to contributing mightily to the success of the Black Hawks, Wharram achieved individual accolades for his play. He was nominated an all-star in 1964 and 1967 and for the Lady Byng Trophy in 1964.

Still skating as well as ever, in 1969 Wharram was forced to leave the game. At training camp that year he suffered a swelling of the heart. He was taken to a hospital in Chicago where the inflammation was halted with medication but the affliction ended his career.

A native of the North Bay, Ontario area, Wharram moved back to that town where he worked for the local school board as a maintenance person. Today, living in retirement, he prefers to maintain his privacy and offers no comment on his athletic past.

Despite Eddie Shack's attempt to check him, Detroit's Gordie Howe scores the first of his two goals against the Leafs in a Stanley Cup play-offs.

DETROIT RED WINGS

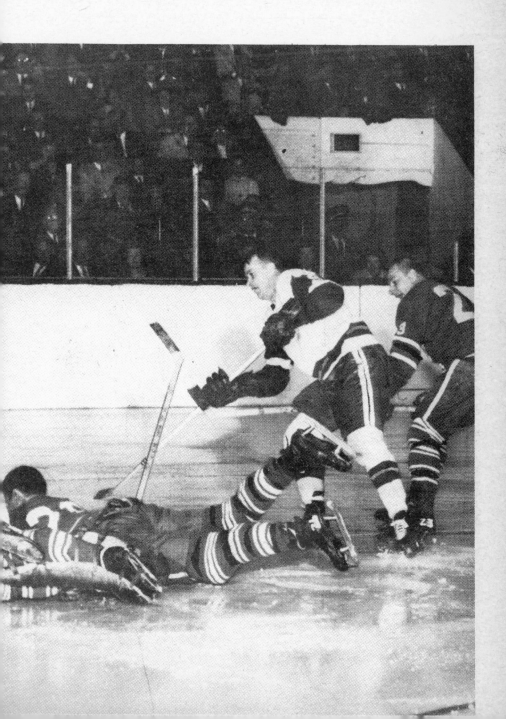

By 1952 the Detroit Red Wings were more than simply a hockey club. They had become a dynasty. Beginning in 1948-49 the team registered seven consecutive league awards, an unprecedented feat that has yet to be matched. Four times during those years, it took the Stanley Cup as well.

Managed by Jack Adams, coached by Tommy Ivan, the Red Wings played a tough, bruising, tight-checking brand of hockey. The nucleus of the club was the Production Line: Sid Abel, Ted Lindsay, and Gordie Howe, the man referred to by many as the greatest ever to play hockey. By the early 1950s the club featured a strong defensive corps. Red Kelly, Bob Goldham, and Marcel Pronovost stood guard in front of the great goalie, Terry Sawchuk. And there were the checkers, Johnny Wilson, Marty Pavelich, Tony Leswick and Glen Skov.

Jack Adams, who began his 35-year association with Detroit in 1927, maintained a policy of constant rejuvenation for the Red Wings. Almost every season, he would make trades that would bring new faces and fresh bodies to the club. An ever-changing Red Wing world revolved around the Production Line and the strategy seemed to work. But in 1956, Adams made the one trade that sapped the club's strength rather than enhanced it. He traded Tony Leswick, Johnny Wilson, Glen Skov, Benny Woit, Marcel Bonin and Vic Stasiuk, giving up quality that was not replaced by the players who joined the Red Wings.

That season, the dynasty showed its first cracks. The team finished out of first place, just barely in second. It rebounded the following season to take first, only to bow out in the semi-finals to Boston. It was not until 1965 when Ted Lindsay made a spirited comeback with the club that the Red Wings once again vaulted back into top spot. The team appeared in the Cup finals three times in the post-dynasty years, 1961, 1963 and 1964, losing each time. Until expansion, it was led by Howe, Alex Delvecchio and Norm Ullman.

Just before expansion, Detroit began a slide into the lower echelons of the league. Some observers feel that the decline was precipitated by the tragic eye injury that removed Doug Barkley from the lineup. A proven performer, he bolstered the defence after the departure of the solid veterans, Bill Gadsby and Marcel Pronovost. A void was created that has yet to be filled. The club has not rediscovered the formula for consistency, to say nothing of greatness, in the post-expansion era. One thing seems certain. The sense of family that former Red Wings talk about when reminiscing about the dynasty years is absent.

Al Arbour

Detroit Red Wings

(b. 1932, Sudbury, Ont.)
Games played 626
Goals 12
Assists 58
Total points 70
Penalties in Minutes 617

Al Arbour

In a hockey career that stretched from 1953 to 1971 Al Arbour became known as the itinerant defensive defenceman who dared to wear eyeglasses on the ice. "That's how people still remember me," he laughs. " 'Hey, aren't you the one with the glasses?' they say." He jokes about bouncing between the minors and four NHL clubs. "I just tell people that I was such a good hockey player that everybody wanted me. Actually I wasn't a great hockey player. I was just a fringe player. I had to bust my ass just to stay around."

One of the advantages of having moved around the six-team NHL, Arbour observes, was that he sipped champagne from Lord Stanley's trophy on four occasions with three different teams: Detroit, Chicago and Toronto. "Not too many people can say that," he adds.

Today Arbour is recognized as one of the most successful coaches in professional hockey. He led the New York Islanders to four consecutive Stanley Cup championships, a streak that began in the 1979-80 season. He has given the Islanders a tough, grinding style that has carried them into the play-offs for all but one of the 11 years he has led the team.

Arbour insists that his stern, bespectacled, gum-chewing countenance has become synonomous with success only because Islander management, coaching staff and scouts share the same philosophy on how to build a contending club and what type of players they need.

The team has been stocked with draft choices who demonstrate not only hockey ability but also strength of character.

In his native Sudbury where he is a partner in a hockey school (the oldest one in Canada, he claims) and a sporting goods store and where he owns a summer retreat, Arbour is known as "Radar" because of his notoriously poor night vision. His players also call him "Radar" but more for his insights than any lack of them. Commenting on Arbour's success as a coach, Mike Bossy, the stellar right winger of the Islanders says, "It takes a combination of discipline and humanity. I don't know of too many guys that don't like him."

Arbour began dabbling in coaching in Rochester of the AHL where he assisted Joe Crozier. He was also an assistant under Scotty Bowman at St. Louis. After he retired from playing, he assumed the coaching reigns with the Blues, but when front office meddling became intolerable, he left that organization.

In 1973, he considered several coaching offers, one of which was from Bill Torrey and the Islanders. "No way! I didn't want the job [with the Islanders]," he recalls. "I thought Long Island was like New York City. I didn't want my wife and four kids living in a place like that." Only after Torrey took him on a tour of pastoral Nassau County did he change his mind. He became the third coach of a team that had sunk to new depths of incompetence.

The man who started coaching because "it is the next best thing to playing" took the Islander position knowing "it would be a heck of a challenge". Everyone thought he was crazy for taking charge of what was the on-ice equivalent of the Keystone Kops. He has proven otherwise.

Doug Barkley

Detroit Red Wings

(b. 1937, Lethbridge, Alta.)
Games played 253
Goals 24
Assists 80
Total points 104
Penalties in Minutes 382

Doug Barkley

Many hockey analysts trace the demise of the Detroit Red Wings to a fateful game in 1966. An accidental blow from a stick blinded defenceman Doug Barkley in one eye and prematurely ended his hockey career. Having come to the Red Wings' camp in 1962, he had grown into the club's number one defenceman. He was ready to fill the void left by Bill Gadsby's retirement and Marcel Pronovost's departure to Toronto. With the loss of Barkley, the defensive corps was robbed of its heart and Detroit's long decline began.

Barkley describes his entry into the pro game as "potluck". He was in Brooks, a small town in his native Alberta, when he happened to spot a small notice in a restaurant advertising tryouts for the Medicine Hat Tigers. "I went over and tried out. I skated one day and the guy in charge said they were going to keep me. That's the way my hockey career started," he remembers. "Otherwise I may not have played."

The property of the Chicago Black Hawks until 1962, he played only three games with them in 1957 and three more in 1959, spending the balance of the time with farm clubs in Calgary and Buffalo. Detroit acquired the 6'2", 185-pound rearguard just when he had decided he might finish his career in the minors. "When I came up with Detroit I seemed to fit right in," he says. Detroit was still a force to be reckoned with in the ranks of the six-team league, Barkley adds. "We went to the finals three out of the four years I was there."

Though he had established himself as an offensive player in the minors, Barkley had no problem adjusting to the tight defensive game in the NHL. "When you got to the six-team league you had to think defence first," he explains. An excellent shot from the point netted him a few goals. In fact, his 11 goals in the 1963-64 campaign were the most scored by any defenceman in the league that season.

Three operations after the accident could not save the sight in Barkley's eye. He had vision after each round of surgery but then the damaged retina would tear again. Finally, he could see nothing out of that eye. At the peak of his career, just before expansion, when the possibility of earning bigger wages was very real, Barkley found himself on the sidelines. The Red Wings gave him a place in the organization. "They didn't give me a lot of time to sit around and mope," he says. "They put me to work. They gave me a job in coaching. You had to work hard at learning how to coach and how to do things I had never really thought of because I thought I'd be playing for another five or six years." He adds, "I think if I had to get out of the game it would've been extremely hard. It was really fortunate that I could stay."

Barkley coached and managed in Fort Worth and Virginia for Detroit's farm teams. He was also at the helm of a squad of Detroit farm hands sent to England to become the London Lions, part of owner Bruce Norris' futile attempt to establish a European league. He put in two brief, unsuccessful stints as coach of the Red Wings, although he preferred to coach in the minors where he had a winning record and always made the play-offs. Ideally, Barkley would have stepped in as a coach of the Red Wings with a long-term contract, a mandate to make changes and the time to build a club through draft choices. "I have to give credit to Detroit," he adds. "They were very good to me, they got me coaching and made a career for me on the other side of hockey."

Barkley scouted for Detroit and then returned to Calgary where he managed a junior club for a season. He invested in a Tier II club, the Calgary Canucks, which he sold four years ago to begin work as a colour commentator for a Calgary radio station broadcasting the Flames' hockey games. It's still like being part of the game, he says, only without the pressures.

In addition to the radio work, Barkley operates a hockey school each summer. "I don't make a lot of money," he laughs, "but I'm not starving."

Alex Delvecchio
Detroit Red Wings

(b. 1931, Fort William, Ont.)
Games played 1549
Goals 456
Assists 825
Total points 1281
Penalties in Minutes 383

Alex Delvecchio

After 23 years of playing hockey with the Detroit Red Wings and another four seasons as coach of the club, it is little wonder that Alex Delvecchio suffered withdrawal symptoms when it was all over. "You miss the game after all those years," says the three time Lady Byng Trophy winner. "You get into a routine — getting up in the morning, having your breakfast and then you go to the shop shall we say, the arena. Then you practise, skate or have a meeting. That goes on every day. All of a sudden you're out of it, the next day you wake up . . . where do you go? You've got to adjust, find a new life. It's a hard adjustment for a person to make."

Delvecchio turned to an ad specialty business that he and a partner started in 1969. Since then, he has taken over the business and five years ago expanded into engraving, plaques and identification signs. His "little shop" in Detroit employs a staff of 11.

During his long tenure with the Red Wings Delvecchio tasted the sweet victories of the powerhouse teams of the early 1950s. He holds a special spot in his heart for the 1951 team that annihilated Toronto and Montreal in eight games to win the Stanley Cup. Many years later he suffered the ignominy of defeat and the abuse of the fans frustrated by the Red Wings' inability to make post-season play. In his prime, he was a highly regarded centre who was a gifted playmaker. Of the 1,281 points he garnered, 825 were assists.

When Delvecchio retired in 1974, he accepted the head coaching position offered to him by the Detroit management. It lasted four losing seasons. "I have different feelings about that now after I look at it," he says in retrospect. "I don't think I would go from a player to coaching in the National Hockey League. There's no doubt in my mind that you should try and gain some experience in the minors and get away from the players." The step from playing to coaching is a big one that cannot be undertaken easily. "There are things you do as a player that, when you become a coach, all of a sudden you have the skate on the other foot. It's a big change."

"Fats" as some of the older people still call him, is active with the Red Wing alumni and plays in several charity games a year. "I'm still pretty much a hockey player," he laughs.

Bill Dineen

Detroit Red Wings

(b. 1932, Arvida, Que.)
Games played 323
Goals 51
Assists 44
Total points 95
Penalties in Minutes 122

Coach Bill Dineen finds that his job as coach of the Adirondack Red Wings, a Detroit farm club, in Glen Falls, New York deals with two areas, the competitive and the developmental. "In the AHL you've got a thin line between winning, which is really important naturally, and developing players. This year we sent five guys up to Detroit from here. It's usually the guys who are going best but that's the nature of the system today. A player playing well down here deserves the opportunity of going up there and playing. It's what the player wants, it's what we want, it's what I want. I think you get a sense of satisfaction from developing somebody to the point where he now has an opportunity to play there. The other end of the spectrum is that you're losing your best player, too."

Unlike most rookies stepping into the NHL in the days of six teams, Dineen did not have to serve an apprenticeship in the minors. He arrived in Detroit in 1953 from St. Mike's College in Toronto. "It probably wouldn't have been a bad idea to spend a couple of years there," he reflects. "In your overall development I think maybe it's not the worst thing to do to play a year or so in the minors. Then you appreciate being in the National League a bit more." Today, he notes, there seems to be a hurry to get graduating juniors right into major league lineups. "I think they're forcing kids to play who aren't really ready to play."

A journeyman forward, Dineen formed a line with Alex Delvecchio and Johnny Wilson. "I contributed the least to that line," he remarks. In his first two seasons with the Red Wings, Detroit won the Stanley Cup. In 1957 he was traded to Chicago for what turned out to be his last NHL season. For the next 11 years he played in the AHL and the WHL. Whenever he did have an opportunity to come back up, injuries intervened. "There was a lot of guys in those days, great hockey players, who never did get the opportunity of playing in the National Hockey League. Now at least I had the good fortune of being there."

Dineen hung up his skates in 1971 in Denver of the WHL where he had been a playing coach, although he continued to coach. The following season brought a change in ownership and a new coach, and he went to Penticton, British Columbia to coach Tier II hockey. Partway through the season he was offered the coaching position for Houston of the WHA and, with it, the opportunity to put an entirely new team together from scratch. "I walked in there and they just gave me a credit card and said, 'Go anywhere in North America you want to and put together a team. Do whatever you want to do.' So they sort of gave me carte blanche to go ahead and do it."

Dineen had never given a lot of thought to continuing in hockey. "It was just sort of a coincidence," he states. In British Columbia, he could have operated a sporting goods store and a summer hockey school but the money and prestige associated with the Houston job made it more attractive. And, "it's the one thing you know best of all, it's the only thing you've done in your life."

Dineen's Houston club fared well during his tenure as coach and, later, as coach and general manager. His team finished first four consecutive times. Twice it won the Avco Cup, emblematic of the WHA championship. He later moved to Hartford as coach. With the club's record barely over .500, he was relieved of his duties in his first year. He became a scout for Hartford for the next four years, the last three as director of scouting.

Two years ago Dineen became coach and director of player personnel for Adirondack. After holding the reigns for different clubs and different leagues, he is truly in a position to comment on the security, or lack of it, in coaching. "Coaching is never a secure job. Anybody that doesn't work at it, it'll catch up with you." Two of his sons are currently in the NHL, Gord with the Islanders and Kevin with the Whalers. Two others, Peter and Shawn are in the minors. A fifth, Jerry, is a junior with St. Mike's.

Val Fonteyne

Detroit Red Wings

(b. 1933, Wetaskiwin, Alta.)
Games played 820
Goals 75
Assists 154
Total points 229
Penalties in Minutes 26

Val Fonteyne

Val Fonteyne left amateur hockey in Alberta and British Columbia and spent four years playing for Seattle of the old Western Hockey League. Since that club had no affiliations with any NHL team, he had pretty well resigned himself to a fate of a few more seasons at that level of hockey. "When I went to Seattle to start with, the team had no connection to the NHL. So I never thought about going to the NHL."

On the recommendation of Bud Poile, then coaching Edmonton, a Red Wing farm team in the WHL, Detroit invited Fonteyne to a training camp tryout. It took him two attempts but eventually in 1959 he joined Howe, Delvecchio and company. The left winger skated for Detroit, New York, Pittsburgh and Edmonton of the World Hockey Association.

Used primarily in a defensive role and for penalty killing, Fonteyne expresses gratitude for having gotten as far as he did. "I just felt I was fortunate to be there. I was a fringe player, eh? I felt there was a lot of guys who I played with in the WHL, like Guyle Fielder, who had more ability. I don't know what the reason was but I was there and I felt fortunate to be there."

In 1974 Fonteyne hung up the blades. "When you're 39-40 years old you know what's coming," he laughs. "I was 39-40. You didn't take much to figure out." An opportunity arose to work for Canada Post in his native Wetaskiwin, 35 miles south of Edmonton. "I could have gone on into scouting or some other job. I just didn't want to move. This came up and I took it. It turned out really well. I was born here. I'm just a small town boy. I've been to big cities and I just don't care for them too much. That's why I decided to stay here."

Bill Gadsby
Detroit Red Wings

(b. 1927, Calgary, Alta.)
Games played 1248
Goals 130
Assists 437
Total points 567
Penalties in Minutes 1539

Bill Gadsby

The unpredictable nature of sports as Bill Gadsby discovered, often leaves its adherents stunned and wondering, "What kind of a world is this anyway?" In 1969, three games into his second season as head coach of the Detroit Red Wings, Gadsby was inexplicably fired by owner Bruce Norris. "He had his arm around me in Chicago the night before. We beat Chicago 4-2," Gadsby recalls. "He said, 'Boy, you sure got these guys going.' I said, 'Yeah, we're going to have a good year, Bruce.' Twenty hours later it was the hoochee. I got fired."

The closest thing Gadsby got to an explanation was that he wasn't "sophisticated enough". "Whatever that meant," he adds. "It was the biggest shock of my life. I couldn't believe it. I didn't bounce back from that for a long time. I had a few chances to get back in hockey but I didn't. I said the hell with it. It's not worth it. I got burned once and I didn't want to get burned again."

Gadsby went into the rental crane business in Detroit where he stayed for 14 years after his brief coaching experience with the Red Wings. More recently he started his own business, a firm called Autometrics that distributes metric fasteners, bolts, tabs, dies, drills, etc. to the automotive trade in the Detroit area. "I'm going to call my own goddamn shots for a while," he says.

Gadsby, a Hall of Famer, spent two decades in the NHL playing a steady brand of defence for Chicago, New York and Detroit. Five times he was named an all-star. The trade that brought him to Detroit in 1961, he says, gave him new life. "I was going to come here for a year and then go back to Edmonton where I lived in the off-season. I was going to coach the farm club out there. I got new life and I lasted another five or six years here."

In 1966 Gadsby retired. "I could have played a couple of more years but the body was talking back to me. When the body starts talking back to you and you can hardly get the legs out of bed next morning, it's time to quit." He returned to Edmonton where he coached junior hockey for a couple of years before returning to the Motor City and a fateful rendezvous with the uncertainties of the professional coaching ranks. If he were ever to accept another coaching position, unlikely as the possibility seems to him now, he would insist on signing a long-term contract, "five years or something, for security."

Warren Godfrey

Detroit Red Wings

(b. 1931, Toronto, Ont.)
Games played 786
Goals 32
Assists 125
Total points 157
Penalties in Minutes 752

One story, as told by former NHLers who know Warren Godfrey, goes that some time after his retirement from hockey, he got into the restaurant business in Florida. When things didn't go too well with it, he answered an advertisement for a cement truck driver. Although he didn't know the fundamentals of the trade, he still accepted the job because he needed the money.

Because Rocky Godfrey is the likeable sort that he is, the other drivers took him under their collective wing and taught the ex-Red Wing the basics to prepare him for his first solo run. The day arrived and he successfully manoeuvered the big truck out of the parking lot, past the cheering fellow drivers urging him on. He wheeled out onto the highway on what seemed to be a flawless maiden voyage. The wail of a police siren brought the run to an unexpected conclusion. Godfrey, it seems, had forgotten to press a certain control, and had motored down the road leaving a liberal wake of wet cement. Fortunately, the story concludes, he did not lose the job.

It is not always easy to substantiate the tale of one hockey player's adjustment to life after the sport. Finding the defenceman who retired in 1969 is no simple matter. Most of his former teammates answer the question, "The Rock? Well, I hear he's down in Florida in the restaurant business."

Apparently Godfrey operated a pool hall in Detroit before moving to the Sunshine State where he indeed got into the food and beverage business.

At one point Godfrey operated a franchise of the Clock Restaurant chain in Florida. Harold Kite, owner of the chain, says he sold out in 1984. He moved to a small town called Otto, North Carolina near Franklin in the west part of the state. The sports editor of *The Franklin Press*, Eddie Sutton, was an acquaintance of Godfrey's. He wrote an article introducing the ex-pro to Franklin on April 4, 1984.

The article begins with and answers the question, "How did a man from Toronto, Canada end up in the restaurant business in Franklin, North Carolina?" In it Godfrey talks about moving from junior hockey to a minor pro club on the west coast to the NHL. Records show he broke in with the Bruins in 1952.

The topic of injuries and fights arose in the interview and Godfrey admitted "to a lot of the former and probably his share of the latter." Mr. Sutton wrote, "The doctors in Detroit and Boston must have made a bundle off Godfrey." The list of injuries includes 200 stitches in the face, a broken jaw, a broken nose, dislocated shoulders, damaged elbows, cracked ribs, broken fingers, five knee operations, broken toes and 12 lost teeth.

"The press and TV overemphasize fights. They are for real, but you never see anyone get hurt. It's hard to fight on skates," Godfrey remarked. "When you first start out, you more or less had to fight quite a bit to gain a reputation. In later years, you don't have to fight as much."

Godfrey explained that during his career he had been with first place clubs but had never been fortunate enough to be on a Stanley Cup winner. "I was a bridesmaid in the Stanley Cup ten times, but never a bride."

Godfrey's last full season in the NHL was spent with the Bruins in 1962-63. The following season he was traded back to Detroit where he played irregularly until 1968. The next year, spent in the minors, was his last. Then, according to the article, "my knees wouldn't let me play anymore."

Godfrey moved to Florida after hockey and opened a restaurant, one of four with which he eventually became involved there. He was also a food and beverage manager for Sheraton Hotels. Franklin, North Carolina, had been a vacation spot for Godfrey and his wife and after "she fell in love with the place", they moved there "permanently". At the time the article was written, he was about to open his new restaurant, The Red Fox.

Conversations with Mr. Sutton in May, 1985 revealed that Godfrey had suddenly and without notice left Franklin earlier in the spring. Rumours have it that he went to Marietta, Georgia, near Atlanta.

Pete Goegan
Detroit Red Wings

(b. 1934, Fort William, Ont.)
Games played 383
Goals 19
Assists 67
Total points 86
Penalties in Minutes 365

Peter Goegan

Pete Goegan played 382 games over ten seasons in the NHL with Detroit, New York and Minnesota. With his career split between the minors and the major league, he knew too well the vicissitudes associated with the game. "If you didn't produce, you were gone for a month or two and called back up," he says, "up and down, up and down."

The combination of a broken ankle suffered when he fell off a ladder while painting his home and "old age" prompted Goegan to retire from hockey in 1969. He returned to his hometown of Thunder Bay, Ontario where he is now a carpenter. His only connection with the sport since then has been a short stint as a coach of a midget hockey team. He left because "the parents got to me."

Bob Goldham
Detroit Red Wings

(b. 1922, Georgetown, Ont.)
Games played 650
Goals 28
Assists 143
Total points 171
Penalties in Minutes 400

Four years ago Bob Goldham had a heart attack that he calls "a blessing in disguise". Says the former star defenceman with Toronto, Chicago and Detroit, "If I hadn't had it I would've gone on the same old way, eating, not exercising, putting on a little more weight." He follows an exercise and diet program developed by physician Terry Cavanaugh and jokingly refers to himself as "a born again athlete". Eating properly and jogging four and five miles a day near his Toronto home, he declares, "I'm probably in better shape now than I've been in the last 35 years. I used to watch these guys jogging down the street and think they were nuts. Now I are one!"

Between 1941 and 1947 Goldham belonged to the Toronto Maple Leafs, although three years of that time was spent in the navy during the war. He went to Chicago in the famous Max Bentley deal in 1947. Another major trade found him wearing a Detroit uniform in 1950. "Going to Detroit was the greatest thing that ever happened to me," he reminisced. "I got there at a time when everything seemed to come to perfection." He had joined a Detroit dynasty that won three Stanley Cups in the time he was there. "We really didn't know what made us as good a hockey club as we were," he says. It was a few years ago while watching the Pittsburgh Pirates win the World Series with their "We are family" theme that he put his finger on it. "We had a family. We just didn't know how to classify it at the time.

It's strange to hear guys say it, but I think there was a good amount of love with each other."

Originally a rushing defenceman, Goldham changed his style when he joined the Red Wings and their other rushing defenceman, Red Kelly. "It just seemed to evolve that way. I decided that this was a better way I could help Detroit and probably further my career by playing that way." Aware of Kelly's great abilities, he chose to stay at home. He learned how to block shots by watching and imitating Bucko McDonald. "I see some of the young guys do it now and I shudder," he notes. "It's more of a desperation move. With myself it was something I studied and perfected."

A broken arm led Goldham to the work he pursued after he retired from professional hockey. While receiving treatment for his broken arm from Dr. Smerley Lawson in Toronto, the physician asked him what he intended to do for the summer. Goldham replied nothing so the doctor got him a job through a friend at Caterpillar Tractor. Goldham stayed in the construction equipment business until his retirement four years ago.

Realizing that he "had had enough and wanted to be home with my family" Goldham at 34 retired from the NHL at the end of the 1956 season. "I could have played longer. When I look back now in retrospect I wish I had. It would have been nice to play longer. The longer you play, the more they recognize the fact." For almost a dozen years he kept in close contact with the game he left by commenting on Hockey Night in Canada broadcasts. He now works for them only four or five times a year.

Retired, Goldham is active enough with his exercising, golf and his hobby of cooking that he often wonders "Where the hell I had time to work before," adding, "I'm too busy to die."

Paul Henderson

Detroit Red Wings

(b. 1943, Kincardine, Ont.)
Games played 707
Goals 236
Assists 241
Total points 477
Penalties in Minutes 304

Paul Henderson's heroics in the 1972 Canada/Soviet Union hockey summit made him an instant legend. "It amazes me that I'm recognized," says the man who rescued a nation's pride. "It doesn't matter where I go, people recognize me. I have a tougher time understanding what that did now more than ever. I played 18 years of professional hockey and I'm remembered for one ten-second shift."

Henderson broke in with Detroit of the original six. His 18-year career stretched through the expansion era into and beyond the World Hockey Association years. A left winger who combined an ability to backcheck with a scoring touch, he played with Detroit, Toronto, Toronto Toros (WHA), Birmingham Bulls (WHA) and Atlanta. In 1980 he quit. "I could have played a couple of more years," he adds. "Atlanta offered me a three-year contract which I turned down." Content with his athletic accomplishments and not wanting to move his family from its home in Birmingham, Alabama, Henderson chose to retire.

Early in 1984 Henderson returned to Toronto where he is a full-time staff member with Athletes in Action, a division of Campus Crusade for Christ. The former star has travelled throughout the nation carrying the word of God to people and conducting workshops on prayer, evangelism and discipleship.

Henderson traces his involvement in Christianity to 1973. "It was at a time of really searching in my life. I was looking for something," he recalls. "I didn't know what I was looking for." Having accomplished all the goals he had set for himself in life, he was unable to answer the question, "Why are you alive?" "It was a really confusing time for me in a lot of ways."

It was in March, 1975 that he became a Christian and stopped being "the classical hypocrite", one of those "Sunday type" worshippers. "I quit fooling around with the Lord," he says. "Accepting Jesus Christ as my savior was the missing ingredient. The Lord's put it all together for me, I'll tell you. I don't think I've ever been more content in my life." Following retirement, he joined the Church Resource Ministry in Birmingham where he trained for his present position.

Though Henderson travels extensively he prefers to stay in the environs of Toronto where there "is enough work to keep me busy for 200 years." Athletes in Action has worked among American football players and Henderson as its spokesperson intends on being its message to hockey players. Dean Prentice, Ron Ellis and Dave Burroughs number among those ex-players who are now born again Christians.

Reflecting on that heroic moment in Moscow in the light of today, Henderson admits "that one period, that one goal has given me a platform that's incredible." From that platform he estimates that he has been able to show hundreds of people the Christian way.

Gordie Howe

Detroit Red Wings

(b. 1928, Floral, Sask.)
Games played 1767
Goals 801
Assists 1049
Total points 1850
Penalties in Minutes 1685

In every field, there exists a standard by which all else is measured. In the game of hockey, the standard was set by Gordie Howe. He has been called the greatest ever to play the sport. He excelled at every element of the game: desire, talent, toughness, shooting, skating, stickhandling, durability.

The desire to play in the NHL develops at a very young age in most players. Howe was no different except perhaps in how confident he was of making it as a professional player. "I started signing autographs about four or five different ways when I was about seven and showed them to my mother to find out which one was the best one," remembers the native of Floral, Saskatchewan. "There was no doubt in my mind."

Dit Clapper, the famous right winger with the Boston Bruins, retired in the 1946-47 season after establishing a new longevity mark of 20 years. That season, coincidentally, happened to be Howe's inaugural campaign. Four seasons later, the first in which he scored 35 goals, he remembers deciding to attempt to break Clapper's record. By the time his career ended in 1980, he had played 32 years in the NHL and the WHA.

Howe had an annual ritual of setting a production goal each season, usually one to three goals more than he scored the previous year. "If I doubled up [scored twice his production goal]," he recalls, "I'd be successful." Having successfully adapted to the defensive style of the Red Wings in his first few seasons, he then discovered he could score goals. He knew that if he played both the offensive and defensive games well, barring injury, he would be around the league for some time. Ted Lindsay, Sid Abel and Howe formed Detroit's ultimate scoring unit — the "Production Line".

Flip open the NHL record book and Howe's name occupies a great many places: most seasons played (26), most games (1,767), most goals (801), most assists (1,049), most points (1,850), most years in the play-offs (20), most points in a final series (12). Add to his records a lifetime of silverware and commendations: four Stanley Cups, six Hart Trophies, six Art Ross Trophies, 20 all-star nominations and induction into the Hockey Hall of Fame in 1972 to name a few.

Howe retired after the 1971 season. The Red Wings, no longer the powerhouse they had once been, entered a new lacklustre period of instability. "The fun had left," he says. "Things weren't going anywhere, especially in Detroit. Things were going pretty rough." He then accepted a post with the Detroit organization. The experience was not a pleasant one, he agrees. "Not when you're totally involved for all those years and then all of a sudden you're into a front office position. You have no goals, no nothing, really. I wasn't learning. That was the sad part about the whole thing. I just felt I wasn't learning anything." He explains that he desperately wanted to help the club on the ice by lending a hand instructing the younger players. The opportunity to help the Red Wings never arose but another one did two years later.

For some time Howe had dreamt of playing on the same team with his two sons, Mark and Marty. The chance came when the Houston Aeros of the WHA offered to sign the whole family. The accomplishments of a lifetime in the NHL took a rear seat for Howe. He immediately tells you that his greatest thrill in the game was "playing with the boys, especially for seven years." For four seasons in Houston, two in New England and, the crowning touch, one season in Hartford of the NHL, father and sons were teammates.

Howe retired for good at the end of the 1980 season, his first in the NHL since his retirement almost a decade earlier. "I had had enough," concedes the seemingly ageless right winger. "I was what? Fifty-two years of age? I guess my timing was perfect. I came along when the stress wasn't on youth like it is now."

Today Howe acts as a special assistant to Howard Baldwin, chairman of the Hartford Whalers. He occasionally lends a hand with coaching. One of his main functions is to represent the NHL in presenting the Emery Edge Awards for the league's leader in the plus-minus category. Living in Gastonbury, Connecticut, he and Colleen, his wife, also manage his successful business, Howe Enterprises.

Talent, ability and strength have made Howe the superior athlete that he is and allowed him to excel in his field. A little good luck along the way helped. One suspects in talking with him that many of his accomplishments, both on and off the ice, are to a large extent the product of the strength he finds in his family. He readily credits Colleen with helping him when he played. Re-evaluating his illustrious career, Howe would change one thing, "I'd have Colleen sign my contract. She's honest but she knows the value of things." He agrees her role has always been significant and remains that way. "We have an arrangement. It's been that way since we got married. She has a master calendar. When anything comes my way, it goes through her and everyone thinks I'm henpecked. Henpecked? Hell, I'm being assisted by a very able young lady. It's not a fairy tale like everything's rosy because every now and then you have arguments. But, all in all, when I look at other lives I think I've really been very fortunate."

Larry Jeffrey

Detroit Red Wings

(b. 1940, Zurich, Ont.)
Games played 368
Goals 39
Assists 62
Total points 101
Penalties in Minutes 293

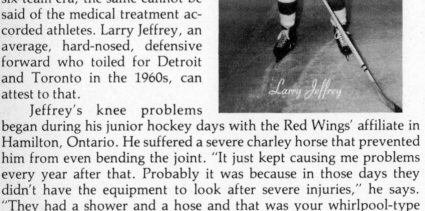

While the calibre of hockey was considered top notch during the six-team era, the same cannot be said of the medical treatment accorded athletes. Larry Jeffrey, an average, hard-nosed, defensive forward who toiled for Detroit and Toronto in the 1960s, can attest to that.

Jeffrey's knee problems began during his junior hockey days with the Red Wings' affiliate in Hamilton, Ontario. He suffered a severe charley horse that prevented him from even bending the joint. "It just kept causing me problems every year after that. Probably it was because in those days they didn't have the equipment to look after severe injuries," he says. "They had a shower and a hose and that was your whirlpool-type thing. You held the hose to cause stimulation to the charley horse."

Later, adhesions developed on his leg. He was sent to Detroit to have them broken, in a scene that might have come from the Marquis de Sade. "One doctor got my shoulder and held me, the other got on my leg and just literally grabbed it and bent it with his weight. They gave me a mild sedative. I remember everything about it. When he gave my knee the pressure, it was just like breaking bones. It was very painful. I heard the cracking. I thought they broke my leg rather than the adhesions. I thought it was a rather cruel way of doing it."

When Jeffrey turned professional, he was disappointed to find that clubs simply had nothing in the way of sports medicine facilities. Braces were tested with his knee. He remembers one that locked his knee in position, allowing him to skate sufficiently well but not permitting him to stop normally. "You had to make the big circle," he explains. "I really look back now and I was like a guinea pig, trying out all these different braces, sending me to hospitals, having the knee drained and cortisone put in to go out and play that night."

Nine operations later, the most recent in January, 1985, his knee still swells up each morning. Jeffrey bears no malice to the game or his former employers. "I'm disappointed they didn't look after my knee properly, but I have no hard feelings. I have a lot of good memories of playing in the National Hockey League," he comments, referring to winning seasons in Detroit and playing on Toronto's Stanley Cup team in 1967.

A final knee wound suffered at the Cleveland Barons' training camp in 1970 finished his career. Jeffrey returned to his 127-acre farm near Goderich, Ontario where he raises cattle and a few standardbred racing horses. He also owns a concession stand and a thriving ad specialties business. For a time he scouted for the NHL's central scouting office.

Red Kelly

Detroit Red Wings

(b. 1927, Simcoe, Ont.)
Games played 1316
Goals 281
Assists 542
Total points 823
Penalties in Minutes 327

Over his 20-year NHL career, Leonard "Red" Kelly established himself as one of hockey's most accomplished players. A graduate of St. Michael's College in Toronto, he came to Detroit in 1947 and blossomed into one of the finest rushing defencemen in the sport. While a Red Wing, he played on four Stanley Cup championship teams, won the Norris Trophy once, the Lady Byng Trophy three times and was an all-star eight times. He was traded to Toronto in 1959 and, before he retired in 1967, shared another four Stanley Cups and won the Lady Byng Trophy another time. His excellence was acknowledged in 1969 when he was inducted into the Hockey Hall of Fame.

Kelly's career almost ended prematurely in 1959 when Detroit traded him to New York. He refused to go to the Rangers because the team was out of contention. "I was told I was blacklisted out of hockey for life in any capacity," he reports. "I said 'that's fine, nobody can force me to do anything,' so I went to work. I told them [Detroit] I could dig ditches to make a living if I had to. They were trying to blame me for the club not playing as well. I thought 'you guys aren't God,' so I went to work for a tool company." Detroit worked a deal with Toronto, a team Kelly was willing to play for. "The only place I could prove myself was by going to a team that still had a chance," he says. The record shows he had a lot of hockey left in him.

Kelly combined hockey and politics between 1962 and 1965 when he served as a Member of Parliament. "I thought that the greatest stickhandlers were in hockey but I found out they were in Parliament. The floor of Parliament was slippery, as slippery as any ice surface that hockey is played on," he laughs. The dual role was tough to handle, he adds, so he decided not to run for re-election. "It was like taking two big 150-pound bags of fertilizer off your shoulders," he sighs.

In 1967 Kelly ended his distinguished career even though he was offered a four-year contract. "I had thought that I couldn't do what I used to do," he explains. "I could still play but I couldn't please myself so it was time to get out. I didn't have the extra overshift I used to have."

Kelly decided to stay in hockey as a coach in the NHL. Over the next decade he was at the helm of Los Angeles, Pittsburgh and Toronto. His most significant addition to the sport was the introduction of "pyramid power" to professional hockey. Competing against Philadelphia's good luck charm, singer Kate Smith, and Harold Ballard in his home Toronto rink, he needed to introduce positive thinking to his charges. Having read about pyramids in literature about Egypt, he put the structure to work for his team. Pyramids were placed under the bench. Players were given pyramids to take home to bed with them. There was even a large one in the dressing room for three players to sit under together for four or five minutes before a game. It worked for awhile, he remembers. Twice the Leafs knocked off the superior Flyers on Philadelphia home ice.

After Kelly left hockey, he went into business in Toronto. Today, he is a director of Camp Systems, a computerized aircraft maintenance program. "The technology originated in the United States," he elaborates. "I brought it back to Canada to employ Canadian people. We service 1,600 aircraft worldwide . . . we are the tops in the world. There isn't anyone who does exactly what we do. We tell you what to do, when to do it and how — preventative maintenance." He is also involved with other maintenance-oriented companies throughout the U.S. and has an interest in a tobacco and cattle operation in Port Dover, Ontario. It has been a Kelly family farm for six generations.

Tony Leswick

Detroit Red Wings

(b. 1923, Humboldt, Sask.)
Games played 740
Goals 165
Assists 159
Total points 324
Penalties in Minutes 900

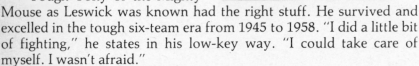

When Tony Leswick turned professional, his 5′6 1/2″ frame carried 137 pounds of bone, muscle and sinew. Asked if he thought a player of that stature could make the grade today in the NHL, he replied, "Depends on the person . . . what you have inside of you."

Tough Tony or the Mighty Mouse as Leswick was known had the right stuff. He survived and excelled in the tough six-team era from 1945 to 1958. "I did a little bit of fighting," he states in his low-key way. "I could take care of myself. I wasn't afraid."

No shrinking violet, Leswick took his place with the bigger men on the ice and needled them into distraction. His barbs were trained on two targets in particular: "Richard and Gordie Howe, both friends of mine . . . today." How did he taunt them? "I couldn't tell you now. These things just came out of the blue in the game and when it's all over you're still friends, you don't hold a grudge."

A swift skater who owned a good shot and an ability to find the scoring range, Leswick led the Rangers in goal production in four of the six years he was with them. When he came to Detroit in 1951, it was his checking abilities that were coveted. He became one of the Red Wings responsible for keeping the opposing guns silent. "That took away from my ability to score, but I did the job." He agrees it was frustrating work. "The headlines are who scores the goals, not who checked whom. The awards are in scoring, not stopping them."

Leswick is still best remembered for his overtime goal in 1954 that clinched the last Stanley Cup the Red Wings won. "Truthfully I got it [attention] more in the last couple of years than I had in a few years. I'm at a loss as to explain why," he ponders.

In the late 1950s, Leswick retired "about three times". He left to become a playing coach with Detroit's Edmonton affiliate only to find himself called up to help the parent club in times of need. He coached in the minors, including Indianapolis. That team's home rink was devastated in a gas explosion that killed over 80 people. Fortunately he and his charges were on the road that day. Had they been in the arena in the vicinity of their dressing room, they would have met the same grim fate.

Finally, in 1965, Leswick left the game altogether and returned to his home in New Westminster, British Columbia where he worked in the hotel business as a bartender and a manager. "I'm semi-retired. I'm not doing very much," he says about his activities these days. He did purchase the local Legion hall and has plans of getting into the restaurant business. He golfs in the summer and curls in the winter.

Ted Lindsay

Detroit Red Wings

(b. 1925, Renfrew, Ont.)
Games played 1068
Goals 379
Assists 472
Total points 851
Penalties in Minutes 1808

His determination and will to win on the ice is a subject that can be described only in superlatives. Ted Lindsay, Detroit's 5'8", 160-pound left winger, earned a reputation as one of the most competitive and fearsome individuals ever to lace on skates in the NHL. But with all his accomplishments, he says he is too often remembered only for his penalties.

"When I played, I only wanted to be the best left winger in the National Hockey League. This is part of my nature. At the time there were a lot of good left wingers in the National Hockey League. With the help of my teammates and with a very good competitive spirit, I was able to become the best left winger in the National Hockey League. I think probably penalties don't bother me but that's all people ever talk about. These are people now who weren't even born when I was playing. I can understand that part of it. All they do is look at the numbers."

Lindsay, Art Ross Trophy winner, eight time all-star and Hall of Famer, was once at a speaking engagement. He was told something he had not realized before. The Red Wings won the Stanley Cup in 1955, two seasons before Lindsay was traded to Chicago because of his leading role in the formation of a players' association. The next time the Wings did as well was in 1964 when Lindsay made his one-season comeback. Perhaps Lindsay and success were synonomous for Detroit. "That means something more to me even though no one has ever said anything about it," he confesses.

Lindsay and various other hockey players made a revolutionary attempt to form a players' association in the NHL in 1957. The people involved in conceiving the union, Lindsay, Tod Sloan, Jim Thompson, Dollard St. Laurent to name a few, did not really need the protection offered by an association because they were better off than most players in the league at the time. As he points out, "These guys didn't need it. I didn't need it. The run-of-the-mill hockey player needed it."

Lindsay continues, "People like Connie Smythe and Jack Adams, who were the pioneers of hockey and to whom I will be eternally grateful because they gave me an opportunity to make a fine living, were scared we were going to take over the game. Unfortunately they didn't recognize we had a brain and we had a love for our game. All we wanted to do was to form an association to be able to represent all players. If a guy was sent down and he had a lease on a house, he was committed to that lease, and the club had no responsibility to him. Back in those days we didn't make very much money and they could send you here and there and hither and yon." They wanted to be able to approach management on a collective rather than an individual basis. If a player were shipped out the team would pay for his lease or his travel expenses.

The association did not survive and those who had participated were reprimanded. Many of the players were sent to Chicago, the cellar dweller club. "A lot of these young guys playing today don't realize the price that some of the guys paid," Lindsay says. His biggest disappointment is that Alan Eagleson is in charge of today's players' association. "I don't like seeing people like that using my game."

"It's no different than our pension. Clarence Campbell was a joke. He talked about the greatest pension plan in the world, in professional sport. That was a farce. The owners never put in one nickel. We put in $900 of our own money. The owners put in approximately $600, so they said. But they got that money when we played the all-star game which we put on. So it was basically our money. So the whole thing was our money," Lindsay elaborates. A pension cheque, he adds, might pay the phone bill and buy stamps for the month. "The saddest thing about it is the younger players today don't understand what the older veterans sacrificed for the lucrativeness that they have now as part of their pension."

Lindsay skated three seasons in Chicago. "I didn't play the hockey I was capable of because mentally, I guess, I was still a

Detroit Red Wing," he admits. "I was existing, I wasn't living, so I quit and came back to the business in Detroit." He retired and worked at the injection molding plastics business he had started with team-mate Marty Pavelich.

Four years later, Sid Abel, coach and general manager of the Red Wings, talked Lindsay into making a comeback. "It surprised a lot of people and I probably surprised myself, too," he laughs. Twenty-five games into the season he played like the Lindsay of old. He would have played another season if he could have remained with Detroit but Toronto, he found out, would not pass him up in a draft so he retired for the second and last time.

In addition to his business, Lindsay worked in television for a time, including "an exceptional, wonderful three years" providing the colour commentary for NBC's Game of the Week hockey broadcast. He became known for his no-punches-pulled approach. "If you feel something, you've got to say it. It gets you into trouble a lot of times, but you can live with yourself," he advises. He also put in a three-and-a-half-year stint as general manager of his beloved Red Wings. "I was disappointed it ended the way it did," he says. "It was only because I wanted to take them back to what they were when I was there. You can't do in three years what has deteriorated for so many years." He was dismissed in 1981.

Recently Lindsay has been doing volunteer work in Detroit area schools addressing students on alcohol and drug abuse. "I speak to young people to try and make them aware that in this liberated, sick, free society drugs and liquor are not a part of life," he explains. If his message gets to only one youngster, he says, the time he has invested will be well worth it.

After Pavelich and he sold their business, Lindsay set up his own sales consultation service, representing various companies in the automotive industry. Working seven days a week, he vows that he will never retire. "I hope some day maybe to get down to a three-day week, maybe when I'm 80 years of age."

Leonard Lunde

Detroit Red Wings

(b. 1936, Campbell River, B.C.)
Games played 321
Goals 39
Assists 83
Total points 122
Penalties in Minutes 75

Len Lunde

While many professional hockey players turn to coaching after they retire, very few turn to coaching overseas like Len Lunde did. Lunde, a centreman, spent five seasons in the NHL with Detroit and Chicago before expansion and with Minnesota and Vancouver after 1967. A regular in his first two seasons with the Red Wings, he spent the rest of his time as a pro bouncing between the NHL and the minors. He retired from the Canucks in 1971 and went to Finland.

Through a Finnish player who had attended the Canucks' training camp, Finnish hockey people learned that Lunde would be available. They invited him to play for a year there, an invitation he accepted. He played one season, after which he coached the Finnish national team. The squad played in the world championships at Moscow that year. "We got beat for a medal by Sweden," he recalls. He would have stayed in Finland, but his family was young and adequate English schooling wasn't available for them.

Lunde returned to Canada and put in one more year in professional hockey in the WHA with the Edmonton Oilers, his last as a pro. For two years after, he ran the hockey program on an Indian reserve near Edmonton. He was offered the job after he played for the reserve team at a national old-timers' tournament.

Europe beckoned once more and Lunde found himself coaching there again, this time with a club in the Swedish first division. He took the following year off and then rejoined the coaching ranks in the Swedish first division. At the same time he acted as a Baltic scout for the Edmonton Oilers. Players he reported on included Jarri Kurri, Risto Siltanen and Esa Tikkanen all of Finland.

In 1983 Lunde returned to Edmonton where he now works in the leasing business. "You get tired of the travel," he remarks about his departure from the game. "I'd like to stay around here now. You're gone six or seven months away from home every year for 20 years. That's a long time away." All the travel hockey calls for would have been much easier without a family. "I'd be single," he states when asked how he would change his hockey past. "It's a tough life when you drag your kids all over hell's half acre. It's hard on them. I'd be single a lot longer. It was too tough."

Parker MacDonald

Detroit Red Wings

(b. 1933, Sydney, N.S.)
Games played 676
Goals 144
Assists 179
Total points 323
Penalties in Minutes 253

Parker MacDonald

Parker MacDonald stepped into major league circles for the first time with Toronto in 1954. But it was not until six seasons later, after he had arrived in Detroit via the New York Rangers, that he discovered some semblance of permanence with a club.

MacDonald, a son of Sydney, Nova Scotia, was a journeyman left winger who was fortunate enough to play on a line with Gordie Howe and Alex Delvecchio. With them in 1962-63, he managed his best-ever totals — a very respectable 33 goals and 28 assists.

MacDonald was claimed by Minnesota in the expansion draft. He put in one and a half seasons with the North Stars until, at the age of 39, he had had enough. An offer to coach a minor league club came from Minnesota and he accepted. In 1973-74 he coached the North Stars, a year in which they fared poorly. Following a stay in New Haven as a coach and general manager of the minor league club there, he joined Bob Berry as an assistant coach with the Los Angeles Kings. He assumed the head coaching duties when Berry moved to the Canadiens. After 42 games and 24 losses, he was fired.

For a time MacDonald managed a soccer team in Los Angeles. Preferring to be in hockey he left Los Angeles for the east coast and his New Haven home. Semi-retired, he does some instructional work with hockey schools in the area and spends time helping a friend in the construction business. More often than not he can be found pleasure fishing.

The world of hockey is still alluring to MacDonald. If a job was offered to him in something such as scouting, he would consider a return. Coaching though is out. The inherent pressure and insecurity of the position are just too much.

Bruce MacGregor
Detroit Red Wings

(b. 1941, Edmonton, Alta.)
Games played 893
Goals 213
Assists 257
Total points 470
Penalties in Minutes 217

"Blessings in disguise" have punctuated Bruce MacGregor's life in hockey and taken him to the assistant general manager's position he now holds with the Edmonton Oilers.

MacGregor came out of Detroit's amateur ranks in Alberta in 1960 to join the Red Wings. Like most players he was intro-

Bruce MacGregor

duced gradually to the professional game, filling in for injured players and seeing spot duty as a penalty killer. "You kind of had to bide your time, get established a bit and show you could play in the league," he reports.

MacGregor developed into one of the better penalty killers in the NHL. Once he began playing regularly, his role, he recalls, was as a checker, a defensive position instead of the offensive orientation he had as a junior. So it remained until 1964-65 when Ted Lindsay made his one-season comeback and MacGregor found himself playing right wing on a line with the great forward.

MacGregor credits the influence of Lindsay with helping him rediscover the offensive side of his game. "Through a lot of his talking with me, he got me changed around. That was the first year I scored 20 goals in the NHL. He was a big part of that," he states. "He was something I needed to get me going back in the offensive role of playing the game."

With Lindsay's departure, MacGregor was united with Paul Henderson and Norm Ullman to form a very productive scoring unit known as the HUM Line. "We had a little bit of everything on that line," he recalls. "We blended in and we were good friends, that was the other thing. We had that kind of relationship. It was really nice to be involved with them."

The turmoil associated with the arrival of Ned Harkness to Detroit, fostered MacGregor's first blessing in disguise. He was traded in 1971 to a team and city with which he thought he would never be happy — New York. The Rangers became a respectable force in the NHL and he had a significant part in their resurgence, playing on a line with Pete Stemkowski and Ted Irvine.

An opportunity to return to his hometown of Edmonton, reduce his family's travelling, money and the apparent security of a long-term contract prompted MacGregor to jump to the Edmonton Oilers of the WHA in 1974. "I sometimes wonder if it was that smart a decision," he queries. "I was really established as a hockey player in New York. We had a great hockey club. I was on a good line. It was a difficult decision to make."

MacGregor discovered that, "the WHA was not the NHL. You came to a team that doesn't have near the talent of players. For me, who needed to play with other people who were talented to be successful, I found it tough coming back [to Edmonton]."

During his second season with the Oilers, MacGregor found himself in a contract squabble with the team's new bosses, owner Nelson Skalbania and coach Bep Guidolin. He was released from the club after training camp, a decision he feels they made before the camp had even started. "It was a hard time for myself and my family. I knew I could still play. They were trying to get rid of a contract that was more than they were willing to pay. Rather than trying to trade me or do something like that, they tried to do it by degrading me and cutting me, telling me I didn't have the ability to play."

An out-of-court settlement was reached whereby MacGregor joined the Oilers' public relations department. He remained aboard after Peter Pocklington bought the team and former teammate Glen Sather arrived to manage and coach. "It's the same old story," he says reflecting on the dispute. "It's something that was negative and turned out to be a very positive thing for me." As assistant to the general manager, he oversees the administration of the Oilers' business office.

William McNeill

Detroit Red Wings

(b. 1936, Edmonton, Alta.)
Games played 257
Goals 21
Assists 46
Total points 67
Penalties in Minutes 142

Billy McNeill's opportunity to play in the NHL came as it did for so many players when misfortune hit others. "Of course in those days you didn't get to the National Hockey League unless there was some reason for you to get there," he relates. "Billy Dineen broke his ankle. So did Alex Delvecchio so that left room for Billy Dea and myself to join the club. It always seemed to happen that way."

When McNeill stepped into the Red Wings' fold from its Edmonton farm team in 1956, he was a natural centreman. Instead he found himself on the right wing. "The right wing wasn't where I was supposed to play," he says. "It's where Jack Adams wanted me to play. It was one of my misfortunes there that I didn't play centre ice in the National Hockey League. One of my big arguments, of course, with Adams was that he had four right wingers. With Gordie Howe being there playing 45 minutes a game, it didn't leave much ice time for the rest of us."

Consequently McNeill found himself back in the minors several times where "you'd get hotter than a firecracker and come back up again." Looking back at the experience, he suggests with no bitterness, "Maybe in my particular case I was with the wrong team at the wrong time. Centre ice was the logical spot for a river skater from Alberta. But we had no choice."

McNeill left the Red Wings for the minor leagues in 1964, never to return. He performed well in the Western Hockey League where he was twice voted league MVP. He retired in 1971 to pursue his business interest in a Vancouver hotel. For the last seven years he has been a representative with Carling-O'Keefe Breweries, a company with which he has been associated on and off over the last 25 years. He and his family live in Vancouver.

Martin Pavelich

Detroit Red Wings

(b. 1927, Sault Ste. Marie, Ont.)
Games played 634
Goals 93
Assists 159
Total points 252
Penalties in Minutes 454

Ex-Red Wing forward Marty Pavelich offers one piece of advice to players leaving the game and going out into the business world: "If you apply the same kind of effort that I had to to become a hockey player, to make myself a National League player, the same kind of effort I applied in the business world, you know what? It works."

Pavelich retired from Detroit in 1957 and in partnership with teammate Ted Lindsay operated an injection molding plastics firm. It wasn't easy, he reports. "The first five years I didn't put a red cent in the bank but I didn't go in the hole either. We were a pretty good sized company. We sold it for a pretty good price. It worked out well because we worked at it and put in the hours, the time, the effort."

Pavelich played ten solid seasons with the Red Wings, a good part of the time with Glen Skov and Tony Leswick, the team's ace checking line. For a decade his assignment was to check the man he calls the greatest goal scorer ever in hockey, Rocket Richard. He and his cohorts went up against the top scoring units in the NHL at the time. Toronto's Kennedy line, Chicago's Bentley line, New York's Raleigh line. They checked, Howe and Lindsay provided the offensive punch and the result was a team that owned the NHL title for seven years and won four Stanley Cups. "If we'd done just a few things differently, we should have won two or possibly three more Stanley Cups," he says.

When Ted Lindsay was traded to Chicago in 1957, he announced that his partner Pavelich would look after business in his absence. "Jack Adams didn't like that. They didn't want you to have any outside interests. He wanted you to give strictly 100 per cent to hockey. I just thought ahead . . . I'm 29 years of age, this is a good time to get out. I might have been traded or sent down to the minors," he explains. He had had a very enjoyable and successful career.

Swapping a Red Wing sweater for a business suit had its trying times, Pavelich admits. "You're kind of hero-worshipped. You get kind of a false feeling about yourself. Once you get out of the game you've got to think of yourself as a human being like everybody else. You got to get out and start a whole new program."

Success has followed him out of hockey into the business world where he now acts as a sales consultant for a number of companies. "It's just enough to keep me busy," he says. Every chance he gets, he goes skiing in Europe and throughout the United States and Canada. His favorite spot is the Bugaboos in British Columbia where he takes in helicopter skiing. He and his family live in the Detroit area.

Marcel Pronovost

Detroit Red Wings

Marcel Pronovost

(b. 1930, Lac de la Tortue, Que.)
Games played 1206
Goals 88
Assists 257
Total points 345
Penalties in Minutes 851

Any changes Marcel Pronovost, a blue chip defenceman with Detroit and Toronto for 20 seasons, would make in the course of his long, productive athletic career relate strictly to its financial side. Today he works for an investment firm in Windsor, Ontario and his reflections on the past are flavoured by the outlook and language of that profession.

"We only thought of hockey," Pronovost states. "I believe and I hope that the kids today are better businessmen than I was. I'm not speaking for everybody else but speaking for myself. I don't think I was oriented that way [towards business]. If I had known then what I know today, I wouldn't have to work today. From 1950, it would have been very easy for me to stash $800, $900 or $1,000 a year away. I would look for some investment even if it was just ten per cent of what I earned. If I had invested ten per cent of what I earned, I wouldn't have to work today."

Pronovost is critical of the NHL pension plan which he says was invested at 2 3/4 per cent in Canadian securities. "I think we could have done better than that with our pension plan," he adds. Today he rolls over his annuity into an RRSP to realize a better return. "Right now I'm drawing a pension of less than $9,000 a year and that's after 23 years of battle," he comments. "Someone's made a lot of bucks off our sweat, I'll tell you that. It's like anything else. The pioneers always do the sweating," he says about the beginning of the plan. "Whoever comes behind, they get a little bit more of the gravy. I hope they know how to take care of it."

Pronovost came up through the Detroit organization and landed with the Red Wings in 1950. Used primarily as a defensive specialist, he was one of the league's most consistent players at his position. He played in Detroit until 1965 when he was dealt to Toronto. Though he had shared in three Stanley Cups with Detroit, the one he won in 1967 with the Maple Leafs is special to him. Considered an "over-the-hill" bunch, Toronto was the overwhelming underdog. "Everyone thought we should grab our canes and crutches and go home," he recalls. "The one thing they didn't count on was the heart, how big the heart was."

In 1970 Pronovost went to the Leafs' farm club in Tulsa to act as a playing coach. "I think I was dreaming a little bit because I realize now it would never happen," he states. "I thought I could better my lot if I wanted to stay in hockey to learn something at the coaching level." He had two tries at coaching in the NHL, first under Punch Imlach in Buffalo and then under Ted Lindsay in Detroit. When those two general managers were dismissed, so was their man behind the bench. He coached the Windsor Spitfires of the Ontario Major Junior Hockey League. "We had a little slide and they let me go. They've been letting coaches go ever since," he notes.

He enjoys his work with the investment firm, but hockey remains Pronovost's first love. He volunteers with a junior C team now in Windsor. He talks about having a good rapport with players at any level. "I can identify with them easily. I know I can help them not only hockeywise, but lifewise. I've gone through some of the stuff they wouldn't want to go through. I went to the university of life."

The one legacy of being involved with professional hockey for so many years, he says, is camaraderie. "What you got was the fellowship of the game. It's like people that have gone to war together. It brings people closer. Veterans tend to look at life a little bit the same way."

Metro Prystai

Detroit Red Wings

Metro Prystai

(b. 1927, Yorkton, Sask.)
Games played 674
Goals 151
Assists 179
Total points 330
Penalties in Minutes 231

"If I had a chance to do it over again I would like to do it over again the same, even the same bloody way, even though we didn't get paid a lot of money or anything like that. But you know I came from a little town. We had nothing. It was just after the Depression. Nobody had any money. Then all of a sudden, bang-o, you're living first class, you're travelling first class, you're making pretty good money. It was pretty damn good money. We were making close to $10,000 a year but I had buddies at home who worked for 12 months for 3,000 or $4,000." So the pride of Yorkton, Saskatchewan, Metro Prystai, describes the lure of professional hockey when he broke into the NHL in 1947.

Originally a Chicago Black Hawk, Prystai developed into a versatile forward who spent most of his career in the crimson garb of the Detroit Red Wings. Though he was a little sad to leave the Black Hawks, he came to a "good organization" where winning a pair of Stanley Cups made the deal even sweeter. His sojourn in Detroit was interrupted for a year when he became the Red Wings' contribution to a kind of sporting "Marshall Plan" the NHL had devised to save the sinking Chicago franchise. "Chicago was down in the doldrums," he reports. "The teams got together and said, 'Look, we're going to send one player a piece to help Chicago.' I was part of the help-the-poor deal. I had been there. I was kind of half-popular because I had a fairly good year. I wasn't very happy to go back because I was enjoying Detroit." A year later Detroit dealt Ed Sandford to get him back.

In 1958, with Detroit fighting for a play-off berth, Prystai suffered a cracked bone in his foot. Once healed, he was sent to Edmonton, the club affiliate in the Western Hockey League, to get back into shape. During his fourth game with the farm club he broke a leg. "I was in a cast pretty well all summer. I went back to Detroit's training camp next year and the doctor in Detroit told me I shouldn't play at least until Christmas." He was sent back to Edmonton where he could skate but not twist or take any hits on the wounded appendage. "I'd come down to games and I wouldn't be dressed and the doctor there would ask, 'What's the matter with you? How come you're not playing?' 'My leg isn't right.' " Prystai relates the conversation complete with the doctor's professional sarcasm. " 'Aaaah, you'll never break it in a million years.' " Four games later he was knocked down and the leg broke again in the same place. He was in a cast for ten more months and out of hockey.

Prystai turned to coaching for a few years, first in Omaha and then in the junior ranks in Moose Jaw and Melville, Saskatchewan. He left hockey to become a sales representative for a brewery. Later he got involved in Saskatchewan Government Insurance (insurance in that province is government operated through franchised agencies) in Wynyard, Saskatchewan and stayed in that business 14 years. He sold the operation last fall. He now intends to become involved in real estate and spend more time at the fishing lodge he owns and operates in northern Saskatchewan.

Earl Reibel

Detroit Red Wings

(b. 1930, Kitchener, Ont.)
Games played 409
Goals 84
Assists 161
Total points 245
Penalties in Minutes 75

Earl Reibel

Although tough trades have always been a fact of life, it seems as though they had a greater effect on the men who played in the six-team era. In many cases players developed a loyalty to an organization because they had practically grown up within it. Being removed from it was a betrayal of that loyalty and the men were robbed of their desire to play.

Earl "Dutch" Reibel developed as a player within the Red Wings' organization. He went from his native Kitchener to Detroit's junior affiliate in Windsor, to the farm clubs in Indianapolis and Edmonton and finally to the parent club in 1953. His first game on October 8, 1953 was certainly memorable. He assisted on each of Detroit's goals in its 4-1 victory over New York, establishing a record which still holds for the most assists by one player in his first NHL game.

A playmaking centreman, he eventually found a home on a line with Howe and Lindsay. "They were two of the greatest players," he declares. "You couldn't beat 'em, not only as players but as gentlemen, too."

Reibel enjoyed successful years with the Red Wings. He contributed to a pair of Stanley Cup victories. He was voted winner of the Lady Byng Trophy in 1956. In his best season (1954-55) he scored 25 goals and 41 assists in 70 games.

In 1957 Reibel was part of an eight player swap that sent him to Chicago. "Once I left Detroit, things just went downhill," he remembers. "It just wasn't the same. I enjoyed Detroit . . . you play with an organization for so long."

Following a stop in Boston the next year, Reibel went to the minors where he finished his hockey career. When he was about to be shipped to San Francisco, he decided to quit rather than go west.

Reibel returned to Kitchener and has worked for the Brewers' Retail ever since. Recently widowed, he lives in Kitchener with his two sons.

Terry Sawchuk

Detroit Red Wings

Terry Sawchuk

(b. 1929, Winnipeg, Man.)
Games played 971
Minutes 57,205
Goals against 2401
Shutouts 103
Average 2.52

Terry Sawchuk is one of hockey's tales of triumph and tragedy. He came out of Winnipeg, Manitoba and sharpened his skills in Detroit's farm system until he was called up to the Red Wings for full-time duty in 1950. He capably replaced Harry Lumley and won the Calder Trophy while leading the league with 11 shutouts.

With Sawchuk's superlative goaltending backstopping one of the greatest defensive clubs in NHL history, Detroit won the Stanley Cup three out of the next four years.

The greatest performance of Sawchuk and his teammates came in the 1952 Stanley Cup finals. Detroit swept both the semi-finals and finals in four games. Sawchuk posted four shutouts and allowed a paltry five goals in those eight games. He won the Vezina Trophy in 1952, 1953 and 1955.

However, the game took its toll on Sawchuk. Once a happy, easygoing man, he began to change. Many surmise that the intense pressure goalies undergo game in and game out changed him into a surly, brooding loner, the testy individual he would remain. He was known to insult fans and media people. The Red Wings traded him to Boston in 1955. Partway through the next season he quit saying his nerves were shot. He was traded back to Detroit where he returned to play until 1964 when Toronto claimed him in a draft.

Sawchuk shared the Maple Leaf goaltending duties with another veteran of the cage, Johnny Bower. The two shared a Vezina Trophy in 1965. It was these players, playing the games of their lives, who led their club to an upset victory in the 1967 Stanley Cup play-offs. Sawchuk later considered this series his best performance in a Cup finals.

Sawchuk went to Los Angeles and New York, a shadow of the man who had stepped into the majors 20 years earlier. He was worn and wasted by the job. In 1970 he and his roommate at the time, Ron Stewart, were involved in a scuffle on their front lawn that resulted in some injuries. A month later he died in hospital from a blood clot in his lungs.

Glen Skov

Detroit Red Wings

(b. 1931, Wheatley, Ont.)
Games played 650
Goals 106
Assists 136
Total points 242
Penalties in Minutes 413

If circumstances had been slightly different and Montreal's contract to coach their Hull-Ottawa affiliate offered more money and more security, Glen Skov might have succeeded Toe Blake in leading hockey's most famous and successful team. But security, as any coach will tell you, is an impossible dream.

Skov had played ten NHL seasons with Detroit, Chicago and briefly with Montreal. He, Marty Pavelich and Tony Leswick were a trio that specialized in checking opposing scorers and contributed significantly to the rise of the Red Wing dynasty of the early 1950s.

The role of the checking line in the Red Wing scheme was to smother the scoring punch of enemy shooters such as Richard and Beliveau and chip in with its own goal production. Doing that work effectively allowed Skov to share in three Stanley Cups.

Skov was later traded to Chicago in 1955 as part of the NHL effort to save the crumbling Black Hawk organization, although he didn't recognize it at the time. "I think what we did eventually instill in the players was, 'Let's not be a last place team. Let's make ourselves contenders and work up the ladder,'" he notes. Eventually this happened in Chicago.

Skov's last season as a professional was spent with Montreal as, for the most part, a playing coach in Hull-Ottawa. After enjoying a successful season, he wanted to return to the Canadiens' organization as the full-time coach of the farm club. "I did not want to be a playing coach. We were very successful. We won the championship.

I just felt it would be better to be behind the bench. They did want me there but we could never come to an agreement on a contract," he remembers. "I always heard that I was prominently being considered [as a possible successor to Toe Blake]."

"I had to make a decision to return to hockey or stay with the company I was with," Skov says. He remained with PMS, a firm that manufactures colourants for plastics, and now heads a division of that company in Chicago where he lives with his family.

Skov sometimes appears in old-timers' hockey affairs. His most treasured involvement in hockey is as an instructor at the annual hockey school for the deaf that attracts hearing impaired youngsters from across the USA. He calls the one week he spends each June helping these kids learn hockey "very gratifying".

Floyd Smith
Detroit Red Wings

(b. 1935, Perth, Ont.)
Games played 616
Goals 129
Assists 178
Total points 307
Penalties in Minutes 207

No one in a hockey organization avoids wrath when a club performs poorly including the scouts, points out Toronto's Floyd Smith. "When your team is doing badly like we did this year, there's no one who can escape," he says, referring to the new depths of despair to which the Maple Leafs sank in the 1984-85 campaign. "Everybody has to accept some of the blame. When you're bad, you're bad and you grin and bear it and wait for the day you're good to give everybody who gave you hell back to them then."

Smith, a defensive forward who played with Boston, New York, Detroit, Toronto and Buffalo between 1954 and 1972, has been a Maple Leaf scout for the last four years. His playing career ended in Buffalo where he started coaching, filling in for an ailing Punch Imlach. He moved to the club's AHL affiliate in Cincinnati and later coached that city's WHA franchise. Hired by Toronto to coach, his career ended after he was involved in an "unfortunate" car accident. Since then he has been a member of Toronto's scouting staff.

The draft choices Smith and fellow scout Dick Duff have made since coming aboard, he explains, have just begun playing and developing. "We feel very confident that from our standpoint, the kids we've recommended will do well," he comments.

Smith's hockey and post-hockey career evolved in similar ways. "All in all, it just continued to fall into place," he explains. "Nothing was ever planned or anything. I did a lot of things outside that I enjoyed. I could probably go outside tomorrow and really enjoy it. I've always stayed in it because it's been interesting. There's never been a day when I can truthfully say that it's been dull. It's that kind of business and that's the part I enjoy most."

The attraction of the game in any capacity, Smith adds, is "the winning and the losing, the highs and the lows. That's the name of the game." He never dwells too much on past thrills. "You feel good about it at the time. But once it's over and done with, life goes on . . . and now we're into a new phase where I worry about kids we draft more than I did anything else."

Norm Ullman
Detroit Red Wings

(b. 1935, Provost, Alta.)
Games played 1410
Goals 490
Assists 739
Total points 1229
Penalties in Minutes 712

Norm Ullman

Norm Ullman had spent 20 years in the NHL and two more in the WHA when he decided to call it quits. Leaving the game in which he performed so ably for so long was not difficult because he was prepared for the transition, mentally and otherwise.

"It's not hard, especially after you played all those years," Ullman states. "If you had played only four or five years and, boom, all of a sudden it's over, nobody wants you and you have to quit, that's tough for the player it happens to. I played pro hockey for 23 years. I think I got everything out of it I could have for the amount of time I put in."

Ullman joined Detroit from its farm club in his native Edmonton in 1955. Over 13 seasons he developed into one of the Red Wings' most productive forwards. One season he led the league with 42 goals. He centred a prolific scoring unit known as the HUM line, an acronym for Henderson, Ullman, MacGregor. Traded to Toronto in 1968, he continued to perform in a steady fashion for the Maple Leafs.

Ullman says he was happy in Toronto except for the last season and a half when he sat on the bench much of the time. It was an easy decision for him to make, therefore, when an offer came to play for the Edmonton Oilers of the WHA. It might have been better, he adds, to have gone to the Oilers even earlier if only from the standpoint of making a lot more money. By returning to Edmonton, he had come full circle. Edmonton was where it had all started for him in hockey and after two seasons there he retired.

"I haven't done much since I retired," Ullman says. "I'm kind of semi-retired." During his career he deferred his income through annuities. "I was fortunate. I didn't have to go to work to put bread on the table right away." In the meantime he is "looking at different things" to do down the road.

Ullman is very active in NHL old-timers' hockey, playing as many as 35 games a year. It gives him the opportunity to travel around the country playing hockey and maintaining the camaraderie he has enjoyed with other players over the years. "This way I'm not cut off from what I've done all my life," he states.

It is only the "off-ice things" that Ullman might reconsider in the course of his career. "I'm a fairly quiet person. I didn't get involved in endorsements, public speaking, making appearances and that kind of thing. If I was going to start all over I'd get into more of that and get established in that way."

Johnny Wilson

Detroit Red Wings

(b. 1929, Kincardine, Ont.)
Games played 688
Goals 161
Assists 171
Total points 332
Penalties in Minutes 190

Johnny Wilson cracked the Red Wing roster in 1949 at just about the time Detroit began ruling the NHL roost for several seasons. He became part of the club's checking unit. "That was our responsibility. Keep the guys off the scoreboard. As a result it took a little bit away from your offensive game. You couldn't hang in there till the last minute. You made sure you picked your guy up 'cause we played an airtight game in those days," he says.

At one time Wilson held the iron man record in the NHL by playing 580 consecutive games. "There were a lot of times, just like anybody else," he says, "that I shouldn't have played. The injuries weren't that serious but you probably should have sat out. We were hurt and we were a couple of players short, the coach would ask you if you could go a couple of shifts. And you got in a couple of shifts and all of a sudden got in the game and probably forgot your injury as long as you didn't aggravate it."

Wilson played for Chicago, Toronto and New York before he retired in 1962. He was part of a multi-player deal in 1955 that sent him and several others to Chicago. That and another large deal, he points out, gutted the championship Red Wing club, something from which it was never able to recover.

Though he retired in 1962, Wilson thinks he could have played a little longer. "I could have played until expansion. I quit mostly because, in those days, there wasn't too much security after hockey."

He joined Molson Brewery as a representative for a few years and later returned to hockey as a coach at Princeton University. He went on to a coaching career that took him to the minor leagues, the NHL, the WHA, Team Canada '77, "the whole ball of wax" as he puts it. "I've done it all."

Wilson left the relative security of university hockey for a general manager/coaching job with Springfield, a Los Angeles Kings' farm affiliate. From Springfield, he moved to Detroit where he was involved in the Ned Harkness controversy. (Harkness' strict disciplinarian coaching methods alienated many of his players. As a result, the Red Wings fell to the bottom of the NHL and have never really recovered.) "That was like coming into a hornets' nest." Then it was on to Michigan-Baltimore and Cleveland of the WHA, two franchises that folded. His final four seasons in coaching were spent with Denver and Pittsburgh of the NHL.

He left at the end of the 1980 season: "I was kind of fed up with coaching because of management and also players. Management today listens to too much flak from players today. Years ago, there was no goddamn way you could see the coach and complain that you weren't getting any ice time or see the manager or go talk to the owner. We never second-guessed." It is an attitude that he reckons dates back to the second NHL expansion in the early 1970s. Lawyers became involved and have, he says, taken over the game.

Wilson left hockey, returned to Detroit and became a manufacturer's representative for Klarich Associates International, a firm that deals in automotive parts. He is also president of the Red Wings' Alumni Association and is active in maintaining that old-timers' group.

Benedict Woit

Detroit Red Wings

(b. 1928, Fort William, Ont.)
Games played 334
Goals 7
Assists 26
Total points 33
Penalties in Minutes 170

Other than a reunion with his former Detroit Red Wing teammates in 1984, Ben Woit's contact with hockey has been limited since he left in 1966. The extent of it has been requests he receives from collectors to sign bubble gum hockey cards. "I don't know how they got my address, but they send them down here." Woit, now living in Thunder Bay, Ontario, is surprised that anyone remembers him after all these years. "I'd say I got ten in the last four years."

Though Woit spent only five years in the NHL with Detroit and Chicago he was fortunate to experience three times what some players never do — Stanley Cup victory. "We were fortunate," he says, applying the collective to himself. "I just happened to be with the right guys, I guess; guys like Lindsay, Howe and Sawchuk . . . you couldn't go wrong with that bunch."

Add to his Stanley Cup total a couple of Memorial Cup championships during his junior years, one with St. Mike's and a second with Port Arthur, and Woit came out of hockey with more than his fair share of winning. He was always a stay-at-home defenceman who liked to play the body. Once, in junior, he drilled Ray Gariepy with a check that made the man announcing the game, Foster Hewitt, "nearly jump out of the booth". His victim continued to play though "I don't think he knew who he was for a couple of weeks."

"I tried to hit them in the NHL but they were a little faster and a little better. I caught a few of them, though it wasn't good enough. That was our game."

Woit was traded to Chicago where he spent a year and a half before going to the minors in 1956. He continued his career there until 1966 when he returned to his native city to work as a longshoreman, something he had done over the summers during his hockey years and which he still does today. "The boat comes in. We get on, load the pipes and give him what he wants," he says. Hunting, fishing and working around his home is what he enjoys most these days.

No, the Chicago Black Hawks and Montreal Canadiens have not called timeout to enjoy a game of leapfrog. Gilles Marotte (2) and Doug Mohns (11) of Chicago and Ted Harris (10), Yvan Cournoyer (12) and J.C. Tremblay, whose number is not visible, of

Montreal, are all frantically searching for the missing puck while Gilles Tremblay (5) seems to be supervising the search. Probably most anxious about its loss is Montreal goaltender Gump Worsley (1) who nearly has his toe on it.

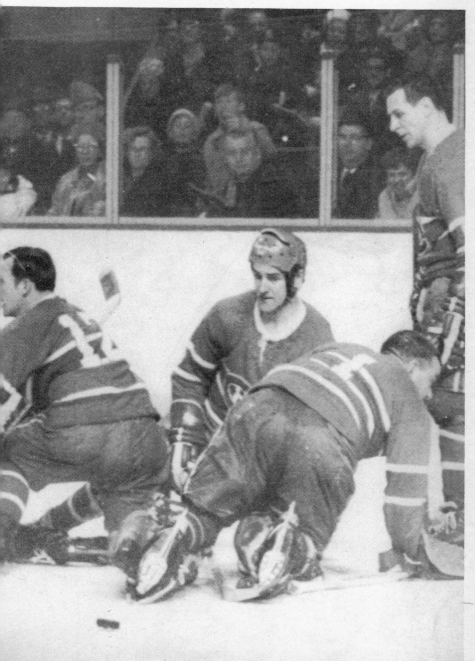

The records show that no franchise in the history of the NHL has enjoyed the success that the Montreal Canadiens have. The club has won the Stanley Cup twenty-one times. Featuring a fast-paced attack that became known as "fire wagon hockey", the Canadiens were truly the cream of the six-team crop through the 1950s and 1960s.

The genesis of Montreal's success lies in the 1940s when Toe Blake, Elmer Lach, Maurice Richard and Bill Durnan revived a club which had been barely mediocre in the 1930s. Frank Selke arrived at the same time to develop a system of farm clubs that would give the team a virtual monopoly on talent coming out of Quebec and continually feed the Montreal team with stars and superstars.

The names on Montreal's rosters of the era read like a list of legends: Maurice "Rocket" Richard, Doug Harvey, Jacques Plante, Dickie Moore, Jean Beliveau, Bernie "Boom Boom" Geoffrion, Bert Olmstead, Henri Richard. At the helm for most of the time was the "Old Lamplighter", Toe Blake, the man with the ability to mold champion teams from his collection of superstars and journeymen. In any sports organization such a collection of big stars and average players could have been a fatal combination. Blake had a knack for controlling them so that everyone played for one purpose — winning. When defining the reasons for the club's success, ex-Canadiens invariably refer to the organization's excellence and how everyone was treated equally. It was a tightly knit group often described as a family.

The Canadiens gave an indication of their impending glory with a Stanley Cup victory in 1953 that interrupted the Red Wings' streak. As Detroit wound down, the Canadiens succeeded them as lords of the league with a string of championships no other club has matched. Beginning in 1955-56, the team won five consecutive Stanley Cups. Those teams may have been the greatest collection of hockey talent the sport has ever known.

With the retirement of Rocket Richard and the departure of Doug Harvey and Jacques Plante in the early 1960s, the Canadiens embarked on something of a rebuilding process. They did not fall out of contention; they merely didn't win the Stanley Cup for a few seasons. Beliveau, Richard, Tremblay, Rousseau, Worsely, Provost and the others surged back in 1965 to claim the championship once more. Had it not been for the Toronto upset in 1967, Blake would have had another five consecutive Cups under his belt.

Montreal was the one club of the original six that carried on successfully after expansion. Sam Pollock, the talented general manager, saved and traded for draft choices which would build the title teams of the 1970s. The traditionally smooth organization faltered in the early 1980s when the club's ownership changed hands. Recently it has rediscovered some of the tradition of *Les Glorieux*.

Ralph Backstrom

Montreal Canadiens

Ralph Backstrom

(b. 1937, Kirkland Lake, Ont.)
Games played 1032
Goals 278
Assists 361
Total points 639
Penalties in Minutes 386

"I thought that after I played for 19 years, I was ready to step into head coaching," comments Ralph Backstrom, coach of the University of Denver hockey club. "You really have to serve your apprenticeship somewhere. I feel with eight years under my belt, four as an assistant, four as head coach, that I'm finally learning something about coaching. Coming out of playing you're not ready for it."

As a collegiate coach, Backstrom finds that communicating with his players is the most important aspect of coaching today. Players nowadays are willing to cooperate with their coaches, he says, if coaches provide logical reasons for what they are doing. Players really want to know why coaches do a certain thing.

When discussing the idea of one day stepping behind the bench of an NHL club Backstrom says, "I'm not dying to get back at this point. I'm here and I'm enjoying it at the University of Denver. If an opportunity came up, I suppose I would have to consider it. I've learned an awful lot in the last eight years about coaching. I suppose I'm getting to the point now when I would like to accept the challenge of a professional hockey team. If not coaching, then the management/development area."

Backstrom's hockey days ended when he was with the New England Whalers of the WHA in 1977. Nineteen years earlier he played his first full season with Montreal. A gifted skater and playmaker, he had the misfortune of being on a team overstocked with good forwards. "I was considered the third string centre unless there was an injury or something," he states. "I was pleased to be part of that organization. I was pleased to play on six Stanley Cup teams. I often thought I could have been a lot better, on an individual basis, if I was playing elsewhere. I couldn't have done better teamwise playing anywhere else."

After 12 years with the Canadiens, Backstrom asked to be traded. When the club refused him his wish, he quit. A couple of months later Montreal completed a deal that sent him to Los Angeles. "In those days you didn't question your authorities. You were taught to respect the people in authority. Finally in my early 30s I got enough nerve to do something about it," he says. "I can remember players in junior hockey who were assigned to check me that were playing regularly and here I was on the bench in Montreal. That bothered me a lot. I got very frustrated, but I never had anything against the organization."

Backstrom spent two and a half seasons on the west coast before being traded to Chicago. He eventually jumped to the WHA where he finished his playing days. His stint at Denver was interrupted for one year when he assisted Bob Berry, the coach of the Los Angeles Kings.

Jean Beliveau
Montreal Canadiens

(b. 1931, Trois-Rivières, Que.)
Games played 1125
Goals 507
Assists 712
Total points 1219
Penalties in Minutes 1029

Jean Beliveau

Never before had the arrival of a player been so eagerly anticipated by a hockey club and its fans than when Jean Beliveau arrived with the Montreal Canadiens in 1953. It had taken four years to entice the accomplished, rangy centre away from Quebec City where he had starred in both junior and senior hockey and where he had enjoyed immense popularity.

Sitting in his Montreal Forum office, Jean Beliveau, former Canadiens' captain and star centre and now the club's senior vice-president of corporate affairs, remembers those early days. "It's probably true that I could have joined the Canadiens two or three years earlier in 1949-50," he recalls. "The context was a little different then. That kind of life was all new to me. I came from a small city [Victoriaville]. Everybody supported you. Everywhere I was going, I was well received. My last year of junior they gave me this big day where they gave me this car. I never had a car in my life. It was a great thing. So I said, in appreciation, I'll stay another year."

He stayed two years. After that time, even the rabid, Montreal-hating Quebec fans knew that Beliveau would have to leave and fulfill his boyhood dream of playing for the Canadiens. He needed to experience the ultimate test of his hockey mettle. The welcome from Canadiens' general manager Frank Selke was a warm one: "I just opened the vault and told Jean to take what he wanted." Today

Beliveau laughs, "I've always said he opened the vault but there was nothing in the vault, compared to today."

Beliveau understands the pressure that results from great fan expectations. In fact he counselled Guy Lafleur about it after Lafleur joined the Canadiens with a pocketful of rave reviews on his junior career. "There's nothing worse than starting your career in professional sport when you're preceded by all this publicity. That's what I told Guy when he started."

Even to this day the great Beliveau is not sure whether or not he measured up. "Personally, I always had the feeling that whatever I was doing wasn't enough," he admits. "It's very difficult to work under those conditions."

After overcoming an injury that hampered the start of his NHL career, "Le Gros Bill" did better than 'just manage' in professional company. His career with the Habs lasted 18 seasons. He played on ten Stanley Cup winners and was named to the first all-star team six times and to the second all-star team four times. With 507 goals and 712 assists, he is the Canadiens' all-time highest point getter. He was awarded the Hart Trophy in 1956 and 1964, the Art Ross Trophy in 1956 and the Conn Smythe Trophy in 1965. While with the Canadiens, he found himself out of the play-offs only once.

At 6'3" and weighing 205 pounds, the smooth-skating Beliveau made an imposing figure as he cruised centre ice. His strength and deft puckhandling made him a constant threat to either score or pass the puck to a winger in scoring position. Exuding a quiet charisma, he became a natural captain. He was the personification of class both on and off the ice.

Beliveau, stately as ever, still evokes instant respect and fondness. Although he retired in 1971, his popularity has not waned and he is called upon to attend functions across the country. He first started doing promotional work for a dairy while in Quebec City and continued with Molson Breweries after he joined the Canadiens. Today he sits on the board of the company.

These days he is happy maintaining a busy schedule, particularly if it takes him to the smaller cities and more remote districts. He plans to start taking Sundays off, "unless it's a national or provincial event" so that he and his wife can enjoy their grandchild.

Beliveau sits on the boards of many charities, including his own, the Jean Beliveau Foundation. It supplies equipment and materials to associations involved with the care of children.

Marcel Bonin

Montreal Canadiens

(b. 1932, Montreal, Que.)
Games played 454
Goals 97
Assists 175
Total points 272
Penalties in Minutes 336

Marcel Bonin

In Joliat, Quebec native son Marcel Bonin is well known, respected and almost revered. Two years ago a newly built arena was named for him — Le Centre sportif Marcel Bonin. A medal in his honour is presented each year to the most accomplished athlete in the area. "Everybody knows me around here," he comments, understating the case slightly. He's one of the few people who can be found simply by making an inquiry at the Joliat city hall.

Bonin established two reputations during his nine-year career in the NHL: first, as a physically powerful, tough and aggressive man on the left side and, second, as one of the most colourful characters ever to grace the sport.

When Bonin came to Detroit in 1952 he could barely speak a word of English. He says with a laugh, his accent still tinged with French, "No, I couldn't speak English at all, but on the ice you don't have to talk." He admits that scoring goals was not his forte and describes himself as a team player who enjoyed the defensive, rough type of game. He helped the Red Wings win their last Stanley Cup over 30 years ago. Later, he was traded to Montreal where he participated in three more championships.

To this day Bonin is still known for his off-ice antics. Once, for the hell of it, he wrestled a bear. A circus had come to town, he recalls. Former boxer Joe Louis was travelling with the circus as a referee for its wrestling bear act. "He gave $1,000 to the guy who put the bear down. He came to my hometown and nobody wanted to go up with the bear. I wanted to fight the bear." With a roundhouse punch he tried in vain to flatten the original big, bad bruin. The strategy did not work and when it was over Bonin found himself on the mat, losing one of the few scraps of his career. Afterwards, the circus asked him to become part of the act. He sat in the audience on another ten occasions, taking on the bear when no one else would but never winning.

Bonin impressed his teammates by eating glass and putting a hat pin through his forearm with no apparent ill effects. Both were acts he had seen in night clubs and mimicked. He was trying to break the language barrier with his teammates through a more universal language, laughter. "When I went to Detroit I couldn't speak too much English, so I do these tricks . . ."

A collision with Pete Goegan resulted in a serious back injury in 1962 that ended his hockey career. The spinal fusion that was performed kept him hospitalized for three years. He returned home where his interest in pistol shooting eventually led him to a job with the local constabulary. For years, he had practised pistol shooting with the cops daily, through friends in the police forces of Detroit and Montreal. He developed into a sharpshooter. Not long after his return to Joliat he was asked by the local police who knew of his abilities to help bring in a gunman who had killed a police officer during a break-in and had kept the force at bay for three hours. "I managed to get in with his brother and I went to pick him up there. When he saw me and his brother he quit," he recalls.

Bonin worked as a law enforcement officer for seven years. After that he surveilled area high schools, keeping individuals off the premises who did not belong or were there to cause trouble or pedal drugs. Asthma has kept him off work for the last two years.

Adapting to life after hockey, Bonin admits, was no mean feat, at least for him. "You go home and you don't know what to do. It took me at least ten years, maybe more, to realize I'm like an ordinary man and to make a small living."

Bonin takes great pride in his children. One is an orthopedic surgeon, another a lawyer, a third an architect and the fourth is an artist. To him they are proof that their father was more than a jester with bears, beer glasses and hat pins.

Butch Bouchard

Montreal Canadiens

(b. 1920, Montreal, Que.)
Games played 785
Goals 49
Assists 144
Total points 193
Penalties in Minutes 863

"Age caught up with me," comments Emile "Butch" Bouchard about his retirement from the Montreal Canadiens in 1956 after 15 NHL seasons. "I was 36. With a bad leg I was surprised I played that much. According to the doctors I should have quit when I was 29 years old."

Bouchard, one of the steadiest rearguards in the league, refers to a serious knee injury he suffered in 1948 that required surgery and a three-month absence from the game. The doctors prescribed retirement but, with his quiet resolve, he purchased a stationary bike and set about strengthening his leg by pedalling ten miles a day in his basement. "I guess I was stubborn," he laughs. "I wanted to play." He returned to play effectively but not as well as he had before the operation. "I had been an all-star five times before the injury. After I got hurt I couldn't make it. I was playing good hockey but not all-star standing."

The knee injury prompted Bouchard to begin to think about life after the NHL. "I heard the doctor say he thought my career was over. So that's why when I had a chance to go into business, I said, 'Well, I have a chance to buy into a business with the little money I have.' At the time I was 29 years old. It turned out to be a good investment, but I had to work quite hard at it." Butch Bouchard's Restaurant became a thriving Montreal eatery. He sold it four years ago when he decided to retire. Before becoming a restauranteur he had been a beekeeper on a farm on the south shore of Montreal Island.

Bouchard, a Montreal native, joined the Canadiens in 1942. His size (6'2" and 205 pounds) and love for hockey are two factors, he says, that contributed to his success on the ice. "I was a determined, enthusiastic, young fellow in those days," says the 65-year-old ex-team captain who was a member of five Stanley Cup champion teams. "That's what you need to make a success in life. You work hard, you're enthusiastic and very disciplined at your game." One person may have more raw talent than another, he adds, but it is the one with the discipline and the ambition who will succeed, in any avenue of life.

Bouchard needed that discipline one night in Boston. An over-zealous fan, a woman, took exception to the way he had been manhandling Bruins' forwards and jabbed him in the back with a hat pin as he walked from the dressing room to the ice. A startled Bouchard jumped around suddenly and in turn startled his tormentor who began screaming. The local police were determined to bring the defenceman down to the station for what seemed to be unchivalrous behaviour. Fortunately things were smoothed out and the woman arrived at the Montreal dressing room to apologize to him for her poor manners.

Bouchard now divides his year in half. He spends the winters in Florida, and the summers on his son Pierre's farm outside of Montreal. Pierre followed in his father's footsteps and played defence for the Montreal Canadiens in the 1970s.

Floyd Curry

Montreal Canadiens

Floyd Currie

(b. 1925, Chapleau, Ont.)
Games played 601
Goals 105
Assists 99
Total points 204
Penalties in Minutes 147

"Many games when you were hurt, you should've probably not played, but you didn't say you were hurt because there was a lot of good hockey players around to take your spot." Floyd "Busher" Curry, author of that statement, knew well that premise behind playing professional hockey during the 1950s.

Curry bounced between the parent Canadiens' club and its farm team affiliate in Buffalo in his first two years as a professional. When Grant Warwick was lost for ten games with a smashed nose, he was called in as Warwick's replacement. Curry remained and Warwick was never recalled by Montreal. The new man blossomed into a solid, consistent performer on the right wing who became classified as a defensive specialist. Observers say that his style was comparable to Montreal's most recent defensive specialist, Bob Gainey. Curry and Ken Mosdell formed one of the league's most effective penalty killing units.

During his final season Curry suffered a severed tendon in his foot. "I never skated the same afterward," he says. That season he was informed by Canadiens' general manager Frank Selke that changes were in the offing. "We have to let you go this summer," he was told. "We can't protect you any longer. We have to bring up Backstrom." Though other clubs were interested in acquiring him, he chose to stay in Montreal and retire. He and a number of others were involved in a fuel oil business in that city and he had no real desire to uproot his family.

Curry has remained with the organization ever since in various capacities. He expresses gratitude that Selke, Pollock and other Montreal officials have kept him around. "It was a good break for me as a boy who left school very young. For the chance to stay in hockey it was great." His affiliation with the club dates back to 1945 making him one of the most senior members of the Canadiens. His duties currently include making travel arrangements for the club and selling advertising in the program and the sign space in the Forum.

John Ferguson
Montreal Canadiens

(b. 1938, Vancouver, B.C.)
Games played 500
Goals 145
Assists 158
Total points 303
Penalties in Minutes 1214

John Ferguson

John Ferguson retired from the Montreal Canadiens in 1971 to assume a new career as a businessman involved in knitwear and horses. It was more a matter, he says, of not being able to afford to continue playing hockey. "I was making more money out of the game [from other sources] than in it."

Ferguson comes by his fascination for horses honestly. His father was a trainer on the West Coast. He concedes, "The breeding business is a great game. If I wasn't totally involved in hockey, I'd probably go into horses full time." He still has an interest in 15 to 20 horses in Winnipeg, Toronto, Montreal and New York.

Today, as general manger of the Winnipeg Jets, he states that the game of horses and the game of hockey are very similar from a managerial point of view. "You're going to race a stable, you've got horses for courses, players for leagues, and you've got your handicappers and your superstars. You've got your allowance horses and those are your types of players. And you've got your claiming horses and your claiming leagues. It's almost identical," he concludes.

Ferguson joined the Jets in 1978 when the club was still a part of the WHA, after a stint as coach and general manager of the New York Rangers. When the Rangers changed owners, he found himself out the door. The Jets have shown continual improvement under his management and in the spring of 1985 club directors rewarded him with a five-year extension of his contract. He jokingly says that Winnipeg will win the Stanley Cup "when Gretzky gets the flu." The Jets are bona fide contenders for the honour and their appetite for a championship is sharp. "Now it's even more of a craving because we have a legitimate chance," he says.

Ferguson is no stranger to the Stanley Cup, having shared in five of them in his time with Montreal. An aggressive forward who acted as the club's policeman, his total dislike of opposing players on and off the ice was well known. When another club happened to be travelling on the same train as the Canadiens, he would refuse to even eat with its members. "I acquired a hatred for the other team," he recalls, "I never spoke to them. I wouldn't play golf in the summer time [with them]. I'd never do anything if the opposition was there." About his extremely competitive nature he says, "I didn't want any favours and I didn't ask for any." His policeman's role on the ice was documented in a *Playboy* article after his retirement, probably the first piece the magazine had ever published about a professional hockey player.

Ferguson played minor hockey in his native Vancouver and junior hockey in Saskatchewan. He bypassed scholarship offers from Colorado College and the University of Denver and took a roundabout, minor league route to the NHL via teams in Vancouver, Fort Wayne and Cleveland. In 1963, Cleveland, an AHL club with no affiliations, sold his contract to the NHL. He had the choice of going to either Montreal or New York. Because he was told he could try for the Rangers if he didn't make it in Montreal, he signed with the Canadiens.

For all his pugnacious tendencies, Ferguson did have a knack for scoring. In his first game, playing wing on a line with Beliveau and Geoffrion, he scored two goals. He notched important markers in play-offs as well but nothing would make him alter his rough and tumble style. "There's no other way of doing it. You've got to bite the bullet," he relates. "I was a dirty, rotten bastard."

Boom Boom Geoffrion

Montreal Canadiens

(*b. 1931, Montreal, Que.*)
Games played 883
Goals 393
Assists 429
Total points 822
Penalties in Minutes 689

Bernard Geoffrion

Few men can boast that they have become more popular after leaving professional hockey than before. Bernie "Boom Boom" Geoffrion says that that is indeed the case with him. During his playing days the "Boomer" and the slapshot that earned him the moniker were the toast of six NHL cities. Today his suntanned visage is recognized throughout the continent mainly because of his promotional work for a major American brewery.

Since 1976 Geoffrion has been one of the collection of former athletes who plug beer in the comical Miller Lite television commercials. His life is now one of commercials, speaking engagements, and golf tournaments. He makes his home in Atlanta, Georgia. "I love the sun. I love the south and I'm going to stay there as long as the good Lord wants me to stay."

A native of a considerably cooler Quebec climate, Geoffrion flashed into the NHL with the Canadiens in the latter part of the 1950-51 season. The next season, his first full one in the league, he scored 30 goals and won the Calder Trophy. He remained one of the league's most feared and most consistent shooters right through his 16-year career. Twice he won the scoring crown and in 1961 he was named the league's most valuable player. Other honours included three all-star nominations and induction into the Hall of Fame in 1972.

Geoffrion became the second player in NHL history, after Maurice Richard, to score 50 goals in a season. But that achievement and others pale in significance, he says, to the ultimate victory — the Stanley Cup. "To win the first Stanley Cup was the greatest thrill for me."

Described as flamboyant in good times and moody in other times, Geoffrion says that no one knew the conditions under which he was playing. "I didn't complain to them because they didn't know what it was like to play with a bleeding ulcer. The only guy that knew was Bill Head who was our trainer at the time. I did not complain. It was no use to complain in that league, with six teams," he states. "I came to play."

Geoffrion retired from Montreal in 1964. "When you know you're done, you're done. There's no use staying there," he remarks. "The kids were coming up; they were great players and I couldn't do it any more. So what's the use of me staying there if I cannot help the team?" He became coach of the Quebec Aces and led them to a pair of championships in two years.

"I am very proud of what I did in the NHL. It was a job for me. I was not a natural player. I had to work maybe three times harder. But I think that I did what I had to do in the NHL by hard work and help from my teammates," he says.

It turned out that Geoffrion wasn't quite done and he made a comeback with the Rangers in 1966. After two seasons in New York he retired for the second and last time. He assumed coaching duties with the Rangers for most of the 1968-69 season. When expansion brought the Atlanta Flames into the NHL fold, he was behind the bench. After three good seasons he quit and headed up an athlete representative business. His final coaching stand was with the Canadiens in 1979-80 and only lasted 30 games.

"I really enjoyed coaching down south for the Atlanta Flames," Geoffrion admits. "Better than Montreal and better than New York." The reason lies in the players. They had all been rejected by other NHL clubs and wanted to prove something. "I really enjoyed coaching those guys. I proved to them, with them, that even though the other teams didn't want them anymore, they could still play in the NHL."

Geoffrion might make just one change in his career if he could. "I just love the game and I thank the good Lord today. If it were not for hockey I might still be in Montreal doing something else. I respect the game. I love the game and I hope that kids when they wear the sweater of their team, they give 110 per cent because it's worth it. But every speech I make, I tell the kids to finish college. If you're good enough at 22 to play in the NHL, they'll draft you. Education is more important than hockey or any kind of sport."

Phil Goyette

Montreal Canadiens

(b. 1933, Lachine, Que.)
Games played 941
Goals 207
Assists 467
Total points 674
Penalties in Minutes 131

Phil Goyette

The camaraderie associated with hockey in the six-team era is something that every former player remembers as the most special part of the game, that magical quality that made the sport addictive. So it is with former centre Phil Goyette who says, "We more or less grew up as a family. If you look at the Canadiens in the middle '50s and early '60s, we all played junior hockey together and just grew up in the same organization as a family." That sense of family, he feels, "is one of the things that makes it a very successful team."

Goyette joined the Montreal Canadiens in 1956-57 and shared in four of the five Stanley Cup championships that the powerhouse organization won. A smooth playmaker, he centred Claude Provost and André Pronovost. "If you had a bad game you had to start worrying that someone else would come in and take your place, so you had to play well every game," he says, recalling life on the well-stocked Montreal franchise. "Maybe that's why you sort of watched yourself and stayed more on your toes."

In 1963, Goyette was traded to New York where he played for six seasons. In the post-expansion era he played briefly in St. Louis and Buffalo, winning the Lady Byng Trophy in 1970.

After 16 seasons in the league came the time, as Goyette likes to put it, that "the mind wants but the body doesn't." He retired and was hired as the first coach of the nascent New York Islanders in

1972. It is an experience he would rather forget. "You've got to have time to build something and if you haven't got it you'll never do it," he stresses. With the club setting records for futility, a case of "you can't change the horses so change the coach" arose. He was fired. When time was permitted for that club to develop, he points out, it captured four consecutive Stanley Cups.

Goyette returned to his native Lachine, Quebec where he now works with United Customs Brokers, a custom brokerage business. He has been affiliated with them for the last 27 years, first in the off-season and now full time.

Terry Harper

Montreal Canadiens

(b. 1940, Regina, Sask.)
Games played 1066
Goals 35
Assists 221
Total points 256
Penalties in Minutes 1362

Terry Harper

Terry Harper was going to the University of Michigan on a scholarship. "Then the Pats [the junior hockey club for which Harper played] squealed on me to the NCAA and I was ruled ineligible," he reveals. Having had his room and board paid for by the team, he was considered a professional, according to NCAA standards at the time. "I was very pissed off about it."

Harper joined the Montreal Canadiens in 1962 and for ten years played as part of the defensive corps. Never high scoring, his specialty was defence. Differences of opinion with team management led to him being traded to Los Angeles in 1972, a deal in which he played a large role in negotiating. He retired in 1982 after seeing service with Detroit, St. Louis and Colorado.

Missing out on the scholarship did not deter Harper from acquiring an education. Over the summers he took courses at the University of British Columbia while over the years he developed a business sense. He spent his time thinking about more than just clearing intruders out of his netminder's crease. In 1967 he developed the plastic skate boot for Lang. "I had lots of ideas in those days," he chuckles. "That was just one of them." A skier, he applied the concept of the plastic ski boot to skates. Things were going so well, he says, "I thought of quitting and just designing other hockey equipment and stuff but I couldn't give up playing. I enjoyed it too much."

Harper channelled his energy into examining the income tax laws. Not long afterwards, he discovered he could save a lot of money by incorporating. Perhaps the first athlete in professional sports to do so, for tax purposes, he became Terry Harper Inc. "I was always interested in saving as much of the money I got as I could from the government because I disagree with what they're doing. I learned to use the rules fairly well. I think I do a better job of investing my money than they do."

After continually dabbling in various enterprises, Harper found that they were supplanting his interest in the game. "I just decided I wanted to settle down somewhere and do something else besides play hockey. I had been doing business things for a number of years. They seemed to be taking more and more of my time and they were giving me more and more enjoyment," he says.

Harper and his family moved to Colorado Springs, Colorado where he lives today. "I sort of do a little bit of a lot of different things," he comments when asked to define his work. "Real estate and investment counselling and tax planning and that kind of thing." He has plenty of time to enjoy the lifestyle Colorado can offer — golfing, skiing and backpacking. He regularly flies his plane to Los Angeles (he has held a private pilot's licence for over 20 years) where his two sons attend university. "We seem to survive," he adds.

Doug Harvey

Montreal Canadiens

(b. 1924, Montreal, Que.)
Games played 1113
Goals 88
Assists 452
Total points 540
Penalties in Minutes 1216

His awards and accomplishments can only partly attest to the skill Doug Harvey displayed on the ice throughout his long and distinguished career: member of six Stanley Cup winning teams, all-star from 1952 to 1962, seven time winner of the Norris Trophy, named to the Hockey Hall of Fame in 1973. Few if any defencemen could match his proficiency in every aspect of playing the game from skating to checking, puckhandling, and anticipation. When hockey afficionados discuss who was the greatest ever rearguard, the tossup is between him and Bobby Orr. The nod generally goes to Harvey because of his ability to control the pace of a game as he was always able to do.

Over thirty years ago, Harvey acquired carpenter's papers. He has built some homes along the way. Today he uses those carpentry skills at the Connaught Race Track in Aylmer, Quebec where he performs various maintenance work around the facility. He joined his old friend Joe Gorman there two years ago. Gorman is the son of former Canadiens' manager Tom Gorman and operates the track.

A gifted all-round athlete, Harvey came out of the amateur and semi-pro ranks in Montreal to join the Canadiens. "It was tough going in training camp," he recalls. "The guys in those days didn't welcome you too much. They made you earn your job." By 1953, Montreal asserted itself from a downward slump and won the Cup with Harvey anchoring a solid defensive corps.

By then, Harvey had already established himself as a sort of club quarterback, the man who carried the puck up-ice to set up a scoring play. In 1953 he had four goals and 30 assists. "I never liked to give the puck away too much," he explains. "I used to get hell for it the first few years, cutting in front of the net and playing in my own end with it. I had a few arguments with Dick Irvin, but he was the boss. So I tried to change but I couldn't."

Coach and player arrived at a compromise. "He said, 'Well, it'll cost you a hundred bucks if you get caught, if someone takes the puck off you.' I don't remember paying," he points out. "It [the agreement] was always there through the years. But if that was the only open ice, I'd go there. Often I would be right in front of the net. I'd sort of get somebody to come to me and then I'd get by him."

Former Canadiens' coach Toe Blake once described Harvey's calm, cool approach to the game by saying, "Doug played defence in a rocking chair." Replies Harvey, "It might have looked that way. I played it just as hard as I could but I put it sort of in a direction rather than running all around."

By 1957 Harvey was a well-established star in the league, help-ing the Canadiens win their string of five consecutive Stanley Cups. It was at that point that he got involved with the formation of a players' association with Ted Lindsay, Dollard St. Laurent, Tod Sloan and others. He was warned by teammates that his involvement could only be detrimental. He remembers saying, "What about the guys that are coming along? We can't go on this way. We're just be-ing laughed at [by management]." He is sure that, as happened to the others, his role in the ill-fated project led to his trade to the Rangers in 1961. "It had to do with union activities," he states. "Christ, I was a first all-star and won the Norris that year. You don't give away a player like that. In my opinion that's what it was. Probably in their minds they thought I was finished. But I went on and played nine more years. I didn't think I was finished."

Harvey acted as playing coach with the Rangers for the 1961-62 season. Under his leadership, the club put in a play-off appearance after a four-year absence. The following year he got out of the three-year coaching contract but remained as a player. He later remarked that as a coach he couldn't be one of the boys. Today he says that it was very difficult being a playing coach in the NHL for that reason. "I was used to being one of the boys," he says, pointing to the 18 years he spent in the semi-pro and pro leagues. He couldn't go for a beer with his teammates as a coach. "Yeah, I was always thirsty after the games," he laughs.

In 1963-64 Harvey left the NHL and spent four and a half seasons in Kansas City as a playing coach. After expansion he came back to play briefly for Detroit and St. Louis. "I think I could've been in the league all those seasons [those he spent in the minors]." For a year he was an assistant coach in Los Angeles. He moved on to Indianapolis and Houston of the WHA before finally leaving the game.

"It was very tough," Harvey admits about leaving hockey. "It took another five years to get it out . . . and now it's starting to come back a bit. Sort of thought I wouldn't mind getting back in, possibly coaching or assistant managing."

Bill Hicke

Montreal Canadiens

(b. 1938, Regina, Sask.)
Games played 729
Goals 168
Assists 234
Total points 402
Penalties in Minutes 395

Bill Hicke

There is an old-timers' hockey club in Regina, Saskatchewan called "Hicke's Hookers". Its patron is the self-admitted "happy-go-lucky", eminently successful Billy Hicke, former right winger for Montreal, New York, Oakland, Pittsburgh and Edmonton (WHA).

Hicke was awaiting the beginning of the Edmonton Oilers' training camp in 1973 when he bought a sporting goods store in Regina known as Kyles Brothers. He never did return for his fifteenth season of professional hockey. Instead he established a very comfortable existence in his hometown. Last year, he points out, his store sold $2.4 million worth of sporting goods.

Later Hicke bought the building that housed the sporting goods store. Five years ago the property was expropriated by the government for an urban renewal project. "I made 12 times what I paid for the building," he says. Since then he has been buying real estate. Recently he and his partners invested in a waterslide park. Often he'll be on the lookout for a garage to house one of the 11 antique cars he has collected. "I spoil myself I guess," he laughs. "I like to get away from the business. I like to spend about 60 to 80 days [a year] in Phoenix."

Hicke believes his success is the product of good fortune. "I think a lot of guys are a lot smarter than I was. I was in the right spot at the right time. I got the sporting goods business, I knew I had no money so I had to work and things happened. I think I'm luckier than I'm smart," he says in his good-natured way. In addition to his businesses he is vice-president of the George Reed Foundation for the Handicapped.

Hicke played with the Canadiens from 1959 to 1964 but, in retrospect, thinks that it might have been better for him to have started with another NHL club. "There were seven superstars in the league. Montreal had six of them. They were just a set club. You had to work hard just to stay there."

Traded to New York in 1964, Hicke describes the ordeal as "kind of like going from heaven to hell". The Rangers enjoyed none of the Canadiens' success or the accompanying benefits. "It was a situation where I had to start all over again because the practices weren't as serious, little things like smoking in the dressing rooms, the coach showing up five minutes before us going on the ice. Things like that just never happened in Montreal."

When the time came for him to retire, Hicke says he had no problem adjusting to his new entrepreneurial life. He accepted the fact that he could no longer play, something most athletes find difficult to do.

Charlie Hodge

Montreal Canadiens

(b. 1933, Lachine, Que.)
Games played 358
Minutes 20,593
Goals Against 927
Shutouts 24
Average 2.70

Charlie Hodge today lives in Langley, British Columbia, near Vancouver. His hockey career ended there in 1972 after a contract dispute with the Canucks' management. "That's the only point that really bothers me about my hockey career," he says, referring to the disagreement. He now works in the real estate business and has been scouting western Canada for the Winnipeg Jets since they joined the NHL in 1979.

Hodge, a native of Lachine, Quebec, joined the Montreal Canadiens in 1954. He appeared in 14 games that year. Between then and when Oakland grabbed him in the 1967 expansion draft, he never played more than half the season's scheduled games, with the exceptions of 1963-64 and 1964-65. He won the Vezina Trophy in 1964 and shared another with Gump Worsely two years later but Hodge views his role with Montreal as "filling the gap for a very short period of time when the Canadiens were between goaltenders."

Hodge adopted the stand-up style because he had no choice. "Because of my size," he says, "I couldn't afford to go down. [Toe] Blake used to holler, 'Get up! Get up!' every time you went down." A story circulated that Hodge's popularity in Montreal was so great a street was actually named in his honour. While there is a street that bears his name, Hodge Avenue is, he admits, a product of necessity more than a result of civic pride for a native son. He happened to build on a piece of property that fronted on a road with no name. "It was a case of having to have an address," he laughs. His proposal to have the street named Hodge was accepted by the city.

After three seasons in California, Hodge went to Vancouver in another draft. He reflects on what he could have done differently in his career. "I think I worked pretty hard, but I might have worked even a little harder but hindsight's always 20/20. I would work a bit harder at the game, a little bit harder at certain aspects of the game. Also, I would probably have tried a bit more to understand the game as other than a hockey player. If I was doing it over again I might be a little bit more interested in a career in the game of hockey in a higher capacity than simply scouting and I would have done a little bit more ground work to it."

Tom Johnson
Montreal Canadiens

(b. 1928, Baldur, Man.)
Games played 978
Goals 51
Assists 213
Total points 264
Penalties in Minutes 960

A bowtie and cigar have been Tom Johnson's trademarks for quite a few years. His allegiance to that style of cravat has remained steadfast through the ebbs and flows of fashion and he is prepared if it ever returns to the scene. "They've come back into style a couple of times," he remarks.

As a defenceman with Montreal and Boston from 1947 to 1965, Johnson was recognized for his defensive abilities. "I was classified by some as a defensive defenceman," he says. "I stayed back and minded the store. With the high-powered scoring teams I was with, I just had to get them the puck and let them do the rest." He performed well enough to be twice recognized as an all-star, share in six Stanley Cups, win the Norris Trophy in 1959 and be elected to the Hockey Hall of Fame in 1970.

Johnson's career was ended when a skate severed a nerve in his leg. He remained with the Bruins' organization, first as a scout and then as an advisor to owner Weston Adams. For three seasons from 1970 to 1973 he coached the Bruins, taking them to a Stanley Cup. Now he is the assistant general manager and performs various functions with the Bruins. The sport used to be a winter operation but it has become a year-round enterprise, he points out.

Being a former player in management, Johnson says, gives you a more complete perspective on the situation. "You can see both sides a little clearer." He explains that concerns become slightly broader once in management. "When I played you used to worry about how well you played. Now you have to worry about how 18 or 20 other people perform."

Al Langlois

Montreal Canadiens

(b. 1935, Magog, Que.)
Games played 448
Goals 21
Assists 91
Total points 112
Penalties in Minutes 488

Beverly Hills is the place to be as far as Al "Junior" Langlois is concerned. He went to the west coast in 1983 to join the firm of Merrill-Lynch as a stock broker. "If you want to ski or swim you can go two hours and find it and then you can jump in the ocean," he says citing the advantages of the lifestyle there. "I married a California girl."

Growing up in Montreal, Langlois' ambition, like most Canadian boys, was to play professional hockey, an ambition he realized when the Canadiens called him up from the minors in 1957. Dollard St. Laurent had been traded leaving a vacancy on the defence. He arrived to find a pretty good teacher and partner for the next six seasons in Doug Harvey. Was it difficult to play with the great defenceman? "Are you kidding?" he exclaims. "It was the easiest thing in the world. When in doubt, just give it to Doug. And if you made a mistake, he'd back you up."

In 1961 Langlois and Harvey remained defence partners when they were traded together to the Rangers. Three years later the steady Langlois went to Detroit. His final season in the NHL was spent with the Bruins in 1965-66. He jokes about having to give up the number 4 he had worn to a rookie who wanted it badly — Bobby Orr.

Langlois' next season with Los Angeles of the WHL was his last as a professional. He rejected offers to attend the Bruins' training camp or to sign another contract with Los Angeles. "Sooner or later you got to find a job and work, so I decided I might as well start now," he reasons. "Nobody knew the salaries were going to go the way they went. And, I guess I was ready and injured enough to say, 'I don't know. Is it [a recurring neck problem that affected Langlois' left arm] going to come back?' "

"That first year just about kills," Langlois confesses about life after hockey. "All your life, this is what you've done and you're no good at it anymore, you can't do it. So you have to start from scratch."

Langlois, who had studied to be a real estate broker when he was with the Red Wings, joined a finance firm called FC International after he left hockey. For a time he worked as a sales representative for Canadien Hockey Equipment in Montreal and from 1976 to 1983 was part of a small brokerage firm there. Determined to get to California he joined Merrill-Lynch in 1983 and went west.

"The best years of my life," is how Langlois terms the seasons he spent as a professional athlete. Checking back, he would do one thing differently. "Maybe I'd savour it more, every moment."

Jacques Laperriere

Montreal Canadiens

(b. 1941, Rouyn, Que.)
Games played 691
Goals 40
Assists 242
Total points 282
Penalties in Minutes 674

Jacques Laperriere

Wearing a suit and glasses, Jacques Laperriere looks scholarly standing behind the Montreal Canadiens' bench concentrating on the play, assisting head coach and former teammate Jacques Lemaire. Two decades ago, he was on the ice, one of the better defencemen in the league, protecting the Canadiens' netminders.

The Doug Harvey trade in 1961 left a void in Montreal's defence. The tall, lean Laperriere was brought up by the club the following season. He proved to be more than competent and, after his rookie year, was awarded the Calder Trophy for his effective work in his own end.

Laperriere used his 6'2", 200-pound frame to advantage in performing his rearguard duties. He developed into an excellent poke checker who could play a good, physical style. In 1966 he won the Norris Trophy as the NHL's top defenceman. Four times he was an all-star as well as playing on four Stanley Cup winning teams.

During the 1972-73 season Laperriere suffered a serious leg injury that continued to plague him. By 1975, it was enough to make him officially retire. He became a coach in the Quebec junior hockey circles and in 1984 he was appointed an assistant coach with the Canadiens.

Claude Larose

Montreal Canadiens

(b. 1942, Hearst, Ont.)
Games played 943
Goals 226
Assists 257
Total points 483
Penalties in Minutes 887

Born and raised in the isolated Northern Ontario community of Hearst, it was a stroke of luck that Claude Larose was discovered by Montreal. A Canadiens' scout was on his way home to Fort William when the train pulled into Hearst. Someone suggested, "There's a good kid playing here tonight. Why don't you take a look at him?" The scout did and Larose found himself in the Montreal organization on his way to the NHL. Until then he had only dreamt of playing professional hockey. "There was very little chance that I would get to compete against the best," he says.

Larose played his first full season with the Canadiens in 1964. A right winger, he primarily played a defensive role with the team's checking line. At the end of that year he was fortunate enough to taste victory champagne after the Canadiens won the Stanley Cup, the first of five which he helped win. His first experience with the bubbly was his last. "You know when you're drinking that champagne and you're not used to that," he explains. "I went a little too far. My throat was just raw from that dry champagne and all the screaming and yelling. I couldn't talk for a week. After that I stuck to beer. They call it the champagne of the poor."

Although Larose never found champagne addictive, he enjoyed the victory that was synonomous with it. "It's so much fun when you win [the Stanley Cup]," he says, his voice reflecting the exhilaration.

"There's nothing else you can win. It got so you wanted to win every time you played. It's something that got into your system. You don't want to give up."

Larose spent his last four professional seasons with the St. Louis Blues and retired in 1978. "I think I wanted to play as long as I could," he explains. "I always tried to keep myself in pretty good shape. That's [hockey] what I wanted to do all my life." Understandably he wanted to remain in the game after retirement. "I love the game. I don't know anything else now."

Larose became a scout for St. Louis. When the ownership of the franchise changed, he followed ex-Blues' general manager Emile Francis to Hartford where he has been an assistant coach since 1983.

Don Marshall
Montreal Canadiens

(b. 1932, Verdun, Que.)
Games played 1176
Goals 265
Assists 324
Total points 589
Penalties in Minutes 127

Don Marshall

In 1972, after 19 years in the NHL, forward Don Marshall retired from the game of hockey. He had spent his first ten seasons as part of the Montreal Canadiens' dynasty. For another seven he was with New York, followed by stops in Buffalo and Toronto. "I still thought I could contribute and when I didn't think I could contribute anymore, I stopped playing," he remarks, explaining why his tenure was such a lengthy one and why he retired when he did.

A Montreal native who came up through the Canadiens' system,

Marshall found himself playing with farm clubs in Cincinnati and Buffalo in his first two seasons of professional hockey. "I figured that's where I was going to end up," he says. "I don't know if I gave it a tremendous amount of thought that [playing in the NHL] was my life's ambition or anything."

When the Canadiens did bring Marshall up, they used him more or less as a utility forward. "I was more of a defensive-type forward," he explains. "I killed penalties for them. I filled in whenever anybody was hurt. I played on a variety of lines in a variety of situations."

"In the minor leagues I scored lots of goals. I always thought I could keep scoring goals. It just seemed when I got there, that's where I fit in best. I think that maybe that was the area that was open for someone and was the role I took. Back in those days they didn't have the high-scoring games that we're having now so keeping them out was very important."

Marshall was traded to New York in 1963. Although he was initially disappointed, it turned out to be a good move for him. "I got to play a little more offensive style with New York because they were rebuilding," he says. "I was with a team when they came back to respectability and I played a little role in that end of it."

After Marshall left hockey, he worked full time for a Montreal firm dealing with mechanical power transmissions, a job he had held during previous summers. He was also a regular commentator on Hockey Night in Canada broadcasts. Now he has retired and lives with his wife in Stuart on Florida's east coast half the year and in upper New York state for the other half. Their existence is comfortable enough to permit him to say that "the wolf's not banging on the door. We're very happy. Life is good. I worked hard. My wife worked hard. We're enjoying some of the benefits of what we did before."

Paul Meger

Montreal Canadiens

(b. 1929, Watrous, Sask.)
Games played 212
Goals 39
Assists 52
Total points 91
Penalties in Minutes 118

When Paul Meger stepped onto the ice of Boston Garden on the night of November 7, 1954 he had reason to believe it would be another good night in what would be his best season ever as a professional hockey player. In his fourth season in the livery of the Montreal Canadiens, he was playing left wing on a line with Jean Beliveau and Bernie "Boom Boom" Geoffrion. He had already established himself as a hard-working checker and a good penalty killer. With the superlative playmaking of Beliveau helping him, how could he be anything but optimistic?

In the first period Bruins' forward Leo Labine was lugging the puck out of his own end. Meger moved in to check him. They collided and the two men lay sprawled on the ice. The back of Labine's skate caught Meger near the right temple and, with blood pouring out of the gash, he went to the dressing room where the trainer stitched the wound. After looking at the cut, coach Dick Irvin told him to sit out the rest of the game.

Meger developed a violent headache on the overnight trip back to Montreal. The club doctor referred him to a surgeon who promptly took X-rays and, using a syringe, extracted some of the pus-like substance from the swelling on the side of his head in an attempt to reduce the pain. "You've cracked your skull," he was told. X-rays revealed a hole about the size of a 50-cent piece. The skate blade had smashed through the skull and jabbed an inch and a half into the brain.

Between November, 1954 and June, 1955 Meger underwent four operations on his brain. The fourth, performed by world renowned neurologist Wilder Penfield, saw the removal of a portion of scarred brain tissue the size of an egg. In those eight months he suffered headaches, dizzy spells, epilepsy, memory loss and general weakness. His hockey career was finished. Lying in the neurology ward seeing other patients die, he wondered if he would be next.

The Montreal Canadiens and his wife, Betty, stood by him. When the Richard riots forced the cancellation of a game at the Forum after one period of play, someone suggested that people entitled to a refund on tickets be given the choice of accepting the refund or contributing to the Paul Meger Fund. Over $27,000 was put in trust for him.

The Megers moved to Barrie, Betty's hometown and the place where Paul had played junior hockey. He learned the electrical trade working for an electrical contracting firm owned by Hap Emms, coach and general manager of the Barrie Flyers. Once he recovered, he became an electrician. For the last 15 years he has been a service technician with Sears.

Meger has had a long record of involvement with the community. His contributions to minor hockey, the Red Cross Society and other charities earned him a Citizenship Award from the Ontario Government in 1983. "I couldn't say anything bad about it," he remarks about his shortened hockey career. As for the accident, he says, "It's one of those unfortunate things. I had to be the one it happened to. It's just nice to be alive."

The accident gave him a zest for life he has not lost. "I work on the principle that I'll never have a bad day and, by golly, I don't."

Dick Moore
Montreal Canadiens

(b. 1931, Montreal, Que.)
Games played 719
Goals 261
Assists 347
Total points 608
Penalties in Minutes 652

Dickie Moore, the Canadiens' stellar left winger, today is the proprietor of an equipment rental firm that employs over 40 people. "I started it in 1962," he relates, "which the Canadiens didn't approve of. They wanted you to be a full-time hockey player which I could understand. I asked,'Who's going to look after me when I retire from the game?'" He heeded his own instincts to prepare for a life after hockey. In addition to the equipment rental firm, he also owns a golf club in the Laurentians.

As a rookie with Montreal in 1951, Moore wasn't quite comfortable with his new environment. Once he adapted, he grew into an aggressive, productive forward who, playing on a line with the Richard brothers, captured the scoring title twice. Furthermore, he had three all-star nominations, won six Stanley Cups and was inducted into the Hockey Hall of Fame in 1974.

"It was like a nightmare for me as a young player being around some of those great hockey players," Moore confesses. He soon discovered how so many great players worked together to win. Once when Henri Richard was in the thick of the race for the scoring title, Moore, playing with an injured hand, worried that he was holding his linemate back. He offered to relinquish his spot on the line. Toe Blake called the three men together and asked the Richards if they wanted a replacement winger. They immediately refused saying, "We got here together, we end together." "This is the kind of attitude that made our team the kind of team it was, and is," Moore says. "We climb together and we go down together."

There was a time that some considered him brash and uncontrollable. "I found that very hard to accept," he comments. "Whatever they were assuming, as far as I'm concerned, was wrong. I think I've proven that I played my game of hockey the way I knew best . . . to survive, to win. I did anything I had to do to win and keep my job. I had to play a certain style."

In 1963, the Canadiens talked about trading the veteran. "I resigned," he says. "I couldn't think about playing for someone else." Toronto managed to lure him out of retirement the following season. Injuries permitted him to play only 38 games. He retired again. Two seasons later, he made a comeback with St. Louis where he played well for a year. He then quit permanently. He felt he could leave the game with a bit of pride, having lost it after his unproductive sojourn with the Maple Leafs.

Moore is still a fixture with the Montreal old-timers' hockey club. The esteem in which he is held by Montreal fans was evident recently when, in a poll, they voted him the club's all-time best left winger.

Ken Mosdell

Montreal Canadiens

(b. 1922, Montreal, Que.)
Games played 693
Goals 141
Assists 168
Total points 309
Penalties in Minutes 475

When the New York Americans folded in 1942, the NHL was made up of the clubs that are now termed "the original six". Players who belonged to the Americans were distributed to the remaining clubs through a draft. One of them, forward Ken Mosdell, went to Montreal where he became a steady performer for 15 years.

Mosdell was in the air force at the time of the draft and returned from his three-year stint in 1945 wondering if he had what it took to make the Canadiens. "I thought I probably wouldn't be able to make any of the teams," he says. "I was lucky. I made the Montreal club but every year you went to training camp you had to fight for your position." The best part about it, the Montreal native says, was playing in his home town.

Mosdell was a checker for the Canadiens. "I always played against the best centres in the league," he comments. "Milt Schmidt was just about the toughest centreman I faced. He wasn't dirty or anything, just tough and hard." For two seasons he found himself on a line with Bert Olmstead and Rocket Richard instead of doing a checker's job. The first year he made the first all-star team; the second he was elected a second all-star.

Being a member of a winning club brought with it great expectations from management and fans. "You were under pressure all the time there. They held it over your head. You could be sent down to the minors and all this. They really pushed the winning part of it all the time. You had to win, especially in Montreal. The fans knew their hockey unlike U.S. cities where all they wanted to see were fights and stuff like that."

Many players of the six-team era wax romantic about the train travel. Not so with Mosdell who saw another side of riding the big steel rail. "Once going to Chicago," he remembers, "one of the wheels came off the train. Coming home from Toronto another night we went off the track and the train tipped over. We were sleeping on the side of the train instead of the bunks." He didn't like the travel at all.

Mosdell's career in Montreal was interrupted for one season when he was loaned to Chicago in 1956. Loneliness and playing with a cellar dweller combined to make it his worst year in hockey. "They [Chicago] didn't act the same in the dressing room as what I was used to. I could hear a pin drop if we lost in Montreal," he explains. "But down there they sat and whistled after a game. I happened to mention it to some guy. He said, 'You're not in Montreal now. You're going to have to get used to it.' I couldn't get used to it, just losing all the time and guys being happy about it."

In 1958 Mosdell retired from the Canadiens although he continued playing in the senior ranks with the Montreal Royals. He needed the money to pay off the debts from a jewellery store in which he was a partner. One day he discovered his partner had bolted with a friend taking with him a good part of the stock and leaving Mosdell with the bills. To pay off the $10,000 to $15,000 left owing, he played hockey for a couple of seasons. From then until seven years ago when he sold out and retired, he was involved in the garage business in one form or another.

Mosdell, now 63, splits his time between his Montreal home and a place on the shores of Lake Champlain at Isle Lamothe, Vermont. He played with the Montreal old-timers until three years ago and still skates in local old-timers' leagues. "I don't really push myself," he laughs.

Bert Olmstead

Montreal Canadiens

(b. 1926, Scepter, Sask.)
Games played 848
Goals 181
Assists 421
Total points 602
Penalties in Minutes 884

Driven by his intensely competitive nature, Bert Olmstead
became one of hockey's best left
wingers. He played from 1948 to
1962 with Chicago, Montreal
and Toronto. Often "Dirtie Ber-
tie", as some liked to call him,
would direct that intensity at his
own teammates hoping to spark
the proverbial fire under them. "I
always took the attitude that I could evaluate a lot of players in the
dressing room," he says. "You only go through this thing once. You
might as well give it your best shot and if you can spruce them up a
little bit, who knows, it might win a hockey game."

Olmstead became an important cog in the offensive machinery
of Montreal's excellent squads in the mid-1950s. He wound up with
421 career assists, almost three times the number of goals he scored.
He remarks that it was a source of frustration for him "when you
knew you were a better goal scorer than what the figure showed.
When it was time to sign a contract, the figures were looked at. One
year I broke the assist record. I got not one handshake, nothing. That
record held up for over 20 years. Come contract time they would
look under "g's" and then "a's" and say, 'Considering the players you
play with, you should have lots of assists.' "

Olmstead played on a line with Rocket Richard and that helped
him get a lot of assists. "He would always yell at me to pass the puck
in their end," remarks the two time all-star, his irritation obvious. "I
told him if he yelled for it once more, 'I'll drive it right into your

head.' I drilled it at his head one night and he knocked it down and put it in the net and came over and said 'Nice pass.' The puck was never going to come from him to me. He always shot on net."

Olmstead owned a big wheat farming operation in Scepter, Saskatchewan and was notorious in Toronto for his habit of missing training camps each autumn because, many thought, of the harvest. He corrects that impression. "I told them I'd never be at their training camp again unless I have a contract before I come," he recalls. "They got you 2,500 miles from home; you're dealing in their ball park. They'd try to do the same thing again, round and round."

Olmstead retired from the game on a bitter note after the 1962 season. Left unprotected by Toronto, he was drafted by New York at the advanced age of 35 despite his warnings to the Rangers that he "wasn't the hockey player they thought I was". The Canadiens called and asked him to report to New York, after which they would make a deal to acquire him. "I said, 'You make a deal right now and I'll report directly to you.' They screwed me once when they let me go when they said I'd never skate again in '58. I was playing on a buggered-up knee in Montreal. The medics had me written off in our organization. I'm still mad at that, I'll always be mad at that. That's why I wouldn't go to New York. I never really trusted Montreal," he says, adding that annual contract squabbles did nothing to build a sense of trust.

Olmstead came back to professional hockey as a coach because he "was restless and wanted to do everything in hockey" from playing to coaching to managing. He coached two seasons in Vancouver of the WHL and then accepted the coach's job in Oakland in 1967. Leading a losing cause was too much for a winner like him. "It was either my health or leave hockey. I had ulcers, I couldn't sleep. I took everything too personally. I thought they [the players] could play better."

Olmstead returned to his wheat farm and later moved to Alberta where he turned to sod farming and established a "very comfortable" existence. Eight years ago he got out of the sod business and is now running a barley and hay operation in Black Diamond, Alberta.

His experience with the game, Olmstead says, has left him with no regrets. He would, however, go for more money if he had it all to do over again.

Jacques Plante

Montreal Canadiens

(b. 1929, Shawinigan Falls, Que.)
Games played 837
Minutes 49,633
Goals against 1965
Shutouts 82
Average 2.37

Sierre, Switzerland is now the home of one of the greatest goaltenders in NHL history — Jacques Plante. Having married a Swiss woman, he decided to move there when he retired from the NHL in 1975. The city is about the same size as his native Shawinigan, he says, and points to some of the advantages of his adopted home. The Rhone River flows by. There is a lot of green and flowers. The sun shines 265 days a year. It seldom gets below 0°C during the day in winter. The skiing is great. As far as the seven time Vezina Trophy winner is concerned, he couldn't have done any better.

During his career, Plante bought annuities which are now his source of income. He volunteers his time and expertise to minor hockey associations in Switzerland and helps with their programs and practices. "It's just to help the kids and to give back to hockey a little bit of what I got," he says. "I play tennis three times a week. I go skiing in the wintertime. In the summertime I work with my brother-in-law on the farm."

Growing up in Shawinigan without television or radio, Plante thought the NHL was beyond his reach. "I thought the players who played in the NHL were ten feet tall. I couldn't see these people being human beings." His main goal was to eventually play for the town team. "I said, if I do that, I'll be able to tell my children that your father played for the big team of your city," he recalls.

A member of the Canadiens' organization from 1947, he did not get a chance to play regularly until Gerry McNeil's sudden departure in 1954. He stepped between the pipes and set new standards of excellence for goaltenders, including being in the net six times when the Canadiens won the Stanley Cup. "As far as a goaltender is concerned, the higher up you go the better it is for you to play because the defence in front of you is better," Plante feels. Playing well was easy with a team of players such as those who played in Montreal in the 1950s and 1960s.

Plante is credited with being among the most innovative players in the game. He introduced the roving goaltender style, stepping out to stop a puck and passing it to a teammate. He developed this tactic while playing junior in Quebec City with a very weak club. He began clearing loose pucks, he says, not for the novelty of it but rather for the sake of survival.

Plante also introduced the mask to NHL goaltenders in 1959. "I had my nose broken four times, my jaw fractured five. I had two cheekbones broken," he says. "I was a catcher in baseball and a goaltender in lacrosse where I wore a mask. So I said to myself that if I wanted to survive in hockey I better start doing something about it." Fearing that a mask would make his goalie too relaxed, coach Toe Blake would not allow him to wear the mask he had been working on since 1956. Hurt early in a game against New York, he was asked to finish the game. The wounded goalie agreed on the condition that he could wear his mask. The club went on to win 11 games in a row and the Stanley Cup, proving that the mask would not hinder a goalkeeper's performance. "I was very fortunate to be playing for the Canadiens," he comments. "If I had been with a bad team where we would've lost, they could have said it was the fault of the mask." The Canadiens accepted his new form of protection. As Frank Selke, the general manager, once pronounced on the Plante mask business, "I don't care if he puts a bucket on his head, as long as he stops the puck."

In 1962 Plante was traded to New York. Being with a losing club, not enjoying the life of an athlete in New York, he decided to retire after three seasons with the sagging Rangers. For three years he was outside hockey, working with Molson Breweries. He made a comeback in 1968 in St. Louis where he played well for two seasons. He moved to Toronto and Boston before joining the Quebec Nordiques of the WHA as coach and general manager. He didn't like his new role because of the pressures of a fledgling organization suffering financial problems, he says. For one last year, in Edmonton (WHA), he donned the pads.

Plante places great importance on the Stanley Cup championships he has shared in. In his mind, the most special achievement of his career was in 1965. Out of hockey a year, he joined the junior national team as it locked horns with the Soviet national team at the Montreal Forum. After only a week's training, he helped Canada to a 2-1 victory, the first time the Soviet Union had been defeated by a junior team.

André Pronovost
Montreal Canadiens

(b. 1936, Shawinigan Falls, Que.)
Games played 556
Goals 94
Assists 104
Total points 198
Penalties in Minutes 408

The Montreal Canadiens' machine was in full gear in 1956 when André Pronovost joined them. A left winger, he found himself for four years playing with Phil Goyette and Claude Provost. "We were the third line, they called it," he recalls. "We played mostly defensively." He played on four consecutive Cup winning clubs.

What Pronovost was most immediately impressed with when he got to the Canadiens' camp was the spirit that pervaded it. "It was the kind of attitude we had in junior," he recalls. "They were great guys, guys that were just there to help you out. They'd say you guys [the youngsters] are here to help us out and whatever we can do to help you out, it's better for us. It was a great team spirit all the way." He fondly remembers Rocket Richard, a superstar, often helping him improve his game at practices.

In 1960 Pronovost was traded to the hapless Bruins. The sharp fall from the top to the bottom of the league was shocking enough to make him consider retirement. "That's why when they traded me, I was thinking of quitting hockey and going back to school," he notes. "Maybe that would have been the best move I could have made. You can't go back but you can think about it." Lynn Patrick convinced him to stay. Two years later he was traded to Detroit and his Bruins' teammates envied him his good fortune in going to a contender.

Pronovost remembers the quandry he found himself in when it came to getting a raise in the six-team league. Early on, he asked Montreal general manager Frank Selke for some extra cash. "Well, son," Selke replied, "Wait until you gain some experience. Then we'll pay you." Later, in Detroit, when he thought he had enough experience to ask for a raise, he was warned that for the amount he was asking, two younger players could be kept on the payroll.

During the 1964-65 season Detroit moved him to their farm club in Memphis. He briefly played with Minnesota in 1967-68, but spent the rest of his time until retirement in 1971 in the minors. "I loved the game and year after year, I'd say, 'Well, this is the year I quit and look for something new to do,' and one year, I decided that was it. I was 35."

Pronovost went into the restaurant business and now manages a restaurant in Longueuil, Quebec. The restaurant business is not much different than hockey in the sense that they both cater to the public. One difference is that as a hockey player he had no say in matters, whereas now he can come and go as he pleases.

Pronovost tried his hand at coaching junior hockey in Shawinigan for a season, but found the experience less than fulfilling. "After that I didn't feel like I belonged," he explains. "I guess I was too tough. I was demanding too much. I couldn't believe the guys wanted to be hockey players without working hard."

Getting a more complete education is something he wishes he had done differently. "I'd make sure I finished my schooling," he states. "I wish I'd gone through to university. I could maybe be more relaxed because I had something to fall back on. Maybe I would have quit before I turned 35."

Claude Provost
Montreal Canadiens

(b. 1933, Montreal, Que.)
Games played 1005
Goals 254
Assists 335
Total points 589
Penalties in Minutes 469

Claude Provost

An explosive offence featuring a glittering array of stars like Richard, Geoffrion and Beliveau made the Canadiens' teams of the 1950s and 1960s formidable. The ability of lesser lights like Claude Provost to smother forwards with relentless checking made those teams unbeatable.

Provost broke in with the Canadiens in 1955. He was one of 12 men who played on each of Montreal's five consecutive Stanley Cup winning squads from 1955 to 1960. The big-jawed winger with his peculiar, wide-stance skating style evolved into a very efficient checker. Quiet and introverted, he seemed suited to an unspectacular role on a team filled with spectacular individuals.

The value of Provost's work on the ice is underscored by his longtime teammate Jean Beliveau. "The style on the ice reflects what the man was," he says. "He was doing his job, doing what we expected of him. He was a very important part at that time. We knew whoever we played, any type of game, we could count on Claude."

Hockey fans remember him particularly for the effective way he always covered Chicago's superstar, Bobby Hull. A defensive specialist, he gained his share of points. In 1,005 games he scored 254 goals and accounted for 335 assists. He was named to the first all-star team in 1965. He was further honoured in 1968 when he became the first recipient of the Bill Masterton Memorial Trophy given annually to the NHL player who best exemplifies the qualities of perseverance, sportsmanship and dedication to hockey.

Provost retired from hockey in 1969 to run a small hotel he owned north of Montreal. More recently he operated a health and fitness centre in Montreal. In April of 1984, while playing tennis near his Miami, Florida home, he suffered a fatal heart attack. He is survived by his wife and two sons.

Henri Richard

Montreal Canadiens

(b. 1936, Montreal, Que.)
Games played 1256
Goals 358
Assists 688
Total points 1046
Penalties in Minutes 928

Idolizing one's older brother is certainly understandable when he happens to be the great Maurice "Rocket" Richard. Attempting to follow in his footsteps, many thought, should have been fraught with expectations and pressures too great to cope with. Henri Richard did better than cope. He earned his own moniker, "Pocket Rocket", and a place among the most proficient players in Canadiens' history.

"There must have been lots of pressure but I really didn't feel it," the younger Richard says. "I guess it wasn't easy, but I never thought about that. I was just thinking about playing hockey."

Playing alongside his brother was his childhood dream, Richard recalls, but one he thought would never be realized because of the 14 years age difference between the two. However, the Rocket was still an offensive weapon to be reckoned with when Henri joined Montreal in 1955. When Toe Blake put the rookie centreman on the Rocket's line, his dream was fulfilled.

Richard remembers wanting to be as great a goal scorer as his brother. "I finally found out I really wasn't the same calibre as Maurice was. I was more a playmaker than anything else," he observes. That may have been a little frustrating, "but then I enjoyed making passes, especially the first five years I played that I spent with Maurice. I was looking for him all the time. That's why I never developed as a scorer. Lots of times Toe Blake would ask me, 'Why don't you shoot a little more?' I kept looking after my wingmen all the time."

Richard absorbed more than his share of abuse from opposing players for being the Rocket's little brother. Being a relatively small man, 5'7" and 160 pounds, fighting, he explains, was not his game but one couldn't back down. "I never backed off from anybody," he says, "even if I was scared. I was so proud that I didn't want to show I was scared."

Though Richard never became the clutch goal scorer his brother was, critics think he was the better all-round player. He played on more Stanley Cup teams than any other hockey player — 11. Understating the accomplishment, he claims it was a case of being at the right place at the right time. He was named an all-star four times, won the Masterton Trophy in 1974 and was inducted into the Hockey Hall of Fame in 1979.

Richard calls his final Stanley Cup in 1973 "my favourite one" although during the series he called Montreal coach Al McNeill the worst coach he had ever played for. Richard says he was angry at McNeill for not playing him in one of the games in the final series against Chicago. "I was just mad. I really didn't mean it." Following the controversy that erupted, Richard scored the winning goal in a crucial game. "I could have been a bum and I was a hero," he continues. McNeill was relieved of his coaching duties next season and, Richard points out, hasn't fared very well coaching elsewhere.

Adapting to the life of a hockey player was not easy, especially for a young French Canadian. Richard recalls travelling to away games on overnight trains. When he got up in the morning he would patiently wait for one of his teammates to awaken before having breakfast. "I couldn't read the menu and I was so shy that I waited for somebody to get up so I could go with him."

In 1975 Richard retired having played more seasons (20) and more games (1,256) than any other Montreal Canadien. He also participated in more play-off games (180) than anyone else in the NHL. Earlier that season he broke an ankle which took too long to mend. He thought, "I better quit before it's too late." On his retirement a "night" was accorded him, out of which a considerable amount of money was raised. He asked the money be put in a foundation named for him. Once a year it distributes money to local charities.

Richard still operates the bar he opened 25 years ago that bears his name in downtown Montreal. These days, one of his sons manages it, while he spends more time golfing, playing tennis and skating with the Montreal old-timers.

Maurice Richard
Montreal Canadiens

(b. 1921, Montreal, Que.)
Games played 978
Goals 544
Assists 421
Total points 965
Penalties in Minutes 1285

Two very special native sons of Quebec were in attendance at a game recently at the Forum in Montreal — Prime Minister Brian Mulroney and, acting in his role of special ambassador for the Canadiens through Molson Breweries, Maurice "Rocket" Richard. On one hand there was the man who reached the zenith of power because he found political strength in Quebec. On the other, the hockey hero whose deeds and actions gave strength to Quebeckers.

The sight goalies feared most of all in the 1940s and 1950s was that of Richard striding across the blue line, charging toward the net, eyes almost unnaturally wide and filled with fire. No man who played the game, experts agree, was better at moving from the blue line into a scoring position. That raw, unbridled desire to drive for the net excited the fans who packed arenas to see him and vaulted him to new scoring heights.

Ask the Rocket today about his ability to score goals after one of his dashes and he answers, "I didn't even know myself what I was going to do coming in past the blue line and even when I was alone with the goalkeeper I tried never to make the same move twice in a row. I always tried to make a different play." In 18 seasons he scored 544 goals, a lifetime mark that stood for years. He established a new bench mark for a single season by notching 50 markers in a 50-game schedule in 1944-45. Bernie Geoffrion and Bobby Hull equalled or bettered the total but in schedules that were longer. Ironically, as prolific a scorer as Richard was, he never won the Art Ross Trophy. However, he was selected an all-star thirteen times. In 1947, he was awarded the Hart Trophy. He was inducted into the Hockey Hall of Fame in 1961.

It is not for the quantity of goals that Richard is best remembered but for their timeliness. When the Canadiens needed a goal, it always seemed to be number 9 who came through. He was the consummate clutch performer. In the play-offs, a time when players will tell you it counts the most, Richard was exceptional. Until Mike Bossy of the New York Islanders surpassed his record in 1985, he held the mark for most career goals in the play-offs with 82. He owns the record for the most game-winning goals in the play-offs — 18. He has scored the most overtime goals in the play-offs — six. It is little wonder that he can't pick out one that stands out in his mind. There were so many.

The Montreal native joined the Canadiens in 1945. Injuries in his first two seasons made some wonder whether he would be durable enough. Richard never doubted he would be good enough for the NHL but he never dreamt he would realize the success he did. "I just wanted to be a well-liked hockey player," he says.

Richard was idolized by Canadiens' fans, particularly by French Canadians in Quebec. How much he was liked became evident in 1955 when he was suspended for the remainder of the season and the play-offs for striking a linesman. The acrimony exploded on March 17, 1955 when fans attending a Canadiens/Red Wings game at the Forum tried to assault NHL president Clarence Campbell. A tear gas bomb was set off and the spectators streamed out onto the street where they joined thousands of others in rioting and looting. Richard appealed for calm the next day in a radio broadcast although he still feels he shouldn't have been suspended for that year's play-offs. It was only after the riot, he comments, that he realized exactly how much he meant to fans.

Richard had a temper as explosive as his scoring prowess and opposing teams attempted to exploit it in order to stop him. Needlers such as Leo Labine, Tony Leswick and Ted Lindsay would tease, mock, elbow, slash and otherwise harass the Rocket, who more often than not, would erupt into a fury that earned him a penalty. A boxer in his youth, he could do better than fend for himself in NHL company.

Perhaps the most spectacular scorer the game has ever known retired in 1960. The injuries, Richard says, had slowed him down enough to make him decide to quit hockey. The reflexes weren't the same and the younger players were starting to make their presence felt. "Even with injuries I could have played another two or three years," Richard feels. "But they [the Canadiens] offered me a good deal and so I took it." If expansion had come two years later instead of seven, he thinks he would have made a comeback.

For the next four years Richard worked in the Canadiens' public relations office. A flash of the old Richard temper surfaces when he begins talking about why he left the organization. He catches himself in time, just as his voice begins to rise, and instead offers a diplomatic answer. "I just didn't get along with some of the guys, so I quit."

For many years Richard has been involved with a fuel company in Montreal and now holds the position of vice-president of sales. He also handles a fishing line business from his basement. His popularity does not seem to have diminished over the years. He is still in demand for interviews and personal appearances, all of which are handled through his agent. He appears in commercials for hair dye and automobile tires, evidence that advertising executives understand his enduring recognition.

The Rocket is now a 62-year-old grandfather. He has limited his on-ice activities to refereeing old-timers' games rather than playing in them. When he looks back on one of the most accomplished careers in the NHL, he says he would do one thing differently: "I would try to do better."

Jim Roberts
Montreal Canadiens

(b. 1940, Toronto, Ont.)
Games played 1006
Goals 126
Assists 194
Total points 320
Penalties in Minutes 621

Jim Roberts, the quintessential journeyman player during his 15-season career in the NHL, defines the way he approached the game: "I kind of played every year in a desperate sort of way, thinking it would be my last if I ever slipped a little bit. Before I knew it, I had a number of years behind me. There was a lot of pressure because I wasn't that great a hockey player. You knew there was always somebody there who was probably capable of taking your job."

Raised in Port Hope, Ontario, Roberts graduated from Montreal's junior affiliate in nearby Peterborough. He found a place with the Canadiens in 1964 after serving a three-and-a-half-year apprenticeship in the minors. While other players had definite roles in the club's game plan, Roberts had to wait for his role to come up, one that called upon his abilities as a defensive specialist. He was mostly used for killing penalties or checking another line late in a game. Other players can call upon the memory of a particular feat on the ice but he recalls a more general sense of accomplishment. "It's the satisfaction of winning a game or winning a number of games with consistent play," he elaborates, "when the final bell rang knowing that we hung on and I was part of it." Being on five Stanley Cup winners, he adds, was a case of being at the right place at the right time.

Roberts, like many other players at the time, found his career extended by expansion. He moved first to St. Louis, came back to Montreal and finished with the Blues once again. In 1978, at the age of 38, he retired knowing there would be no place on a youthful roster for an aging veteran. "It was getting harder to get ready to play a game. The satisfaction wasn't there because I couldn't do the things I used to be able to do. The time was there. I had had enough," he says.

Roberts left hockey and for a year "fiddled around with a few things in St. Louis," knowing in the back of his mind that he would return to the game. "I just needed a real, good break from it," he comments. He then joined his former coach, Scotty Bowman, in Buffalo as an assistant. He left the Sabres in 1984 to become an assistant coach under Bob Berry in Pittsburgh where he helps with the coaching of young talent. In game situations he is responsible for the Penguin defencemen. After his first year with the team he says, "We've enjoyed it. We've had a good time so far. It's just a little frustrating coming from better teams and being put in a situation where you're really not good enough to win your share of games." With the likes of Mario Lemieux, the club has a good nucleus of talent on which to build, he adds.

Bobby Rousseau

Montreal Canadiens

Bob Rousseau

(b. 1940, Montreal, Que.)
Games played 942
Goals 245
Assists 458
Total points 703
Penalties in Minutes 359

Bobby Rousseau was one of the few players in the era of six-team hockey to play on the Canadian Olympic team before turning professional. He was one of three juniors selected to bolster the 1960 squad at Squaw Valley that placed second behind the Americans. The thrill of competing for Canada, he assesses, ranks "just a little behind the Stanley Cups" he shared in as a Montreal Canadien.

Rousseau's promise as a junior player was fulfilled in the pro ranks. A right winger who was a very capable playmaker, he won the Calder Trophy in 1962. He remembers doubting that he would be a contender for the award because the Canadiens had him killing penalties to strengthen his defensive game. When an injury removed Bernie Geoffrion from the lineup, he filled in and showed the offensive capabilities that won him the rookie of the year award.

An assist is as important as a goal, Rousseau believes, and his thoughts are reflected in his statistics. They show many more "helpers" than goals. He admits to having lacked leg strength. "I used to fall quite a bit," he remarks. "People used to joke about it." Even today, he adds, friends suggest a close affinity between him and a little tot who repeatedly falls on his way to the net in a television commercial. The struggling youngster also happens to be wearing Rousseau's old number, 15.

Traded to Minnesota in 1970, Rousseau spent a season there and felt "politics" at work that he had never known in Montreal. The next year he went to New York and regained his old form. Chronic back problems led to surgery and finally retirement in 1975. "I could have come back," he explains. "It would have taken me a year at least and there was the possibility I could have reinjured it." With his mind on a second career as a golf pro, he retired. Today he is a golf pro at the Dunes Golf Club in Sorel, Quebec.

Dollard St. Laurent
Montreal Canadiens

(b. 1929, Verdun, Que.)
Games played 652
Goals 29
Assists 133
Total points 162
Penalties in Minutes 496

Dollard St. Laurent joined the Montreal Canadiens in 1951, part of a wave of players that included Dickie Moore, Jean Beliveau, Boom Boom Geoffrion, Jean-Guy Talbot and Claude Provost. They became the bones and sinew of a new hockey dynasty. He found a niche on the left side of Montreal's defensive corps in tandem with the great Doug Harvey.

"I could rush when it was time to move the puck and get it going," St. Laurent comments. His strengths, he adds, were in "playing the man and hitting pretty hard." He helped the Canadiens win four Stanley Cups before being traded to Chicago in 1958. There he was part of another championship team "which was a tremendous effort for, not cast-offs, but just about."

The "cast-offs" to whom St. Laurent refers were the many individuals traded to the last place team because they were involved in the first futile attempt to organize a players' association. "I think I was traded because I belonged to the association," he says. "They tried to split up the gathering by shipping players to other teams. We weren't as powerful as we should have been at the time, but we started the ball rolling for the younger kids."

Chicago sold St. Laurent's contract to a minor league club, the Quebec Aces, in 1962. At the time Doug Harvey, then coaching New York, attempted to orchestrate a deal that would have brought his former partner to the Ranger camp. St. Laurent guesses that "there was something going on between Montreal, Chicago and Quebec" that prevented his acquisition by New York. "I still had the capacity and the potential to play in the NHL."

St. Laurent broke a leg while with Quebec, an injury that brought about his retirement. He then joined a brother in Montreal with whom he operated a successful insurance business. Having sold that enterprise in 1978, he now is a representative with Primaco Limited, a company involved in the financing of insurance premiums. Just recently he retired from old-timers' hockey in order to spend more time with his wife and seven children.

Jean-Guy Talbot
Montreal Canadiens

(b. 1932, Cap Madelaine, Ont.)
Games played 1056
Goals 43
Assists 242
Total points 285
Penalties in Minutes 1006

Jean Guy Talbot

Jean-Guy Talbot got his wish when he retired in 1971 after 17 seasons in professional hockey. He assumed a position with the St. Louis Blues' organization. The job had been promised to him when he agreed to be traded to Buffalo for his final season rather than retiring as he originally intended. "I had a job. I didn't know what it was but I wanted to stay in hockey," he explains. "I started as a scout. I went all over the place. I wanted to learn from the bottom because changing from player to management was quite difficult."

Talbot found himself in Denver, Colorado at the helm of a Blues' farm team. There he enjoyed success, leading the club to a championship. The following season the Blues called upon his coaching services but when opportunity knocked, he was not sure he wanted to answer. "I wasn't ready," he confesses. "I didn't want to go. There were too many guys on the team that I played with. That's the worst thing that can happen to a coach. I wanted to stay in Denver for a few years until most of the guys I played with weren't there."

Talbot took over the Blues in the 1972-73 season and made the play-offs with them. Partway through the next season he resigned. "It was too much for me," he explains. "It was too many chiefs and not enough Indians. If I couldn't do it the way I wanted to, I said, 'get somebody else. I want to do it my way. If I lose, fire me. If I win I want the credit for me and the players.' "

Talbot returned to Denver of the Central Hockey League the next season as a coach. He coached Denver of the WHA until that franchise folded in 1975-76. The following year he accepted an invitation from John Ferguson to be an assistant coach with the New York Rangers and took over the coaching reigns in his second season. When management decided the Rangers were not developing into contending form fast enough, both he and Ferguson were purged. Talbot had had enough of hockey and six years ago accepted a position in the promotions department of Carling O'Keefe Breweries in Trois-Rivières, Quebec where he now lives.

Talbot is still well known in that part of Quebec for the 12 seasons he played with Montreal beginning in 1954. In combination first with Tom Johnson and then with Terry Harper, he played defence on a team that was a hockey dynasty. His name is on the Stanley Cup seven times. "They say you have trouble when you have too many superstars on one team," he says referring to Richard, Beliveau, Harvey and the others. "These guys were like everybody else. They were each just one of the boys."

In the 1967 expansion draft Talbot was first picked up by Minnesota, then sent to Detroit and finally went to St. Louis although he played little in the first two places. "I was thinking of quitting," he says. After 12 years on the same club it looked as if he would not play for the watered-down expansion clubs. Fortunately he was put to work in St. Louis and helped that team to the Stanley Cup finals three times before finishing in Buffalo. Tired of moving and having "had enough" he quit at 38 years of age.

Gilles Tremblay

Montreal Canadiens

(b. 1938, Montmorency, Que.)
Games played 509
Goals 168
Assists 162
Total points 330
Penalties in Minutes 161

Gilles Tremblay

At the peak of his career, Gilles Tremblay, a speedy left winger with Montreal, was prematurely and permanently sidelined by a serious case of asthma. "I went to training camp in 1968 and the Hong Kong flu was around," he recalls. "So they offered the boys at training camp a flu shot. Some of them took it. Some others did not. I took the shot but I was never able to beat the virus. So I got the flu and then I got worse and worse."

"It got to be bronchitis. I kept playing with pills. It was a vicious circle. You take one pill. It doesn't go. You take a stronger pill and keep going. So the first thing I knew, it turned out to be asthma and I had to quit in February '69." Tremblay figures the debilitating asthma cost him more than $1,000,000 in lost wages. Still an effective performer, he could have cashed in on the sky-rocketing salaries caused by expansion and a rival hockey league.

By the time Tremblay was forced to the sidelines, he had spent ten seasons with the Canadiens. An excellent all-round, two-way player, he spent most of his years playing on a line with Jean Beliveau and first Boom Boom Geoffrion and then Yvon Cournoyer. The accomplishments he relishes most, he says, are the team ones: six league titles and four Stanley Cups.

Tremblay became a colour commentator with the Canadian Sports network on French language radio and television broadcasts. Fourteen years later he still finds the work enjoyable. "I'm still travelling with the boys. I'm always part of the game," he says. "You're still talking about what you know the best. You're well respected because of your credibility, the way I played, the example you gave when you were on the ice. The people still remember you and they're still watching you on TV. I'm probably more recognized today than when I played, because I'm always on the screen. That's good. It must be tough for somebody to leave the game and be forgotten."

In addition to broadcasting, Tremblay does public relations work for a skate manufacturer in the Montreal area where he lives.

J.C. Tremblay
Montreal Canadiens

(b. 1939, Bagotville, Que.)
Games played 794
Goals 57
Assists 306
Total points 363
Penalties in Minutes 204

Jean-Claude Tremblay

Recent reports on Jean-Claude Tremblay have the former Montreal defenceman travelling between North America and Europe, having a good time, and, according to one ex-teammate, "working hard at it". Constantly on the move, he is a difficult man to pin down.

Tremblay played for Montreal between 1959 and 1972, occupying an important spot on the team's defence. Although he was never a high-scoring defenceman, he always managed a substantial number of assists, evidence of his playmaking abilities. In his final two seasons with the Canadiens he tallied 63 and 57 points, most of them assists. Over the years he was part of five Stanley Cup efforts.

Wooed by the Quebec Nordiques, Tremblay jumped to the WHA in 1972. He led that league with assists in 1973 with 75 and in 1976 with 77. He retired in 1979 after 20 years as a professional hockey player. Having invested his income in annuities, he turned to a new life of leisure after hockey.

Bob Turner

Montreal Canadiens

(b. 1934, Regina, Sask.)
Games played 478
Goals 19
Assists 51
Total points 70
Penalties in Minutes 307

Bob Turner

The best thing he ever did, Bob Turner decided, was to get into real estate nine years ago. At the time he was coaching the Regina Pats junior hockey club and operating a vending business as well. He happened to be putting a coffee machine into a new real estate office and the owner, an acquaintance, invited him to join. He became a partner in Crown Real Estate and enjoyed "eight excellent years". Last year he sold out "at a nice profit" to a major real estate chain of which he is now an employee. He and his wife now have the chance to holiday in Hawaii and Phoenix. "You could never do that when you played hockey," he laughs.

Turner played six of his eight NHL seasons with the Canadiens. He joined Montreal in 1955 and was part of the five-consecutive-year reign that the club enjoyed as Stanley Cup champions. A defenceman on a team that was as powerful defensively as it was offensively, he says the rearguards were provided with an incentive to keep the puck out of their end. They were paid a bonus of $1,000 each if Jacques Plante won the Vezina Trophy. "We always looked forward to that," he says. "I wasn't one of the stars on the team," he admits. "I was just hanging on by the skin of my teeth."

Turner was traded to Chicago in 1961 where he spent two more seasons. He was then demoted to Buffalo, a minor league affiliate. "I think it was more of a move to embarrass you. That's one of the reasons there's a union in the league now," he explains. "They didn't want me to quit. I think they wanted to cut my salary. So I said I was packing it in."

Turner returned to his native Regina where he worked for a time with Carling O'Keefe Breweries. For ten years he coached the Regina Pats, taking them to a Memorial Cup victory in 1974.

While linemate Frank Mahovlich watched in the background, Andy Bathgate certainly proved his ability to play with the Toronto Maple Leafs as he centred the puck for Red Kelly to score against the New York Rangers.

EW YORK RANGERS

In the 1950 Stanley Cup final, the New York Rangers fought with the Detroit Red Wings through seven games. Tied at 3 in the final game, the clubs battled into a second overtime period when Pete Babando captured the Cup with his goal. The heartbreaking loss perpetuated the Red Wing dynasty and took the wind out of the Rangers' sails for the next 15 years.

The Rangers never fulfilled the promise they showed in their first few seasons after joining the NHL in 1926. In their inaugural campaign they finished first in their division. The following year they won the Stanley Cup, a feat they repeated in 1933 and 1940. "Post-war blues" is the common diagnosis of the sag that afflicted the Rangers. Unable to replace the talent they had lost during World War Two, they found themselves slipping in the six-club order.

Fifth was a familiar place for the Rangers in the time leading up to expansion. Under coach Phil Watson, a member of the 1940 championship contingent, the team made the play-offs for three consecutive years, in 1956, 1957, and 1958. Players like Bathgate, Prentice, Howell, Henry, Fontinato, and Evans, products of the Rangers' farm system, brought the club back to respectability but the ultimate goal, Lord Stanley's trophy, eluded them.

Whatever element makes the good into the best was missing in the Big Apple, at least for its hockey club. One thing is certain. It wasn't, players point out, the easiest city in which to play professional hockey. The Rangers could never practise in their own rink. They had to settle for a reasonable facsimile on another level of Madison Square Gardens. They never enjoyed home ice advantage in the play-offs because the Gardens were reserved by Ringling Brothers' Circus every spring. The city with its size and attractions made concentrating on hockey difficult. Ex-Rangers still remember with annoyance the long commuter rides just to get to and from practice. Hockey in New York, unlike other NHL cities, did not command the undivided attention of the sporting public, detracting from the players' sense of belonging. It is hard to know what intangibles might have helped their cause.

With Doug Harvey at the helm, the Rangers ended a play-off drought, appearing in the 1961-62 semi-finals. But they finished out of the spring ritual again until 1966-67 when Emile Francis, who had taken the club over three seasons before, guided them to another semi-final berth. Francis fashioned a rebirth of the Rangers which led to consistent post-season play and a shot at the Stanley Cup in the 1972 final. They bowed out in six games to Orr, Esposito and the rest of the Bruins. The club last appeared in the Stanley Cup final in the spring of 1979. They lost to Montreal in five games.

Dave Balon
New York Rangers

(b. 1937, Wakaw, Sask.)
Games played 775
Goals 192
Assists 222
Total points 414
Penalties in Minutes 607

Dave Balon

A 22-ton, steel-hulled replica of a paddle wheeler churns its way through the waters of Lake Waskesiu in Prince Albert National Park in northern Saskatchewan. Accurately outfitted, the *Neo Watin* acts as a cruising convention and party centre. Its captain is Dave Balon, a left winger who saw duty with New York and Montreal in the six-team era and who was later active with Minnesota, Vancouver and Quebec of the WHA.

"At one time all we did was scenic tours," Balon says relating the history of his *Neo Watin* enterprise. "All we did was just four tours a day." It was originally built as an attraction for Edmonton's Klondike Days and Balon bought it 10 years ago. He spent $15,000 "to make it look beautiful". Before investing in this ship, he had been involved with marina operations in the same park. Conducting the charters is something he finds enjoyable and "It's something I can handle." He adds that he is disabled; he has M.S., multiple sclerosis.

Always a strong athlete, Balon knew something was the matter when "I lost all the power in my legs. There was a numbness in my face and tongue. Finally they sent me over to Winnipeg for tests. I was glad when I did find out," Balon states, astonishing the listener. "At least now I know, I can face it myself." Coping with the disease, Balon says, is a matter of not physically overdoing it, a difficult thing for a man who had always pushed himself. A couple of years ago he was Saskatchewan's M.S. ambassador to the rest of Canada. Saskatchewan is the province with the highest incidence of the disease in Canada.

Balon developed his hockey skills on Ranger-sponsored teams in northern Saskatchewan. He joined the parent club in 1960 where he was known for his "good hands", as they say in the hockey business, and his excellent wrist shot. His habit of scoring near the crease earned him the tag "garbage collector". Standing near the net, he says, is not without perils. "I had to pay for a lot of my goals," he chuckles.

His game having deteriorated noticeably, Balon retired in 1974 and returned to Prince Albert. In one of his last years, his coach benched the once productive journeyman saying that he had "lost his legs" and accused him of being out of shape. Years later he came to realize that it was more than age that had robbed him of his vigour.

Andy Bathgate
New York Rangers

Andy Bathgate

(b. 1932, Winnipeg, Man.)
Games played 1069
Goals 349
Assists 624
Total points 973
Penalties in Minutes 624

"I think playing in the six-team league was a great honour," says Andy Bathgate summing up the sentiments of a generation of hockey players and fans. "Even today people remember you because they really followed hockey then and they knew everybody in the league. But now, you know the local boys and that's about it."

Bathgate, a four time all-star with New York, Toronto and Detroit before expansion in 1967, was certainly one of the most accomplished and better-known players in the NHL. In New York, where he was team captain for many years, he was the club's most potent offensive weapon. He regularly led the team in scoring and was frequently among the top ten in the league. In 1959, the season he won the Hart Trophy, he scored 40 goals and added 48 assists playing for a fifth place club. In 1962 he tied Bobby Hull for the league points title at 84 although Hull won the Art Ross Trophy for having scored more goals.

Bathgate became the focal point of one of the biggest trades of the 1960s when he and teammate Don McKenney went to Toronto for Dick Duff, Bob Nevin, Arne Brown, Bill Collins and Rod Seiling. The two Rangers were instrumental in bringing the Stanley Cup to Toronto in 1964. He finished his NHL career with Pittsburgh.

Bathgate left the Penguins to play and coach in Switzerland. Management was about to send him to Vancouver of the WHL when the European offer came. "I just felt I didn't want to go into the minor leagues at that time," he says. "I had played two seasons before in Vancouver before my final year in Pittsburgh." With some trouble, he was reinstated as an amateur so he could take the Swiss opportunity.

"So I went there and I enjoyed it very much. It was a good experience. I would've gone back but it was at the tail end of my career and I didn't want to drag it on and possibly get hurt over there because they used their hockey sticks more than I was used to over here." He returned and coached Vancouver of the WHA for the 1973-74 season. He played 11 games in the next year and then retired.

His 18 years of professional hockey have been good to Bathgate. It seems unlikely, in retrospect, that he found a spot in the Rangers' lineup in 1954, his third attempt to make it. Turning pro may have been a dream of every Canadian boy, but he recalls doing so very reluctantly. When he was playing junior in Guelph he earned money both as a player and from a good job he was provided with. Going to the Rangers or one of the farm teams meant less money. "I actually took a cut in pay to go to New York," he remarks. But, he adds, you didn't have a choice.

Bathgate lives in Toronto where he operates a golfing range in Mississauga. Business has been so good, he reports, that he might have to expand. Fans still see flashes of that old brilliance when he skates with a team of NHL old-timers based in Toronto.

"I would have liked to have been on more Stanley Cup winners," Bathgate muses in hindsight. "Especially one in New York would have been great. It was unfortunate we didn't have the management there to really put things together because they had the personnel but never got it together properly."

Larry Cahan

New York Rangers

(*b. 1933, Fort William, Ont.*)
Games played 665
Goals 38
Assists 92
Total points 130
Penalties in Minutes 700

Larry Cahan

Larry Cahan spent 22 seasons as a professional hockey player starting in 1954 with Toronto and finishing with the Chicago Cougars of the World Hockey Association. A defenceman of large proportions, 6', 200 pounds, he recalls being involved in three separate, historic drafts: the first ever held by the NHL in 1955 when New York drafted him from the Maple Leafs, the expansion draft of 1967 when Oakland claimed him, and the first held by the WHA. "I've seen it all," he states.

It is almost inevitable that an athlete who has participated in a sport for nearly a quarter of a century can come up with a bit of trivia concerning his career. "Howe and I are the only two guys that were captains in the NHL and the World Hockey league," Cahan declares.

Cahan spent most of his career with the Rangers. "With the Rangers we always had pretty good teams. It was our misfortune that we played Montreal in the play-offs. We'd give them some good series, though." It was particularly hard for the Rangers who were forced to play all their play-off games on the road because the Ringling Brothers' Circus took over Madison Square Gardens each spring. "You can imagine having to play all your play-off games in the Forum in Montreal!"

The NHL expansion was a good break for Cahan, as it was for other veterans, because they could play longer in a diluted league. A stop in Oakland was followed by four years in Los Angeles. "Lo and behold, I thought I was all finished and the World Hockey league came," he remembers. A combination of his 40-year-old body not "responding anymore" and the loss of a lot of salary money owing to the bankruptcy of the Cougars franchise (a loss big enough that "I don't even like to talk about it", made him decide to retire).

Cahan operated a sporting goods store in Vancouver for about nine years. "It was exciting. The only problem was you became a slave to the business. Everybody wanted to come to see me and a lot of people were calling me at home and what have you." He eventually sold out and turned to working for Prudential Insurance. He still skates with old-timers in Vancouver every week.

Peter Conacher

New York Rangers

(b. 1932, Toronto, Ont.)
Games played 229
Goals 47
Assists 39
Total points 86
Penalties in Minutes 57

Pete Conacher

Being the son of former great Charlie Conacher may, Peter Conacher agrees, give spectators inflated expectations of how he would perform as a forward in the NHL. "I think that maybe the fans expected it because of my name," he says. "I think I had to make my own way. I wasn't nearly the player that my dad and uncles were. It's not often that happens."

Conacher, who played 229 games over six seasons with Chicago and New York, spent most of his decade-long professional career in the American Hockey League. Looking back on it, he notes, "I would have liked to be able to contribute more, but it didn't work out that way. I regret not having won a championship."

Conacher retired from hockey when he was dispatched to San Francisco from Hershey. "I really didn't want to go. I decided I had had enough and I quit," he explains. "All the time I was playing hockey, I worked at the Toronto Stock Exchange as a broker. I'm still there now for Burgess-Graham Securities. I've been there off and on for 30 years." He is still involved in organizational aspects of old-timers' hockey in Toronto.

Jack Evans
New York Rangers

(b. 1928, Garnant, South Wales)
Games played 752
Goals 19
Assists 80
Total points 99
Penalties in Minutes 989

Jack Evans

Jack Evans, coach of the Hartford Whalers, says he enjoys holding the most insecure, pressure-packed job in hockey. "It is a very high pressured way to make a living," he agrees, "but there are many satisfactions to it." Insecurity is part of the job. "You don't concern yourself about the insecurity of it. You just try and do your best. That's the way I've looked at it."

Evans took over the Whalers in 1983 when the club ranked among the worst in professional hockey. It has improved significantly since then and the rebuilding program has brought it to about "tenth or eleventh best in the league". Motivation, he comments, is one of the major keys to coaching success in professional hockey. "One of the biggest things is to have your players working for you. If you don't, you're dead."

Hartford is Evans' second coaching stint in the NHL. In 1975, he was at the helm of the hapless California Seals. He remained with the club for two more seasons after it moved to Cleveland. When it merged with Minnesota in 1977, he was out of a job. He then coached the Salt Lake City Eagles, a St. Louis Blues' affiliate, for five seasons. Emile Francis became Hartford's general manager in 1983 and hired Evans for the head coach's job. He remarks, "I feel very fortunate to have had two tries at it."

Born in Wales, raised in Drumheller, Alberta, Evans played first for New York (1948 to 1958) and then for Chicago (1958 to 1963). A solid defender, he played on the power play and killed penalties. In those days, he recalls, fighting wasn't the intimidating factor, it was body checking. "You'd throw a good body check. That's how we intimidated. There was very little fighting."

Because Evans was one of the Rangers involved in attempting to establish a players' association, he found himself shipped to Chicago, "the Siberia of hockey". Owners dispatched anyone involved in the premature union to that ailing, last place club. Eventually the Black Hawks reversed their fortunes and grabbed the Stanley Cup in 1961, a victory he describes as "very gratifying".

Evans retired in 1963 and intended to return to Calgary where he had operated a sod nursery/landscape business for a number of years. Instead he accepted offers to play in the Western Hockey League and remained there until he became a coach in San Diego where he now makes his home. From there he went to Salt Lake City and then the California Seals.

Lou Fontinato

New York Rangers

(b. 1932, Guelph, Ont.)
Games played 535
Goals 26
Assists 78
Total points 104
Penalties in Minutes 1247

Lou Fontinato

Hockey, Lou Fontinato's first love, gave him the means with which to pursue his second love, farming. Today he single-handedly runs a dairy farm on a 265-acre spread near Guelph, Ontario. A farmer for the last 22 years, he comments, "It doesn't pay a helluva lot but it's challenging."

Fontinato staked his spot in the NHL as a policing defenceman with the New York Rangers in 1954. "We just practised what we were told to do right from junior on. They always want a guy out there hitting, being a policeman," Leapin' Lou comments. "There are no regrets. What the hell. You're in the big top and you play the only way you know how. Mind you, on the way up, you had people encouraging it [the hitting]."

The Rangers of that era proved to be mediocre at best. Fontinato thinks that the environment had a lot to do with their lack of success. "A lot of those years with the Rangers, if we were playing in a city other than New York, we'd probably end up in first place," he says, citing the "different" New York atmosphere. The team's lack of success eventually prompted his trade to the Montreal Canadiens. "There was a time when we lost out on some play-off money and I questioned a few things. That was the only time in my career that I questioned management, the only time. They'd say, 'Jump', I'd say, 'How high?' They'd say, 'Cut your hair,' I'd get it shaved off for fear it wasn't short enough. You can't say I was a shit disturber," he points out.

Fontinato had decided that the 1963 season would be his second last in the NHL before retiring to his farm. Fate intervened cruelly. He suffered a broken neck during a game and it finished him. "I knew I wasn't going to play hockey again," he remembers. "All I said to the doctor was to get me better so I could lift a bail of hay." For a month he was paralyzed. The use of his legs returned first and then, four months after the accident, the use of his arms. "Sometimes I can say I never really fully recovered, but I'm not complaining."

There is still something of the fighter in Fontinato. For the last dozen years he has been battling the government over the money he was offered for some land expropriated from him. While the prices have been upped, he says he is not totally satisfied yet. "It's a helluva lot better than what they first figured on. We still haven't come to a real agreement." The battle, he feels, might suggest that he is "hard-headed and stubborn, but I'm just standing up for my rights, eh?"

Jean Guy Gendron

New York Rangers

(*b. 1934, Montreal, Que.*)
Games played 863
Goals 182
Assists 201
Total points 383
Penalties in Minutes 701

Guy Gendron

Only in the world of athletics could an honest-to-goodness French Canadian like Jean Guy Gendron acquire the unlikely nickname of "Smitty". When he joined the pro ranks with New York in 1955, his teammates had difficulty pronouncing his surname properly. One of them, Wally Hergesheimer, pinned him with something more manageable. "Just imagine a guy with a name like that calling me 'Smitty'," Gendron laughs. "Smitty" he remains to hockey chums he meets in his travels as a member of the NHL's central scouting staff.

Gendron, a native of Trois-Rivières, Quebec, was a journeyman forward with New York, Boston and Montreal in the six-team era. "I was a hard worker," he states, "not a star or anything like that. I must have been not too bad to play 13 years in the NHL."

Whenever it seemed as though he was about to retire, circumstances would change and Gendron found himself staying in the game. When Boston sold his contract to the Quebec Aces in 1964, he was resigned to finishing his career there. Expansion came, Philadelphia invested in the Aces as a farm team and, eventually, the veteran Gendron was one of the players they brought up. Retiring again from the NHL in 1972, he was lured back by Quebec of the WHA for two more seasons.

Gendron became the Nordiques' coach when his term as a player ended. "You want to see what's going on on the other side [of the bench]," he explains. "But it's pretty tough, I can tell you that." After a pair of respectable seasons and with one more season left on his contract, he quit. "I said this was too tough for me, so I decided that's it."

Gendron has been a golf pro in the Quebec City area since he left hockey and now works each summer at the Club Lac St. Joseph course. Two years ago he joined central scouting and spends his winters travelling the land looking at the hockey stars of the future and providing data on them to the clubs. While his line of work is not without its rigours (his car engine packed it in a mile from home returning from one trip), he finds it very satisfying. "You're happy, especially if you see that a kid goes on to play in the NHL and does very well. You say, 'Jesus Christ, look at this kid. I knew he was going to be a good hockey player.' "

Rod Gilbert

New York Rangers

(b. 1941, Montreal, Que.)
Games played 1065
Goals 406
Assists 615
Total points 1021
Penalties in Minutes 508

Rod Gilbert

The man singing the song "New York, New York" could very well have been Rod Gilbert. Since the right winger with the matinee idol looks joined the Rangers in 1960, he has developed an infatuation with the city. After he retired from the Rangers in 1978 he chose to remain in the heart of the "Big Apple" to make his post-NHL life. He holds the city more dear to his heart, he says, than his own native Montreal.

Gilbert skated 18 seasons with the Rangers. He was a consistently good player who now owns the career points record for that venerable organization. The man who became an all-star, a member of Team Canada '72 and a Hall of Famer almost didn't make it in professional hockey when he fell and broke his back in his last game of junior hockey. "I was paralyzed for four months," he remembers. Amazingly, he came back and played with the Rangers for four years with a back brace before hurting his spine again. The graft of vertebrae required put him out of commission again for almost an entire year. "That's all I knew how to do," he comments explaining his iron resolve to return to the game. "I had a taste of the NHL. That was my goal in life, to play in the NHL."

When the end came, Gilbert remarks, "It was over too soon." A decade and a half had flown by. A number of circumstances contributed to his decision to leave the sport. "It was a combination of losing interest, different management, different players . . . [Emile]

Francis left, they traded Ratelle, they traded Vic Hadfield, Brad Park, all the players I felt we could win a Stanley Cup with in the early '70s. My goal of winning the Stanley Cup for the Rangers seemed impossible. They started rebuilding and I was an older player. I just didn't feel that enthusiastic about it."

Gilbert remained with the Rangers as a vice-president doing marketing, scouting and television work. Three years later he accepted an offer to coach the Ranger farm team in New Haven. "It was a great experience," is his assessment. "I was sort of preparing myself to coach for the Rangers." The Rangers hired Herb Brooks instead. "That took care of me. I'm not coaching anywhere else and I'm not coaching in the minors."

After leaving the coaching ranks, Gilbert ran his own restaurant for a couple of years. Although initially he did well, he did not enjoy the business. "It was a little too involved at night. We'd close at four o'clock in the morning and a lot of people were involved in drinking and that wasn't my sort of thing. It wasn't my style. I was just married. I had a couple of young kids. I didn't get to see them too much during the day."

The high finance district of Wall Street is where Gilbert can now be found. He is employed with a firm called Fundamental Brokers "doing brokering and public relations". Former New York Yankee pitcher Whitey Ford holds a similar position with the company. He does promotional work that involves, among other things, taking customers to sporting events in New York.

Gilbert has lost none of his appeal to New Yorkers. "It seems I got more popular when I terminated my career than when I played."

Vic Hadfield

New York Rangers

(b. 1940, Oakville, Ont.)
Games played 1002
Goals 323
Assists 389
Total points 712
Penalties in Minutes 1154

Vic Hadfield

Had he not undergone serious knee surgery in 1976, Vic Hadfield feels he might have been able to play "another couple of years". Instead, he was forced to retire and the knee is still a source of aggravation. "I can't play golf, that's how much it bothers me," he says, which is quite an annoyance for the operator of a golf course.

Hadfield donned a Rangers' uniform for the first time in 1961. Just being there is still the thrill of his career, he says. An unspectacular left winger who dug the puck out of the corners, he also staked out a reputation as an aggressive player. One season, 1963-64, he led the league in penalty minutes with 150. The ability to fend for himself, he says, "is what kept me there."

Later in New York, Hadfield formed the GAG Line (goal-a-game) with Jean Ratelle and Rod Gilbert. In the 1971-72 season he scored 50 goals, a mark which still stands as the most goals by a Ranger in one season. The low point of his career arrived in 1974 when he was traded to Pittsburgh. "You had New York Ranger embedded on your chest," he remarks. "It was quite a blow."

Hadfield remembers thinking as a rookie that retirement was a long way off. "When you're that young you're not thinking about retirement." Later on, he planned for the inevitable and invested in 160 acres of land near Burlington, Ontario, along with Harry Howell and Andy Bathgate. It was "something to fall back on". Eventually his partners sold out and he became the sole proprietor of land that has increased its value tenfold over the last decade.

Hadfield built the Indian Wells Golf and Tennis Club on the land and the enterprise keeps Hadfield occupied full time. In addition to the successful golf side of the operation, he has thriving food and beverage facilities. "There's always something to do," he states.

Ted Hampson
New York Rangers

(b. 1936, Togo, Sask.)
Games played 676
Goals 108
Assists 245
Total points 353
Penalties in Minutes 94

"My only claim to fame, or shame," jokes Ted Hampson, "was that I scored on the final buzzer that would have sent the game into overtime in the sixth game of a final for the Stanley Cup." Unfortunately for him and Minnesota it didn't count.

Hampson from Flin Flon, Manitoba played 12 seasons in the NHL. Before expansion, his career as a forward was split among Toronto, New York, Detroit and the minors. After arriving in the major league in 1959 he discovered the game was slightly more defensive than in junior hockey. "I found I wasn't scoring very big in professional hockey. Fortunately I was able to still play a good checking game and kill penalties."

The promotions, demotions and trades were all an accepted part of the game Hampson agrees. "I think we were pretty naive in those days. I think we just kind of let things fall where they may and hope you played well enough that someone would give you a chance or you'd get promoted. I felt if I played well enough I'd get a chance and if I didn't, I didn't deserve to."

Hampson, like many others, found new hockey life after expansion and played more regularly with Oakland, California and Minnesota. In 1972 he jumped to Minnesota of the WHA. He retired in 1976 after playing his last games with Quebec. His age, 39, and wanting "to be a family man a little more than I had been" were the factors that helped him arrive at the decision to quit.

Hampson went into the hockey equipment business as well as coaching at the junior level in Bloomington, Minnesota. After being in the business world for a while, he decided that he really wanted to be back in hockey full time. "I was just about 40 so I really hadn't done anything else for twenty-some years and I found it tough to get into something else," he says. Looking back at it all today he wishes he had gotten a college education either before or during his career.

Through Lou Nanne of the North Stars, Hampson got a job coaching a minor league affiliate in Oakland for three seasons. He then joined the NHL's Central Scouting staff. More recently he has been chief scout for the St. Louis Blues, looking at young talent in rinks across North America and Europe. Part of his challenge lies in making up the year's talent they lost when the Blues, then undergoing an ownership crisis, missed the 1984 draft selection.

Andy Hebenton

New York Rangers

(b. 1929, Winnipeg, Man.)
Games played 630
Goals 189
Assists 202
Total points 391
Penalties in Minutes 83

Andy Hebenton

Andy Hebenton laughs when asked about what he would change if he could play his nine-year NHL career over again. "I might have got an agent a lot earlier," suggests the former New York Ranger and Boston Bruin. "We were kind of stupid. I think for the amount of money we played for and the amount of money the owners were making at the time, we should have done a little better."

Other than that, he would have "minded his Ps and Qs off the ice", alluding to the spare time Hebenton and other players had on their hands when they "had a few beers and a few laughs". The time, he thinks, might have been more constructively applied "doing something".

Hebenton, from Winnipeg, Manitoba, spent his first five years as a pro toiling for Montreal's farm teams. He figured if he didn't make it into the major league by age 25 he never would. Just after he turned 25, New York acquired him from the Canadiens. "I wasn't a really outstanding hockey player," he adds, offering "just a plugger" as a more apt description of his style. "I went both ways. I was fortunate to get picked by the New York Rangers and stay there." In 1957 the "plugger" won the Lady Byng Trophy.

Hebenton played 630 games between 1955 and 1964, nine complete seasons in the NHL. He went to the minor leagues on the west coast after his NHL career drew to a close and continued that reliability. In fact he only missed two games in 26 years of professional hockey, both to attend his father's funeral.

Hebenton's retirement in 1974 from Portland of the Western Hockey League was not really of his own volition — the league folded. At 45 years of age and still enjoying playing hockey, he thinks perhaps he should have pursued it a little longer by asking one of the new World Hockey Association clubs for a tryout.

Instead Hebenton and a partner started a cement business which they still operate today in Portland, Oregon. "We're doing pretty good this year," he comments. "We've had our ups and downs like everybody else in the construction business in the world."

Hebenton coached Vancouver's affiliate in Tulsa briefly in 1974 on an interim basis. He enjoyed his three-month term and the team wound up in the league final. Why did he not continue coaching? "Nobody phoned me," he laughs. "I guess I really didn't push myself. I'm like all the other old-time hockey players. You figure that somebody is going to pick up the phone and give you a call."

Camille Henry

New York Rangers

(b. 1933, Quebec City, Que.)
Games played 727
Goals 279
Assists 249
Total points 528
Penalties in Minutes 88

Camille Henry

Camille Henry first donned a New York Rangers' uniform in the autumn of 1953 and immediately laid to rest the criticism that had been made against him all along. His detractors claimed that his slight 5'8", 152-pound frame would not permit him to play in the NHL. Even when he was only 16, "I was damn sure I was going to play in the NHL," he says. He won the rookie of the year award for the league in his first season, scoring 24 goals and adding 15 assists in 66 games.

Wanting him to develop his defensive game and, Henry suspects, being nervous about playing such a small centre, the Rangers demoted him to their Quebec and Providence farm clubs for part of the following two seasons. He returned to New York and for seven seasons centred Red Sullivan and Andy Hebenton. His scoring touch made some observers declare that, pound for pound, he was the greatest scorer in the league. Except for 1959-60 when he was injured for part of the season, Henry scored no fewer than 23 goals per season from 1957-58 until 1963-64 — and this during an era when an output of 20 goals a year was considered excellent. With 32 goals, 24 assists and two minutes in penalties he won the Lady Byng Trophy in 1958. "It's something you're born with," he says about scoring ability. "You can practise to make it better, but you have to be born with it."

The game exacted a physical toll on Henry. Injuries resulted in surgery on his back, forearm and wrist. Once after a crushing check, he suffered a concussion that paralyzed him for 20 seconds and put him in the hospital for two weeks. Today he wears braces to support his ailing knees.

His bad back led to his departure from New York, Henry believes. "I loved New York and would have loved to finish my career there," he states. During the Rangers' 1964 training camp his back gave out. He could only skate with the aid of a specially designed corset and doctors decided that surgery would be necessary by season's end. Halfway through the year Henry heard the shocking news over the radio that he had been traded to Chicago. "They knew I needed a back operation and at the time I was 32 years old. The end was near."

Henry says he told Black Hawk management that he would be needing back surgery that would keep him off skates for at least six months. He was told not to worry about anything. "Just help us win the Stanley Cup. That's why we traded for you." Chicago lost the Cup in seven to Montreal. When he approached management about their promise, they denied the conversation had ever taken place. "That's when my troubles started with him [Chicago GM Tommy Ivan]."

Henry spent the next year with Chicago's farm club in St. Louis. When he reported to Chicago's training camp in 1966, he was told before the club embarked on a road trip that it might be better for him to get into shape in the AHL. "Right away I knew the writing was on the wall." He returned to Quebec on his own and hoped that Emile Francis, who had said he would try to get him back to New York, could swing a deal with Chicago.

Nothing happened and Henry was out of the game for two years. At home in Quebec he wrote a biweekly column for a French language daily on the NHL, including his experiences with Tommy Ivan. Paraphrasing John F. Kennedy, his approach was, " 'Don't ask what hockey can do for you, but ask what you can do for hockey.' So I said I'm going to try and help the players if it's possible so the things that have happened to me won't happen to them." His columns included criticizing the complete control owners had over their players. "We were a bunch of slaves and whatever they said, they decided, that was it."

Being forced out left Henry bitter, "But what can you do? The players' association wasn't strong enough then. I think if the players' association would have been strong I would have played, somewhere." Francis eventually dealt with Chicago and Henry was brought back to the Rangers in 1967. He played for the club after an injury forced Vic Hadfield out of the lineup. The next year he was traded to St. Louis. His second year with the Blues was spent as a playing coach for their Kansas City affiliate. At the end of the 1970 season, hurt, knees in pain, 39, he "just couldn't take it anymore".

Henry returned to his hometown of Quebec City where he managed a rink for three months. The WHA was born and he was given the coaching job for the New York Raiders. That job lasted until 1974 when the club folded. He stayed in New Jersey for the next four or five years acting as a hockey instructor for youngsters at a local rink. "Depending on how many guys showed up, I worked three or four days a week. I didn't work much." He accepted an offer to host a radio program in Montreal. It lasted a year after which he became a security guard for a time.

"I haven't worked too much since then," Henry comments about a difficult time. "I became a diabetic seven years ago. Stress is not the kind of thing that helps a diabetic. I'm a very nervous person to start with. I do have problems, because I still can't accept the fact that I am a diabetic."

Henry agrees that hockey hasn't worked out too well for him. "It hasn't worked out at all," he states. "I just wish I had a chance to work, anywhere." Looking back he says he would definitely still play hockey but he would make sure he completed his education at the same time. Now biding his time, he concludes, "It's not easy at times but you give yourself a little push in the ass and then you try to do the best that you can."

Walt Hergesheimer

New York Rangers

Wally Hergesheimer

(*b. 1927, Winnipeg, Man.*)
Games played 351
Goals 114
Assists 85
Total points 199
Penalties in Minutes 106

His teammates called Wally Hergesheimer "Fingers" because he had lost parts of two fingers in an industrial accident. For six out of his seven years in the NHL he played right wing for the New York Rangers. A slender 5'8", 150-pound man, he managed to break into the 20-goal circle four times.

His excellent sense of humour, Hergesheimer thinks today, might have helped him "over the humps" during his hockey career. Only now does he admit that his career might have been prematurely ended by the attitudes of club management. He broke a leg in the 1954 campaign which did not mend well over the summer. Though his condition was known, the club put pressure on him to play by insinuating that he was exaggerating the extent of his pain. Fourteen games into the next season he fractured the leg again. Players understood the competition that existed for work in the NHL, he says. That's why they were willing to undertake such risks to continue playing. There was no question about who was calling the shots. Never before has he expressed any of his true feelings on the subject for fear it would sound like "sour grapes".

At the end of the following season, he was traded to Chicago. "That was the low point of my career," he remembers. There he broke a collar bone. "That finished me."

Next year Hergesheimer found himself in the minors where he was bounced back and forth between the Rangers and their farm teams in Buffalo and Rochester. "You wonder sometimes," he comments about the motives of NHL clubs. "They just shifted you around like you were a bale of hay."

His final season in pro hockey, 1961-62, was spent in Calgary. He retired and with his family returned to his native Winnipeg where he began working with the provincial liquor commission. Today he is an assistant manager of a liquor store. He played old-timers' hockey when it first began in Manitoba but today he prefers to devote as much of his spare time as possible to golf.

Wayne Hillman

New York Rangers

(b. 1938, Kirkland Lake, Ont.)
Games played 691
Goals 18
Assists 86
Total points 104
Penalties in Minutes 534

In 1961, rookie defenceman Wayne Hillman was fortunate enough to be part of Chicago's Stanley Cup victory and the five day party that followed. It was the last time he actually helped win the treasured trophy, he says, but he was part of the post-victory festivities through association another four or five times.

Hillman, younger brother of Larry Hillman, was a journeyman rearguard in the NHL. After three and a half seasons with the Black Hawks, he spent another three and a half years with New York, playing more often and more consistently. After expansion, he spent a year in Minnesota, followed by four in Philadelphia. His final two seasons were spent with Cleveland of the WHA.

Through his brother or friends on other clubs, Hillman found himself invited to more Stanley Cup celebrations than the average hockey player ever experiences. While with Cleveland, he returned to Philadelphia to watch his former teammates win the Stanley Cup. Bobby Clarke and company, knowing their old buddy "Mooner" (a nickname he acquired after some post-curfew hi-jinks sometime during his career) would be watching from a favourite hangout, telephoned him at the place after the winning match and ordered him down to the party.

Reflecting on his time in Philadelphia, a team and a town he says are "good", Hillman thinks he might do things a little differently if he had the choice. "If I had to do it all over again I would have stayed in Philly and maybe finished off another couple of years there and then maybe turned to coaching." As it was, the lure of more dollars brought him into the WHA.

Hillman played two seasons in Cleveland and then retired. One problem was his inability to get along with the coach. "He was one of those 'rah-rah' college boys," he states. "I threw my skates into my trunk and never took them out for eight years. I never had them on and I never went to a game in eight years. I just dropped out of sight."

After retirement Hillman took a few years off and just relaxed. Still living in Cleveland, he chooses to remain vague about what he does these days. A mystery man of sorts, he finds it sufficient to state that he is "interested in a number of things" and he is "monkeying around with different businesses."

Harry Howell

New York Rangers

(b. 1932, Hamilton, Ont.)
Games played 1411
Goals 94
Assists 324
Total points 418
Penalties in Minutes 1298

Harry Howell

Fifteen games into the 1978 season Harry Howell relinquished the coaching reins of the Minnesota North Stars to Glen Sonmor and became the chief scout for the team. Since then he has been spotting talent in American high school and collegiate hockey leagues as well as in the junior ranks in Canada. "Years ago it was a 20-year-old draft and you had three years to look at a fellow playing major junior hockey," he says, explaining the expanding role of the scout in the sport. "You didn't have to worry about high school players because they were all underage, so you could concentrate on colleges and junior A."

The merger of the Cleveland Barons and the North Stars brought Howell to the North Stars in 1978. He had been an assistant general manager and general manager with the Barons. He coached for the first 15 games of 1978 but when that didn't work out he swapped jobs with Glen Sonmor, the chief scout. "It's gratifying when a player you picked turns pro and helps the team," he adds. "I enjoy what I'm doing."

The chance to become a playing coach helped convince Howell to jump from Los Angeles of the NHL to New Jersey of the WHA in 1974. He had spent 21 seasons in the NHL, a more than capable defender. The Rangers had promoted the Hamilton, Ontario native to their club in 1952 right from their junior affiliate in Guelph. "They had the post-war blues," he explains of the New York club at the time. "They had a lot of great teams in the '30s and early '40s and the war kind of wiped them out. There was an opportunity for young players to step in. The only thing I really wanted to do was play in the NHL. I gave up a lot of things for it and it paid off well."

After 15 seasons in the league, Howell's defensive skills were recognized and he was voted the winner of the Norris Trophy as the league's top defenceman. Four years later he was known as the last man to win the trophy before Bobby Orr staked his annual claim on the award. Howell owns three club records with New York: most seasons, 17; most games, 1,160; most career penalty minutes, 1,147.

In 1969, Howell's play deteriorated after a spinal fusion operation and he was given a choice of being traded or retiring and holding a job with the Rangers in some capacity. At 36 years of age he decided to continue playing and he wound up in Oakland. Looking back he thinks that it might have been better to accept the Ranger offer to stay in the organization and begin learning the administrative part of the game earlier. "But when I think about it in the long run, maybe it was good to keep playing and earn a little bit more money."

Two dozen years after he had started playing, Howell retired at the age of 43. "I knew the time had come," he says. "The time had come a couple of years before. The players all of a sudden got young."

Earl Ingarfield

New York Rangers

(b. 1934, Lethbridge, Alta.)
Games played 746
Goals 179
Assists 226
Total points 405
Penalties in Minutes 239

Earl Ingarfield

From a hockey player's stand-point, Earl Ingarfield has had the ideal retirement. He has been successful in his post-playing occupation and has also maintained the contact that ex-players so desire with the game as an avocation.

Ingarfield played 13 seasons in the NHL, the most productive of which were spent with the New York Rangers from 1958 to 1967. A journeyman in the true sense of the word, he performed quietly, unobtrusively centring an excellent line that featured Andy Bathgate and Dean Prentice. He assesses himself thus: "I used to think I was a fair playmaker and I think I had pretty good hockey skills and I guess my skating was alright."

Like many Canadian boys, his dream was to play in the NHL and he set his goals accordingly. However, he gave himself an option if he faltered on the way to realizing his dream. "My father was in the International Tractor business and I worked with him in the book-keeping and parts department. That way if hockey didn't work out there was something else for me there, which I also enjoyed."

Ingarfield coached a junior club in Regina, Saskatchewan the year following his retirement. "The next year I went to work scouting for the Islanders in Western Canada. About halfway through the first season, the Islanders' coach was let go so I coached the Islanders," he says. "I enjoyed it. It was a really weak team, though. I coached for that year, then the following year went back to the scouting department."

Ingarfield checked out amateur talent for another year before returning to his native Lethbridge where he became involved in the sport in a bigger way. "There was a team in the Western Junior Hockey League that was moved here from Swift Current," he recounts. "So I left the Islanders and bought into the team here in Lethbridge and I was assistant manager and coach and part owner for a couple of years." Eventually he quit coaching but remained a part owner and became the sales manager for a radio station.

Three years ago, having had enough of radio, he wanted to "start to take things easy, but I really didn't know what I was going to do." He found himself back in the Islander fold as a scout. "I got the itch again."

Ingarfield scouts mostly in Western Canada with an occasional foray to the east. Assessing talent today goes beyond watching a player on the ice, he notes. "It is important to find out about a boy's background, his family, his attitude off the ice as well as on. Kids with attitude problems don't change."

Orland Kurtenbach

New York Rangers

(b. 1936, Cudworth, Sask.)
Games played 639
Goals 119
Assists 213
Total points 232
Penalties in Minutes 628

For 14 seasons Orland Kurten-bach played in the NHL, a big centreman who broke out of junior hockey with a reputation as a high scorer. Expectations were high and, for him, unattainable. It was hoped he would be another Jean Beliveau. The biggest knock against him over the years, he admits, was his slow skating. The company in the NHL was so much faster and stronger than in the junior ranks.

The Rangers brought Kurtenbach out of western Canada in 1960. His first two seasons were spent with New York farm clubs. "It didn't matter how good a player you thought you were, or how good you could be, they always sent you down to the minors," he comments. "I guess they weeded out their products on down the line." Breaking into the Rangers' lineup was no easy matter. "It was like a decision had already been made," he adds. "Some guys got in the minors and just never got out of there."

Kurtenbach played for New York, Boston, Toronto and Vancouver before badly injured knees forced him to retire in 1974. Along with stepping on the ice for the first time in the NHL, he considers another highlight of his career "setting a goal to play in the NHL for ten years and playing for 12 years and all the good things that go with it."

Rather than leave hockey, Kurtenbach chose to stay as a coach. "I enjoyed it [the game] and it's the closest thing to the playing aspect of hockey," he explains. He started as coach of the Seattle Totems, a minor league club which eventually disbanded. He moved to Tulsa where he had some success winning league and play-off championships. After one and a half seasons in Oklahoma, he was called up to coach the Vancouver Canucks. He feels he was ready for the jump to an NHL bench. "I could have stayed in the minors and learned a lot more, but a lot of the job has to do with common sense and making adjustments."

A change in management saw Jake Milford replace Phil Maloney as general manager and Kurtenbach's boss. "It was a frustrating year," he reports about his second season with the Canucks. "I had worked out a deal with Phil for coaching and it worked out well with Phil and then Jake came in. So you had to get used to it." In the end he was fired and turned to scouting for the club.

Today, Kurtenbach lives in Burnaby, British Columbia and works in the insurance business. He still skates regularly with the Canucks' old-timers in charity games. It is generally asserted that hockey disrupts family life. However, Kurtenbach discovered a different story in retirement. "You're closer to the family in hockey because you're with them for three months straight [during the off-season], but in business you're working a lot of hours and you see them less."

Dan Lewicki

New York Rangers

(b. 1931, Fort William, Ont.)
Games played 461
Goals 105
Assists 135
Total points 240
Penalties in Minutes 177

Danny Lewicki

When Danny Lewicki looks back at his nine-year stint in the NHL he has this assessment of himself: "A hockey player who didn't reach his potential. I always felt I could have done better and should have done better."

An excellent skater who stickhandled and shot well, Lewicki played with Toronto, New York, and Chicago. "Possibly I was a little ahead of my time," he says. "I was a very offensive hockey player rather than a defensive hockey player." Does this mean he never backchecked? "Never!" he laughs. "Oh, I did a bit, but at 169 pounds I wasn't able to hurt anybody."

Lewicki scored 105 goals and 135 assists in 461 regular season games. He is one of the few players to have been on clubs that won the Memorial (Port Arthur Bruins, 1948), Allan (Toronto Seniors, 1949) and Stanley Cup (Toronto Maple Leafs, 1950).

After leaving the NHL in 1959 Lewicki toiled in the minors for three or four seasons before calling it quits. Had he known that the league would expand so quickly after he first heard it rumoured, he thinks he would have stuck around a little longer. After he retired he became a sales representative with CHUM radio where he spent 13 years. Since then he has been with Acklands Limited, an automotive supplier.

Nick Mickoski

New York Rangers

(b. 1927, Winnipeg, Man.)
Games played 703
Goals 158
Assists 184
Total points 342
Penalties in Minutes 319

Nick Mickoski remembers only too well his shot hitting the post in an overtime period of the seventh game of the 1950 Stanley Cup final. The miss meant more than a lost opportunity to win the treasured trophy, he says. "Patrick was president of the team then. Before the last game he says, 'I got a cheque for each one of you guys for $1,000 if you guys win it.' They got the champagne and everything else. So we lost in the second overtime about two in the morning. Not only did we lose the $1,000 but we came back to our hotel and there wasn't any champagne, just goddamn beer. The bastards wouldn't even give us the champagne. We went seven games, we did a pretty good respectable job. Goddamn, why did it hit the post and not go in? At least I could've had my name on the Stanley Cup. That's the closest I ever got."

Scouted in his native Winnipeg by the Rangers, Mickoski remembers the first time he attended the club's training camp. To his surprise the team actually paid him expense money for his effort. "I thought the guy was out of his mind," he exclaims, expressing the surprise a $280 cheque inspired. "In those days if I had two nickels to rub up against my ass I was doing pretty good. I couldn't believe I was getting money just to play hockey. I would've done it for nothing."

Mickoski's final stop was Boston in 1960. "I didn't have the enthusiasm any more," he says. "I didn't enjoy Boston, I didn't like it."

He retired to Winnipeg where he operated a taxi cab and hotel business but his absence from hockey was only temporary. He soon became a playing coach with San Francisco of the Western Hockey League where he stayed six seasons. Later he played and coached for a senior team in Newfoundland, the Winnipeg Junior Jets of the Western Junior Hockey League and the Winnipeg Jets of the World Hockey Association.

One of Manitoba's top golfers over the years, Mickoski has represented that province at national championships. Recently he competed in the national senior gold competition. A 57-year-old, he continues to skate with the Manitoba old-timers. He lives in Winnipeg where he still owns the taxi operation.

Mickoski regards the players of today with their three- and four-year contracts with a little envy. In his day, it was one year at a time. You had to produce to justify next year's contract. "You played with fear, a fear that somebody would get your job. There was a lot of that kind of pressure on you. I could have been ten times a better hockey player under today's circumstances."

Jim Nelson
New York Rangers

(b. 1941, Big River, Sask.)
Games played 1023
Goals 69
Assists 299
Total points 368
Penalties in Minutes 904

As a junior in Prince Albert, Saskatchewan, Jim Neilson played left wing. A rash of injuries forced his conversion into a defenceman and started his success in hockey. In 1962 he joined the Rangers, the club to which he had been bound in his youth by, as he calls it, "the beloved C form."

Neilson, known as Chief by his teammates because of his native ancestry, recalls mostly sitting, watching and learning during his first two seasons. The transition into the professional game came fairly easily to him. "I'm an easygoing guy. I never look far ahead and I've used that philosophy all my life. I just play the game. It's over and there'll probably be one again tomorrow," he says.

"In those days everyone had an assignment and was expected to carry it out rather than the free-flowing style of today," Neilson adds. His role was to play defensively. He did that well enough to stay in professional hockey for 17 years. The big, fine stickhandling rearguard was nominated to the all-star team in 1968. "Now that I look back, it wasn't long at all, it seems like 17 weeks," he comments. "I guess I was able to do the job. I never thought of why I wanted to stay that long. I guess I liked the game. It was fun being with the guys."

In 1974, Neilson was traded to California. He later went to Cleveland and, for his last season, played with Edmonton of the WHA. Chronic back problems caught up with him in 1979.

Deteriorated disks in his back required surgery if he were to continue playing and the operation came with no guarantee. "I had to shut her down," he states, "No choice. I had never thought of retiring but when surgery was mentioned, I took an hour to make a decision and shut her down then."

For the next season and a half Nielson scouted in western Canada for Edmonton. He then moved to California where he became part owner of a golf course. "You learn how to be on your own once in a while, when there's no one backing you up if you make a mistake," he says about the experience in California. After three years he left and returned to Prince Albert.

Since 1984 Neilson has been working with the federal government's Native Economic Development Program evaluating proposals. Recently he has been approached to write a book on his career. If he does go ahead with the project, he jokes, "It'll be one of the shortest books in history, but what the hell, I'll put a lot of pictures like I've seen in the other ones."

Larry Popein

New York Rangers

(b. 1930, Yorkton, Sask.)
Games played 449
Goals 80
Assists 141
Total points 221
Penalties in Minutes 162

Larry Popein

New York bought Larry Popein's contract from Eddie Shore and brought the forward to the Rangers in 1954. He was part of a new wave of talent that saw Worsley, Bathgate and Fontinato arrive in the Big Apple to lend some credibility to the squad.

While being in the NHL was an accomplishment, Popein acknowledges that all that glittered was not necessarily good. "Some things were disappointing," he admits. "I thought some things would be entirely different and more glamourous. The commuting to practices . . . we had to go to Madison Square Gardens every day and it wasn't convenient because we lived out in Long Island. That took about three hours every day." After a Saturday night game in Toronto, the Rangers would take the overnight train back, arriving at 1 p.m. Then they would take the subway to Long Island where most of them lived, "gobble a half-assed meal" and trek back to the Gardens for the Sunday night encounter.

In Popein's case, the problem was exacerbated when the season ended because he lived in Vancouver. He had to drive across the continent to the west coast. The time on the road, he says, was "what discouraged me most."

A hustling, two-way centreman, Popein was flanked for a time by Bathgate and Prentice. The unit was the most effective the Rangers had. The ability to work and the willingness to lend and accept constructive criticism made the line as successful as it was, he adds. He worked on a regular shift, the power play and killing penalties. He says, "As long as I was playing I was happy."

Partway through the 1960-61 season, Popein was sent to Vancouver of the WHL. He played there until 1967 when, at 37 years of age, he was signed by the Oakland Seals. Though he wanted to finish off the season and his career in Vancouver, the Seals made it financially worth his while to alter his plans.

"I knew I wanted to stay in hockey so I sort of prepared myself to jump on the other side of the fence," Popein explains. He coached Omaha of the CHL for the next two years, taking the team to a championship. He moved on to coach in Seattle and Providence. In 1973-74 he coached the Rangers for 41 games. Then Phil Maloney offered him the positions of assistant general manager and director of player personnel with the Canucks for 1974-75. "I didn't hesitate because I thought I'd get the best of both worlds, living in Vancouver and working for the hockey club," he continues.

Popein still enjoys the best of both worlds today. He says he enjoyed every bit of his career, even the last few years in the minors. At the end, the salaries were "pretty good" and his stay in the minors, waiting and hoping for the break he wanted, was worth it because, luckily, it happened.

Dean Prentice

New York Rangers

(b. 1932, Schumacher, Ont.)
Games played 1378
Goals 391
Assists 469
Total points 860
Penalties in Minutes 484

Dean Prentice saw his career stretch from 1952 when he joined the New York Rangers to 1974 when he retired from the Minnesota North Stars. In the intervening years, the iron man from Schumacher, Ontario played in Boston, Detroit, and Pittsburgh and never spent a single moment in the minors. A good skater, although underrated by many, Prentice played his best on a line in New York with Andy Bathgate and Earl Ingarfield. He was voted an all-star in 1960. "I did a lot of work and had a lot of dedication to perfect those skills," he says. "I was blessed to stay that long."

Never having had the fortune of being on a Stanley Cup champion club, his most memorable moments came when he played with one of the great ones. "The highlight of my career was getting an opportunity to play on a line with Gordie Howe and Alex Delvecchio and getting into the Stanley Cup play-offs. I used to check Gordie Howe all the time. Playing against him was a tough battle. To get the opportunity to play with him and see and share his ability, it was a real joy."

Prentice coached in the minor leagues briefly after he retired. He is now a recreation and arena manager in Ayr, a small town near Cambridge, Ontario. He appreciates that job, he adds, because it gives him an opportunity to be with young people. Trim and fit, he also indulges in the occasional game of old-timers' hockey. A born again Christian for several years, he is also involved in spreading the word about "a better way of living".

Don Raleigh
New York Rangers

(b. 1926, Kenora, Ont.)
Games played 535
Goals 101
Assists 219
Total points 320
Penalties in Minutes 96

A newspaper columnist once asked New York Rangers' general manager Muzz Patrick who he thought possessed the hardest body check in the league. "Without a doubt," the Ranger boss replied, "it's Bones Raleigh." Raleigh was the six foot, 145-pound centreman known more for his playmaking than his hit-ting. Once the scribe had time to reset his dislocated jaw, he said, "What do you mean Bones Raleigh? He's the skinniest guy in the league." "That's what I mean," Patrick explained. "When he hits 'em, he cuts 'em."

That tale of legendary skinniness is one that Bones Raleigh still recalls humorously. He broke in with the Rangers during the war. The club's ranks had been depleted by enlistments and they were badly in need of players. At the age of 17, he signed with New York. He lasted half the season, spending the balance with a minor league affiliate. The following season, an unusual wartime law prevented him from crossing the border to rejoin the Rangers. He was promptly reinstated as an amateur and returned to the junior ranks, becoming one of the first, if not the only, NHL player to play a full season of professional hockey and go back to the junior game.

Raleigh spent ten seasons in the NHL. One of the moments he remembers best is being one goal away from the Stanley Cup in the final series of the 1950 season against the Red Wings. Babando scored the winner for Detroit in overtime. Before that decisive incident, Raleigh had a glorious opportunity to win it for the Rangers but the chance disappeared when the puck took an unpropitious bounce over his stick. "Nobody gives a damn for anyone except for the winner," he says. "If we'd won that game, the Rangers wouldn't have had that 50-year dearth they've had now."

During his stay in New York, Raleigh became one of the first to wear a moustache at a time when facial hair was not permitted in the league. "Oh, I don't know," is his reason for flaunting league authority. He remembers for a moment another "incredible" trapping of a long gone era — a league edict stating that players of opposing teams could not be friendly off the ice.

A combination of the Rangers wanting to rebuild and a change in attitude brought Raleigh to the end of his NHL career in 1956. "It was a question of energy," he explains. "It became work to me after a while. When it becomes work it is no longer a good thing to do. You lose your drive. I found it difficult because I was so tired all the time with my small frame. I didn't have the pep."

Raleigh went to the minors where he became a playing coach for a couple of seasons. When it became obvious to him that there would be no place for him in that capacity in the NHL, he turned to his present occupation of selling insurance. "When you're 30 years old and you don't have a trade," says the proprietor of J.J. Raleigh and Company Limited, "it's like the guy coming out of the army. What do you do? I couldn't become an accountant. I couldn't get into an office. All you can do is sell. You can always get a job if you can sell. When I was through with hockey there weren't too many avenues open to go into unless . . . it was coaching or something. So all you can really do is sell. You sort of capitalize on your name at the time. I got into insurance."

Raleigh is active these days in hockey as president of the Manitoba Hockey Players' Foundation, an old-timers' organization that plays for charity and lobbies to have that province's former hockey greats enshrined in a Hall of Fame. He still puts on the blades for those charity events though as he says, "I'm getting too goddamn old for that now. I'm 58 and a half. I didn't have any energy when I was 38. I have even less now!"

Looking back at it all now, Raleigh thinks it would have been nice to do better and to have won a Stanley Cup but he does not express any regrets about the experience. "I had a chance to go into medical school myself in '47 instead of hockey. You often wonder if that might have been the right route. However whatever is is. I've been successful in my insurance business. As long as you're happy in what you're doing, that's all that matters."

Jean Ratelle
New York Rangers

(b. 1940, Lac St. Jean, Que.)
Games played 1281
Goals 491
Assists 776
Total points 1267
Penalties in Minutes 276

Jean Ratelle

In the 1965-66 season, just as Jean Ratelle's career began to show promise, he was diagnosed as suffering deterioration of the lower spine. The condition required spinal fusion surgery which, it seemed, would force him to retire. His attempted comeback the following season saw the lanky centreman score only six goals, the nadir of what had been an up and down stay in the NHL.

"It was kind of touch and go," Ratelle admits about the surgery and its aftermath. "I was hoping I would be able to come back. I was always confident that I would." The operation, he adds, was a complete success and his back "never really bothered me afterward."

Born in Lac St. Jean, Quebec, Ratelle first saw action with New York in 1960 when, still a junior, he was called up for three games. His two goals proved to management that they indeed had a quality prospect. However, during his first two seasons he did not live up to expectations and spent most of his time in the minors. "It seemed like some of the players kind of played there [in the six-team league] for a while," he says. "It was kind of hard to break in. It took me a couple of years before I was able to make it."

In 1963-64, Ratelle returned from the nether world of the farm leagues only to become embroiled in a contract dispute with Rangers' boss Muzz Patrick. He came back the next season to score 14 goals in 54 games. He finally seemed to be on track with 21 goals in 1964-65 when the spinal problem was diagnosed.

Emile Francis, having become the Rangers' coach, put Ratelle on a line between hardnosed winger Vic Hadfield and the flashy Rod Gilbert. The Gag Line (Goal-A-Game) was born and with it, a resurgence in Ratelle's form. His playmaking and scoring skills were used effectively and he became an offensive leader in New York. In the early 1970s, his play earned him the Lady Byng and the Bill Masterton Trophies as well as an all-star nomination. His most significant memory in the game, he insists, was his involvement with Team Canada in 1972. The combination of it being the first confrontation between NHL players and the Soviets, the enthusiasm associated with the series from both players and fans and Team Canada coming back from a deficit to win the series make it very special for him.

One of the biggest trades in NHL history saw Ratelle and teammates Brad Park and Joe Zanussi go to Boston for Phil Esposito and Carol Vadnais. He continued to play effectively with the Bruins. His style was generally described as that of a "classy centreman" by all those who watched.

After 20 NHL seasons, a torn hip muscle that refused to heal forced Ratelle to retire in 1980. "I was 40 years old. I was old enough," he states. "I felt I wasn't cheated as far as playing hockey goes." He remained with the Bruins' organization, first as an assistant coach for four years and more recently as part of the scouting staff. "My only regret is that I didn't win the Stanley Cup," he concludes. "But I worked my hardest at all times. I gave it everything I had. If you've done that, then you've got to feel good."

Ken Schinkel

New York Rangers

(b. 1932, Jansen, Sask.)
Games played 636
Goals 127
Assists 198
Total points 325
Penalties in Minutes 163

Ken Schinkel

Ken Schinkel wishes that the C form, the contract that made many teenage hockey players the exclusive property of one professional club, had never existed. He signed one and became the chattel of Springfield, an AHL team operated by Eddie Shore, which had no affiliation with any NHL club. Consequently he languished in the minors, unable to try out with an NHL club until he was 27 years old.

Schinkel says he threatened to quit unless he was granted at least one chance to crack an NHL lineup. After all, he had established himself as a proficient scorer and he knew that two or three NHL clubs had expressed an interest in acquiring him. By 1959 Springfield and the Rangers reached a working agreement and Schinkel was on his way up.

Schinkel found himself playing a defensive role with the Rangers on the checking line and killing penalties. Because he was a more seasoned player who knew the importance of back checking, he was placed on lines with rookies, so that they might pick up his defensive style. The change from a minor league offensive threat to a major league checker was not frustrating, he says. "I prided myself on my defensive work. I just was hoping the brass would appreciate the defensive part of my game. I got a bigger kick out of making a play than I did out of scoring."

Schinkel played on a mediocre Rangers club that enjoyed only a few successful seasons under coach Phil Watson. Though he feels fortunate to have played in the exclusive six-team league, he wishes that he might have had the chance to skate with a better club. "I would have really liked to have been on a team that was established, where I could do my part and contribute."

When expansion came, Schinkel found new life in Pittsburgh. "It [expansion] gave me the opportunity to play longer than I should have ever played," he comments. In 1974, at 41 years and the top-scoring winger on the club, the Penguins asked him to take the coaching job after Red Kelly's departure. At the time, he says, he had little desire to coach because he felt he had more good playing seasons left in him. He put in two stints, each a season and a half long, as coach of the Penguins. "My main problem was my stomach," he explains. "I couldn't handle the pressure part of it. I thought I would coach very well in the league, but when you don't sleep three or four nights in a row . . . It's not worth your health. I knew my personality would change. It wasn't good for me and it wasn't good for my family. I've got a beautiful wife and great kids. When you're miserable with them, it's not worth the price."

Schinkel has remained with the Penguins as an assistant manager. Recently he has assumed more responsibilities scouting. Thirty years ago he wouldn't have believed it if someone told him he would remain in the game for so long. He believes that the only way anyone can last that length of time in hockey lies in advice offered to him by Muzz Patrick: "Keep your nose clean and work as hard as you can and you'll be in this game a long time."

Irv Spencer

New York Rangers

(b. 1937, Sudbury, Ont.)
Games played 230
Goals 12
Assists 38
Total points 50
Penalties in Minutes 127

Defenceman Irv Spencer, a native of Sudbury, Ontario drafted by the New York Rangers in 1959, quickly discovered the difficulty of establishing an NHL career. "You could be around for three or four years and they could still say you didn't have enough experience," he laughs. "Of course there was only six teams in the league. You had to wait until somebody died to get a position."

Waiting for an opportunity to play had its own perils. One had to have patience and not lose the desire to go on. "If you sat there long enough, it just seemed that you would lose something. I know that's what happened to me somewhat," Spencer admits.

Spencer later moved to Boston and Detroit. He spent ten years in the Red Wing organization playing for various farm teams across the United States. He retired in 1974 after two seasons in the WHA. "Strangely enough," he adds, "the person who brought me into the major leagues, Phil Watson [a former Rangers' coach who held the same job later with Vancouver of the WHA], asked me to quit. I was ready to quit. I was finished." Knees badly worn by years of hockey and unable to keep up, he complied with his coach's request.

Spencer settled in the San Diego area where he had played minor league hockey. Since his retirement he has been involved in the mortgage business. Currently he heads the savings and loan department of a bank.

Explaining some of the bewilderment that accompanies retirement, he says, "At the time I was probably more lost than anything. Years ago, if you were loyal to a club, they were sort of loyal to you. You knew you had a job next year. You were taken care of. That's the way it was basically all my life from the time I was 16 when I left home to play hockey. I was pretty well assured that I'd be doing what I wanted to be doing."

"When you quit hockey, all of a sudden you're out of the house so to speak, out in the cold world. You ask, 'Where do I start?' I was more lost. I didn't have any remorse about leaving. I just started working on a new life and put hockey in the background and left it there."

Red Sullivan
New York Rangers

(b. 1929, Peterborough, Ont.)
Games played 557
Goals 107
Assists 239
Total points 346
Penalties in Minutes 441

George (Red) Sullivan

"It's in your blood," offers Red Sullivan as his reason for staying in hockey in some capacity after retiring as a player. Sullivan spent ten seasons in the NHL with Boston, Chicago and New York. "I don't have any formal education and ever since I was a kid I've always wanted to make my living out of sports."

Sullivan, a centreman, was known for his forechecking abilities and his talent for verbally harassing the opposition. When he got to New York in 1956, he became a regular and found a home on a line with Camille Henry and Andy Hebenton. The 1958-59 season was his best when he scored 21 goals and 42 assists.

A serious spleen injury led to Sullivan's retirement in 1961. During a Saturday night game in Montreal he kicked the skates out from under Doug Harvey. The next night in New York, Harvey exacted his revenge by spearing Sullivan. He suffered a bruised spleen and it looked as though he might die at one point. He was even given last rites.

Sullivan began coaching in Baltimore of the AHL. He stepped behind the Rangers' bench partway through the 1962-63 season. Into his third losing season with the Rangers, he was fired. "I was bitter," he says, "but I had to bite the bullet." Perhaps the youngest man to assume coaching duties in the NHL, he found himself "having to jump on players", many with whom he had played. It was the toughest aspect of the game for him. In hindsight he thinks, "I didn't have the patience that a good coach should have. If I had to go back to coaching I'd certainly do it a lot differently."

For the next several years he alternated between coaching and scouting. He coached Pittsburgh in 1967-68 and 1968-69. Then he scouted for the Bruins until accepting the head scouting position with Washington in 1973. For a brief 19 games, he once again stepped behind the bench, hoping to reverse the Capitals' losing tide. He didn't and was fired again. In recent years he has been on the staff of the NHL's central scouting bureau and ranks and rates available hockey talent. He and his family live in Peterborough, Ontario.

Gump Worsley

New York Rangers

(b. 1929, Montreal, Que.)
Games played 860
Minutes 50,201
Goals against 2432
Shutouts 43
Average 2.91

Gump Worsley

Lorne "Gump" Worsley's career began in fine fashion — his performance in net for the Rangers in 1952-53 earned him the Calder Trophy as the NHL's top rookie that year. However, he never got a chance to suffer the "sophomore blues" because he was supplanted in net by Johnny Bower. In his biography, *They Call Me Gump*, he said, "I figured a guy is good enough to win the Calder, well, that's something and he should be given another whack at it. I was bitter as hell — at Boucher [general manager and coach] and the whole organization."

Worsley returned in 1954 to become the Rangers' goaltender, flopping in front of the twine for a team that was not very defensively oriented. Phil Watson joined the Rangers in 1955 and soon became his tormentor. "You can't play good with a beer barrel belly," Watson said ridiculing the stocky netminder. The irreverent goalie quickly replied, "Beer is a poor man's champagne. I'm strictly a V.O. [rye] man."

Worsley acquired a reputation for drinking and partying in New York. While with a Rangers' farm club, he wrote: "I soon got caught up with the city's fast life and almost ruined my career before I got started with the New York Rovers [the Rangers' farm club]." When the Rangers plummeted in the league standings after 1958, he termed the next three seasons "pure misery for me, the darkest of my career. I was doing a lot of drinking then, using the bottle to chase all those bad games and bad goals." In the end he declared that his reputation as a hell-raiser and drinker was exaggerated over the years.

When the Rangers demoted him to Springfield in 1959, Worsley contemplated quitting. "I was 30 years old and the thought of having to find another job outside hockey did cross my mind. But I went to Springfield anyway. What else could I do?" He persevered and returned to the NHL. In 1963 he was traded to Montreal. He said, "I felt like a man who'd just been let out of prison."

Worsley played in distinguished fashion for a distinguished team. While with the Canadiens, he shared the Vezina Trophy twice, in 1966 and 1968. The championships that were only a dream in New York came regularly in Montreal. He was part of four Stanley Cup winning clubs. The fourth, in 1968-69, was memorable because he had come back from a nervous breakdown to help the club to victory.

Traded to Minnesota in 1970, Worsley played with the North Stars until 1974 when he retired. He remained with the club as a scout, a position he holds today. In 1980, Worsley's long service in the league was recognized with his installation in the Hall of Fame.

It's all over as Toronto Maple Leaf goalie Johnny Bower rushes out of the net to receive the congratulations of his team mates after 4-0 clinching victory over Detroit Red Wings. This victory won the Stanley Cup for Toronto Maple Leafs for the third straight time.

With an apparently "over-the-hill gang" of hockey players, the Toronto Maple Leafs won the last six-team Stanley Cup in 1967. No one figured that a club which featured so many veterans would even finish in the play-offs, let alone defeat Chicago and Montreal to win it all. In terms of professional hockey, the preserve of young legs, the Leafs were a geriatrics ward. Johnny Bower, Allan Stanley, Tim Horton, Bobby Baun, Marcel Pronovost, Bob Pulford, and George Armstrong were all well into their 30s. Helped by younger players like Dave Keon, Jim Pappin, Pete Stemkowski and Ron Ellis, the old men completed an upset that proved to be the last throes of the powerhouse that Punch Imlach built, beginning in the late 1950s.

When Imlach was hired by the Leafs in 1958, he came to a team that had not won a Cup since 1950-51 when the late Bill Barilko notched his famous overtime marker. In fact the club, attempting to rebuild, did not appear in the play-offs again until 1958-59. The glory of Conn Smythe's teams of the late 1940s who had captured three consecutive Stanley Cups, seemed too distant to ever again be repeated.

Imlach brought in Johnny Bower, already over 30 at the time, to mind the net. He added Allan Stanley and, later, Carl Brewer and Kent Douglas to a defence which already had Tim Horton and Bobby Baun. Frank Mahovlich burst on the scene to lend scoring power. By 1962, when the team won its first of three consecutive Stanley Cups, its forwards included the likes of Bob Pulford, George Armstrong, Dave Keon, and Dick Duff. Employing Imlach's brand of conservative, defensive, disciplined hockey, the Leafs reclaimed some of the success the team had known a decade before.

In the post-expansion era, Toronto has sunk to the level of a have-not organization in the NHL. Seemingly on an endless rebuilding campaign, the team has become a stranger to post-season competition. Since 1967, the team's best showing in the NHL's "second season" has been the elimination of the New York Islanders in the 1977-78 quarter finals in seven hard-fought games. The most enduring aspect of the team recently has been the antics of the mercurial man who won ownership of the club from the Smythe family, Harold Ballard.

Gary Aldcorn

Toronto Maple Leafs

(b. 1935, Shaunavon, Sask.)
Games played 351
Goals 41
Assists 56
Total points 97
Penalties in Minutes 78

Garry Aldcorn

The great love for the sport of hockey that every player professes often instills a yearning to stay in the game forever. Some become coaches, others scouts. In the case of Gary Aldcorn, a left winger with Toronto, Detroit and Boston in the late 1950s, he left hoping for a different destiny and now finds himself almost directly involved again as an entrepreneur.

Aldcorn remembers being one of several players including Billy Harris and Bob Pulford who worked on undergraduate arts degrees during their hockey-playing days. "We used to play that as a ploy whenever we were talking salaries," he says, explaining the bargaining leverage the pursuit of high learning could offer. "We'd say, 'We could always go back to school.' Of course the general managers didn't know what we were talking about so they'd get a little frightened." In his estimation the tactic worked. "We were making more money in our second and third year than guys who had been there six or seven years in the league."

Aldcorn's retirement from hockey at the end of the 1960-61 season to attend university full time turned out to be somewhat ironic. The decision was triggered, he explains, by a tragedy when the wife of fellow Detroit player Billy McNeill contracted polio and died. Aldcorn underwent "a little bit of a cathartic experience", an emotional upheaval. "I looked at what I was doing . . . what I felt I knew and how good I was. I think I answered those questions on a hockey level. I just felt I would challenge some other level and be of a little more value to somebody."

Hoping to enter medical school one day, Aldcorn returned to the University of Manitoba in his native province. When he didn't get accepted into the medical program, he completed the requirements for an arts degree and continued to study, earning one masters degree in science and another in business.

Aldcorn was reinstated as an amateur and in 1968 played on Canada's national team. Later he went on to coach the team. In 1970, he became involved with the nascent Hockey Canada, a government body directed to formulate overall hockey strategy, tactics and long-range plans for the participation of Canadian hockey teams in international competition. At the time, he became involved in initiating and developing the national coaching certification program.

Aldcorn left that organization in 1974 and became a sports consultant which, he says, he still does a little. He consulted with groups such as the CAHA and Hockey Night in Canada on film work.

Within five years Aldcorn was turning his energies into another business side of sport. He started Flak Equipment, a company developing protective equipment that uses air to absorb shock. "Basically it's an airbag underneath a plastic shell," he elaborates. "The plastic absorbs the hit and distributes it through the amorphous air underneath." His firm, located north of Toronto and employing 25 to 30 people, manufactures equipment for hockey and football teams in Canada and the United States.

His products are currently being introduced into the NHL. "I haven't utilized any of my sports connections yet. I didn't want to impinge on them. I wanted the product to stand on its own merits rather than trying to coerce someone into using them because of our friendship," he adds.

As it does in the realm of sports, confidence plays a major role in a successful enterprise. Aldcorn is confident. "The reason I know I'm going to be successful is that I'm not going to put a bad product out there just for the sake of putting a product out there and selling it, which is a different tack than Cooper and CCM and all the other guys take. They'd sell pickled lemons if they could." By making a quality product and addressing the "top third" of the market, he feels that Flak Industries will be well on its way.

So, in essence, Gary Aldcorn never left the game of hockey. He has augmented the good intuitive understanding of the game he says he has always had with scientific and commercial knowledge he has gained over the years. He now applies his knowledge to a business that concerns itself with a fundamental part of the game — safety.

George Armstrong

Toronto Maple Leafs

(*b. 1930, Bowlands, Ont.*)
Games played 1187
Goals 296
Assists 417
Total points 713
Penalties in Minutes 721

George Armstrong

The "Chief", George Armstrong's nickname because of the Indian ancestry on his mother's side of the family, played 20 seasons in the NHL, all of them as a Toronto Maple Leaf. A steady two-way player, he was considered unspectacular but effective. Punch Imlach in *Hockey is a Battle* said, "He did more for the Maple Leafs than any other hockey player who played for me." His tenure as Leafs' captain spanned that club's best era — its four Stanley Cup championships. In 1975 his productive career was recognized with his induction into the Hockey Hall of Fame.

Recalling his time in the NHL, Armstrong insists that while certain moments like Stanley Cup victories were happier than others, just being a part of the world's premier professional hockey league was enough reason for satisfaction. "I just liked playing. I have no place for trophies in my house. There's no trophies or pictures of me in my playing days. There's no 50-goal puck," he says. "I just enjoyed playing. I enjoyed the comradeship."

When Armstrong retired in 1972 the Maple Leafs offered him a job as a scout. He scouted for a year before accepting an offer to coach the Toronto Marlboros of the Ontario Major Junior Hockey League. He wanted to see if he enjoyed coaching. In five seasons with the junior club, he led it to two Memorial Cups, the national junior title. The experience helped him arrive at one conclusion. "I found out I didn't like coaching," he remembers, revealing his inability to contend with the fundamental hyprocrisy of most minor level competitive sports. "I didn't have the heart to tell players they weren't good enough to play [in the pro ranks] and then go ask the kid to kill a penalty next game. Kids think that there's some secret potion that will make them good hockey players. Hockey players are born, not made. I can't tell him he's not a hockey player and then ask him to play for me. What I really wanted to do was scout, so I quit."

Since then Armstrong has been head scout for the Quebec Nordiques. Based in Toronto, he now travels throughout the continent to assess up-and-coming talent for his employers. "I like being involved in the game I like, the game I've been involved with all my life, the game I know most about." It offers two luxuries that almost all ex-pros crave — contact with the game and the opportunity to enjoy the camaraderie of a very special fraternity, his former teammates and adversaries whom he meets on the road.

Bob Baun
Toronto Maple Leafs

(b. 1936, Lanigan, Sask.)
Games played 964
Goals 37
Assists 187
Total points 224
Penalties in Minutes 1493

Bob Baun

Bobby Baun, Toronto's hardrock defenceman from 1956 to 1967, is probably best remembered for his heroics in the 1964 Stanley Cup finals. He returned to the ice after suffering a broken ankle to score the winning overtime goal in the sixth game of the series. He finished the series on that wounded leg and helped the Leafs win a third consecutive Stanley Cup.

"I've never dwelled too much on that," Baun says, unwinding after another 16-hour day at the Tim Horton Donuts franchise he owns in Toronto. "I can say it's given me a lot more mileage than I deserved." Baun believes he simply did what was expected of him. The special moments he remembers from his 17-year professional hockey career are connected more to the people he met through the game than in the battles for honours on the rink.

"To me, my greatest moment in sports was having a drink with Mr. Eisenhower on the tenth tee at Augusta National," he reveals. He met the former president at the famous course during a round of golf after the hockey season. The list of celebrities he has met and talked with is long and covers the spectrum of human achievement: Duke Ellington, Louis Armstrong, Richard Nixon, Dr. Wilder Penfield and Norman Vincent Peale, the writer of *The Power of Positive Thinking*. This book has been Baun's "bible for the last 30 years". His interest in politics and his friendship with Senator Keith Davey, a longtime Liberal Party campaign organizer, earned him a job one election keeping Prime Minister Lester B. Pearson busy. "Mr. Pearson and I, all we did was talk hockey and baseball. He was a great New York Yankees' fan and I grew up on the Yankees. That's what we did for hours on end."

Baun went to Oakland in the 1967 expansion draft and then a season later to Detroit. He was traded back to Toronto where he played until the 1972-73 season. After severely straining his neck vertebrae in a fall, he followed a doctor's advice and retired from the game. It turned out to be the second time he had broken his neck. The first time was in Montreal on New Year's Eve, 1967. "I didn't know about it until five years later," says the man with the superhuman tolerance for pain. For the next five years he controlled the constant pain by ingesting 222 tablets.

After his retirement, Baun spent three days in a Toronto hospital undergoing operations to correct the various injuries the bruising checker had suffered during his years on the blueline. "The doctors operated on my right knee, my two elbows and my neck. I had the whole works done. I said, 'I don't want to waste any of your time and I don't want to waste any more time than I have to. Get it all over with.' The only thing I didn't have done was my nose," he comments, refering to his oft-smashed proboscis. "I didn't have the heart to do my nose."

Baun left hockey to continue farming, his off-season job since 1967. At one time, his cattle operation northeast of Toronto encompassed 2,000 acres. The ultra-modern, very automated farm attracted visitors from across the country. "We were forced out by that new proposed airport in Pickering," he says. The government froze land sales in the area and land values plummeted. "If you wanted to sell or you wanted to build, you couldn't do any of these things."

Baun left farming for the real estate business where he "did very well". He then dabbled in insurance and helped establish a company called Pan-American Family Insurance. When his attempt to buy the entire business failed, he moved into the doughnut business as part of the chain that his former teammate, the late Tim Horton, had started.

Located at a busy intersection of Highway 401 in the east end of Toronto, Baun's latest enterprise is providing him with a new challenge. "It's interesting. You have to be an administrator, you have to be a manufacturer and you have to be a retailer," he adds. Baun and his family live in the Toronto area.

Johnny Bower

Toronto Maple Leafs

(b. 1924, Prince Albert, Sask.)
Games played 552
Minutes 32,077
Goals against 1605
Shutouts 62
Average 2.56

The scene could be from any summer hockey school — except that every one of the students is a goaltender. Crouched in one net, demonstrating the fundamentals and moving as carefully as when he minded the twine for the Toronto Maple Leafs, is Johnny Bower. Affable, knowledgeable and patient, he seems to be able to successfully teach the wisdom he acquired over 12 seasons in the NHL to youngsters, some of whom weren't even born when he was backstopping the Leafs to four Stanley Cups.

The school for goaltenders, Bower explains, is something he does each summer for two weeks. The idea for the school was conceived by his daughter Cindy four years ago. As a skating instructor for minor hockey teams in Toronto, Cindy realized this type of service was needed because coaches kept requesting her famous dad's help with aspiring goalies. Now the father and daughter are a teaching team; he shows netminding fundamentals and she gives lessons in "efficiency skating". Says the ex-Leaf, "I have a lot of fun with the kids. If one comes out and makes it, I can say I helped him a little. It's quite a feeling to see someone make it."

Bower knows what it takes to make it. He broke in with the New York Rangers in 1953. Though he played well he found himself in the minors where he stayed until he was scouted and drafted by Toronto in 1958. Initially he had no desire to uproot his family from its comfortable surroundings in Cleveland and exchange relative security for the vicissitudes of the NHL. Nevertheless, he went to Toronto and, at 33 years of age, became hockey's most renowned late bloomer.

The always respected Bower established a reputation as a hard-working player who responded well to pressure — a money goal-tender. The image of Bower at his best endures. In the second overtime period of the 1967 Stanley Cup final against the favoured Montreal Canadiens, Yvon Cournoyer broke in on Bower from the wing unmolested. The maskless, stout goalie lunged out and a certain goal was stopped. The puck went back up-ice, the Leafs scored and completed a great upset. "I always liked to play under pressure," he says, his smile brightened by the false teeth that replaced the casualties of the hockey wars. "I always played best under pressure. I don't know why. Maybe it was the money and prestige that went with the big games."

By 1970 his vision had deteriorated enough to affect his play, though he maintains his reflexes were as good as ever. At 47 years of age he accepted a scouting position with the Maple Leafs which he continues to do today. Often he tutors Toronto's goalies and has even been known to don the pads for the odd practice session. He and his wife Nancy make their home in Toronto.

Carl Brewer

Toronto Maple Leafs

(b. 1938, Toronto, Ont.)
Games played 604
Goals 25
Assists 198
Total points 223
Penalties in Minutes 1037

His head a shiny, shaven sphere; his body, still athletic and covered in a three-piece pin-stripe suit; his conversation, to the point and articulate — the combination of presentation and speech makes Carl Brewer come across as a corporate Mr. Clean.

When Toronto made a re-surgence into respectability in the late 1950s, it was largely due to having bolstered its roster with talented defencemen like Allan Stanley, Bob Baun, Tim Horton and Carl Brewer. Brewer's effectiveness in stifling opposing forwards is well known but he is best remembered among fans for his controversial departures and returns to the NHL and among players for his high-strung, unpredictable nature.

Brewer is not quite sure of exactly how much time he put into professional hockey. "Gosh, I really don't know, possibly 12 [years] . . . there were so many retirements and mind changes . . . I think it's possibly around 12," he replies. He shocked the hockey world in 1962 when, at the height of his career, he decided to quit hockey to study French and Political Science at the University of Toronto.

"It has been suggested that I had some ability and for that fact I am grateful. I like to think that at times I played well but I think under the circumstances, perhaps I didn't reach the potential I might have," he says reflecting on his career. "I think the most effective years I had were my first two years in the NHL when I was 19 and 20 and I think again later in my career when I was close to 30, I believe. I played in Detroit and I think that I played very, very effectively there."

Today, Brewer is primarily involved in real estate investments. "I'm excited with what I do," he reports. The earlier experiences he had in business have prepared him for his current work. "I like to think that I have some determination and some drive and I think I have some discipline and because of that, over a period of time, I've been able to develop some business acumen."

Never afraid to blend a little pleasure with business, Brewer discovered that the name Toronto Maple Leafs had never been registered so he registered it with the Province of Ontario. The Ministry of Consumer and Corporate Affairs settled the controversy that arose by saying that although technically Brewer did indeed own the name Toronto Maple Leafs Hockey Club Limited, owing to prior usage, Ballard and company had a right to retain it. "I just did it for fun," he chuckles.

Barry Cullen

Toronto Maple Leafs

(b. 1935, Ottawa, Ont.)
Games played 219
Goals 32
Assists 52
Total points 84
Penalties in Minutes 111

Like his older brother Brian, Barry Cullen stepped into the NHL from the junior ranks with a lot of promise. When he proved less than successful at hockey, he also turned to the automobile business where he made his fortune.

Cullen played three seasons with Toronto and one with Detroit. He was eventually sent to Buffalo, a minor league affiliate, where he played until he retired in 1964. "I felt that probably, maybe, I didn't get the chance. Maybe all players think that," he says. Once in Buffalo with the intense competition for jobs in the NHL, he was never recalled to the parent team.

At 29 years of age, Cullen quit and went into the car business. He was initially an assistant to his brother and then a leasing manager. He learned the business from the bottom up and eventually got a General Motors franchise in Guelph, Ontario. Like his brother's operation, it is considered among the best in the nation. "I really smile when people say, 'Too bad you're not playing hockey today,' or something like that," he comments. "The best thing that ever happened to us was that we didn't have more success in hockey because we got out early."

In a sense, Cullen adds, hockey and the car business are similar. Both are very competitive pastimes, both involve hard work, both involve getting along with people and both require an ability to motivate others. He considers himself fortunate that he has had the opportunity to apply those skills in the automotive game in a bigger way than in hockey. The returns are much more impressive in one than they were in the other.

Brian Cullen

Toronto Maple Leafs

(b. 1933, Ottawa, Ont.)
Games played 326
Goals 56
Assists 100
Total points 156
Penalties in Minutes 93

Brian Cullen

The luckiest break Brian Cullen got in his six-year NHL career came when he was with Toronto and attended a father-son banquet in Richmond Hill, Ontario. A man whose son could not attend because he had broken a leg asked him and teammate Bob Pulford if they would come to his house and sign the youngster's cast. The hockey players agreed and struck up a friendship with the man, Herb Kearney, a Toronto car dealer.

When Cullen left professional hockey in 1961, Kearney offered him a job as his leasing manager. Eventually Cullen acquired his own dealerships, first in Grimsby, Ontario in 1966 and then four years later in St. Catharines. He has since built one of the largest, most successful General Motors dealerships in the nation with a staff of 80 and annual sales of $25,000,000. "Yeah, I've been very, very fortunate," he agrees. Two brothers, Barry and Ray, also ex-hockey players, are also in the automotive trade.

Cullen, one of the stars in the St. Catharines TeePees' march to the 1954 Memorial Cup, was ushered into the professional ranks with much fanfare and great expectations. He was an offensive player, he maintains, who found himself on a Maple Leaf club oriented to a defensive, bump-and-grind game. His scoring statistics (56 goals and 100 assists in 326 games) might have been better if he had served on a club with a more offensive philosophy, such as Chicago, he says.

After four seasons with Toronto and two more with New York, Cullen retired, opting to go to something that turned out to be slightly more lucrative. Since he left hockey, Cullen has become involved in another sport, horseracing. He has invested in a number of thoroughbreds including one called Pre-Emptive Strike, a horse that finished third in the 1985 Queen's Plate. Until that race, it had earned over $267,000 in 18 starts.

Kent Douglas

Toronto Maple Leafs

(b. 1936, Cobalt, Ont.)
Games played 428
Goals 33
Assists 115
Total points 148
Penalties in Minutes 631

Kent Douglas was acquired by Toronto in 1962 from the Springfield Indians of the AHL. That year he won the Calder Trophy as the league's top rookie. His apprenticeship in the minors and instruction from the legendary Eddie Shore had prepared him for life in the NHL. "It's tough to step out of junior and be able to play in the NHL," he remarks. "It's a different game. It made a big difference to learn what you can and can't do and how to protect yourself because that was important, too."

Eddie Shore's idiosyncrasies and his unusual, sometimes bizarre, methods of instruction are often recalled by his ex-players. Once he tied a rope around a goaltender's neck and then lashed it to the crossbar, explaining that if the goalie continued his habit of dropping down, he would hang. This was Eddie Shore's way of reinforcing the importance of standing up in the crease. "Eddie Shore wasn't what you would call the best teacher in the world," Douglas says, "but he knew what he wanted you to do and how he wanted you to do it. If you could put up with some of what went on, you could learn."

Douglas continues, "He kept me there for two weeks [after the season was over] and paid me full salary and he and I were the only two people on the ice for four hours, two in the morning and two in the afternoon. We went over how to skate, how to handle the puck, where you pass from, everything you could possibly learn about the game of hockey. He realized that I was interested in learning how to play."

Douglas spent five seasons with the Maple Leafs, earning a reputation as a solid, intelligent defender. "It didn't matter how good you were going, they could always put somebody else out there," he comments. The key to hockey or any sport for Douglas is being mentally prepared. "If you're mentally prepared, mentally sharp, you can do a lot more things than what you maybe think you can. If you're ready to do it, it'll happen. You have to make it happen in your mind first."

Musing on his pro hockey days and his attitude at the time, Douglas says, "I might have listened to a few people maybe a little bit more." He continues, "I've had discussions with management at different levels. Quite often I didn't agree with them. Maybe I might have changed my mind and then I might not have either. I'm a pretty stubborn person. I believe in what's right and what's wrong. I was always able to look in the mirror and know who the hell was looking back and I think that was important to me." Without doubt that attitude shortened his career. "If you were coach or general manager who would you rather have on the team, someone who you got along with or someone who was giving you static?"

"I guess everything was business in those days, as much as it is today," Douglas comments. "I just liked to have a little fun while I was playing. Maybe that's what bothered them. I think a game's a game. It sure is wonderful to win. Like I say, it's an awful lot easier to win than it is to lose, but you have to enjoy what you're doing. You've got to have fun while you're doing it. If you don't, it's never going to happen."

Douglas used to question Imlach ("I used to call him George because he didn't like that. He wanted to be called Punch.") about his frequent, intense practices. "His theory was that you had to go out there and you had to work as hard as you could every day. The travel schedule was set up so we could practise. For some people who like to practise, that's wonderful, but, like I used to tell him, some guys have ability. It's not all just hard work. What the hell would a guy like Keon need to practise skating for? At 160 pounds, all he was doing was tiring himself out. There were guys who just liked to skate. That's what Imlach liked. Not everybody had to do that. I think that's one of the reasons there was a lot of problems. His theory was you practised twice a day [in training camp] to get in shape for the season. Three weeks before the end of the year, you started practising twice a day again. You can't knock the guy's record. He was very successful. I guess it worked. But it sure as hell takes the fun out of it."

Douglas played with Detroit and Oakland before leaving the NHL in 1969. His final pro season was with New York of the WHA in 1972-73. For a time he was a playing coach in Baltimore. Today he lives in Baltimore where he is a real estate agent as well as the coach of the Annapolis Naval Academy hockey club. There he applies a coaching philosophy that he says espouses not only hard work but also injections of fun and relaxation.

Richard Duff
Toronto Maple Leafs

(b. 1936, Kirkland Lake, Ont.)
Games played 1030
Goals 283
Assists 289
Total points 572
Penalties in Minutes 743

Dick Duff

There comes a time in all athletes' lives when the demands of their chosen sport exceed their capabilities. For Dick Duff, those demands were self-imposed. He expected a high standard of play from himself. When he felt he was consistently falling below that standard, he quit. "I can't stand pat and play," he said and, with that, retired from hockey in 1971.

Duff's final two seasons were split between Los Angeles and Buffalo. He wonders if the time to retire should have been at the end of the 1969 campaign when he had helped Montreal to another Stanley Cup victory. "After I left Montreal, I was never the same," he comments. "I never had the same enthusiasm to play." By then he had accomplished what some players only dream of — eight consecutive appearances in the Stanley Cup finals and his name inscribed on the trophy six times. He had realized, as he defines it, "hockey's own rewards. The team collectively wins."

A native of Kirkland Lake, Ontario and a product of St. Michael's College in Toronto, Duff was brought up by the Maple Leafs in 1955. Compact, tough, productive, he became a fixture on Toronto's left wing from the doldrums of the mid-1950s to the club's resurgence into respectability in the early 1960s. After helping the club win a pair of Stanley Cups, he was part of a big trade to the Rangers in 1964. Adjusting to New York after being in Toronto all those years proved too difficult. He didn't fit in with the Rangers. When Montreal acquired him the following season, he was reborn as a hockey player. Canadiens' general manager Sam Pollock, Duff says, knew that with a little motivation and a little time in the hockey-oriented atmosphere in Montreal, he could again play up to his former level.

Duff once felt that either injury or the intense competition for jobs would allow him at best ten years in the NHL, but he stayed for 17 seasons. Then, with a back pocket stuffed with those collective wins and a political science degree he had completed over the years, he left hockey. "I was happy to be out. I felt a sense of relief," he reports. He took two years off because he didn't feel like working although, during that time, he ran unsuccessfully for federal election in a Northern Ontario riding. It was then he discovered that people's political ideals and associations run much deeper than the respect and admiration they might have for a former athlete.

After working for the school board in Kirkland Lake, Duff returned to Toronto to live and settle down. For five years he worked with Canadian Manufacturers. Then he came back to hockey as a full-time scout with the Toronto Maple Leafs. Now he says he lends his experience and expertise to finding the kind of players he knows it will take to turn the club around.

Billy Harris

Toronto Maple Leafs

(b. 1935, Toronto, Ont.)
Games played 769
Goals 126
Assists 219
Total points 345
Penalties in Minutes 205

Billy Harris

A letter from a depressed Maple Leafs' fan to the sports editor of *The Globe and Mail* begged owner Harold Ballard to improve the club's hapless ways by replacing coach Dan Maloney. "We have suffered 17 brutal years with your feeble-minded attempt to ice a competitive hockey team," wrote the man. "The second-best coach in hockey is sitting idle — Billy Harris. Look what he did with the Edmonton Oilers before Glen Sather dumped him. Please, Mr. Ballard, we devoted Maple Leaf fans have suffered enough."

Living in Toronto, Harris is accessible to the Maple Leafs although it's not certain he would accept the head coaching post. Reflecting on his experiences in coaching, his job since he quit playing in 1969, he has decided that the ideal position is assistant coach rather than head coach. "That's the only job I'd be interested in now," he remarks, "an assistant coach in the National Hockey League." An assistant, he points out, is not on the firing line yet can be very important. "You can help an organization."

Harris spent 12 seasons in the NHL, most of them with Toronto in the six-team era. This slightly-built centreman also played later with Detroit, California and Pittsburgh. A good skater and playmaker, he was part of three Stanley Cup efforts with the Leafs. He is one of the rare individuals in professional hockey who continued to pursue an education while in the NHL through the University of

Toronto's extension department. "If you have a chance to play pro," he advises, "it's not the end of your educational career." Busy with marriage, children and vacations, it took him 14 years to complete his economics degree.

Two seasons with losing teams proved to be his final ones in pro hockey as a player. Those fruitless years, he says, sapped the joy of playing the game from him. The decision to retire was an easy one to make. "I wasn't sure what I was going to do after retirement," he comments. Coaching is something that "99 per cent of all professional hockey players" would like to do if they had the opportunity. His varied involvement in coaching began with Hamilton of the Ontario Major Junior A circuit. He went to Europe in 1971 to coach the national teams of first Sweden and then Italy. The European experience was a valuable one he maintains. "I felt rather guilty because I learned an awful lot more about coaching than I was able to teach. I was really impressed with my experience in Europe. I think they were a little more advanced in coaching than we were in North America."

Harris returned to Canada to coach the Toronto Toros of the WHA from 1972 to 1975 and that league's Team Canada in 1974. He moved to Laurentian University in Sudbury where he coached the hockey club and lectured in sports administration. For two years he was an assistant with the Edmonton Oilers of the NHL. Originally hired by Bryan Watson, then coach of the Oilers, Harris remained after Watson was fired and replaced by Glen Sather. He fulfilled the obligation of his two-year contract and was not rehired.

"I challenged Sather," Harris recalls. "I told him I didn't want to come back as an assistant unless there was some assurance that I'd be the next head coach and he wouldn't give me that assurance. I have no regrets. The reason I challenged him was because I could see the team was going to win the Stanley Cup. I didn't know in how many years. They had the nucleus to be a very successful organization. So I was probably the only employee with the Oilers' club that wasn't handpicked by Glen Sather and I was very honest with my answers [about the Oilers]. Often I gave answers he didn't like to hear."

A stint in Sudbury as coach of that city's struggling Ontario Hockey League franchise ended with his dismissal. "It was the only time in my life I've ever been fired," he says. It is somewhat gratifying to him that the team has performed even worse since his departure. Harris is now a member of Pat Stapleton's Fundamentals In Action instructional crew teaching hockey basics to youngsters and coaches across Canada.

Larry Hillman

Toronto Maple Leafs

(b. 1937, Kirkland Lake, Ont.)
Games played 790
Goals 36
Assists 196
Total points 232
Penalties in Minutes 579

Larry Hillman

At one time, Larry Hillman says, he held the record for being the most travelled player in professional hockey. From the time he set foot in the NHL with Detroit in 1954 to the time he retired from the Winnipeg Jets of the WHA in 1976, he had played with 17 different teams in four different leagues. On one occasion, he recalls, his father mentioned the difficulty he had keeping track of his son. "I said that I can't help it if everybody wants me. I took the positive attitude rather than the negative."

Hillman sees himself as having been an average defenceman, "not great or anything" who "could handle most situations". During his stay in the NHL, he perfected the method of clearing the puck by lifting it high above everyone into the centre ice area. He learned this trick playing in the tight confines of the Boston Garden. His knack for being in the right place at the right time earned him a share of four Stanley Cups, two of them with Toronto.

It was his goal, Hillman states, to last as long as he could in professional hockey. He wanted to emulate the great Gordie Howe. "I took good care of myself both on and off the ice. I took care of myself off the ice better than most guys did. Most players liked the big lights in those big cities. I wasn't there for the big lights."

Hillman would have continued playing had it not been for a contract dispute with the Winnipeg Jets of the WHA. It went to court where he lost. While appealing the decision, he sat out the season and then joined the Calgary Cowboys as an assistant coach. After winning the appeal, Winnipeg offered him the head coaching position if he dropped the lawsuit. He accepted and led the team to two championships. When management changed and John Ferguson became the general manager, Hillman found himself out of a job.

Hillman sold a fly-in fishing camp he owned in northern Manitoba and returned to his hometown, Kirkland Lake, Ontario. For four years until 1984 he conducted hockey schools for the town. Four years ago he bought a fishing-hunting lodge on 140 acres of land at nearby Charleton and runs it six months of the year.

In the spring of 1984 Hillman was struck with a rare and often fatal disease called Guillain Barré Syndrome. A paralysis slowly spread into his legs and arms. He spent ten days receiving treatment in Toronto. For another two months he underwent therapy in Englehart, Ontario. He credits his good physical condition with helping him resist the disease. Except for the tingling he feels in his feet and hands, he says he has fully recovered.

Tim Horton

Toronto Maple Leafs

(b. 1930, Cochrane, Ont.)
Games played 1446
Goals 115
Assists 403
Total points 518
Penalties in Minutes 1611

Tim Horton

On the evening of February 20, 1972, Tim Horton was driving back to Buffalo following a game between the Buffalo Sabres and Toronto Maple Leafs. Then 44 years old, he was still performing yeoman service as an NHL defenceman for the Sabres. His club had lost that evening though he had played well enough to be chosen one of the stars of the game.

Maple Leaf Gardens had been the scene of many of the triumphant moments of a long productive career. A native of Cochrane, Ontario, Horton joined Toronto in 1952 just after its dynasty of the late 1940s began to crumble. He remained as the club was refashioned into a new dynasty in the 1960s. He played an important role on the new Leafs and was chosen an all-star four times. A powerful, strong man, he never had to rely on fighting. All he had to do was grab another player and, as one former teammate recalled, "You'd turn blue." Playing along Allan Stanley over those halcyon days in Toronto, he participated in four Stanley Cup victories.

Horton was traded to New York in 1970. A season later he was in Pittsburgh and finally in 1973 joined his former coach Punch Imlach in Buffalo. During the off-seasons he began to build the chain of doughnut shops that bear his name. He was successful in both athletics and business.

Horton drove towards Buffalo following the game in the Gardens. He lost control of his car along the way and died instantly in the ensuing accident.

Ted Kennedy

Toronto Maple Leafs

(b. 1925, Humberstone, Ont.)
Games played 696
Goals 231
Assists 329
Total points 560
Penalties in Minutes 432

That Ted Kennedy is now associated with the regal sport of horseracing is fitting because the former Toronto captain was considered a thoroughbred of the ice wars when he led the Maple Leafs through their glory years in the 1940s and 1950s. For the last ten years he has been an official with the Ontario Racing Commission in Toronto.

"I've always been a great admirer of the thoroughbred race horse," Kennedy says. "Even when I was playing I would have a horse of my own, not for racing, but as a pleasure horse. After I quit playing and bought a farm, then I started to raise my own horses. It's just because of my fondness for the thoroughbred race horse that I got involved."

"Then it became so expensive to be in the racing game," Kennedy continues. "To make it worthwhile you had to have very expensive stock or be extremely lucky . . . and I couldn't afford to depend on luck , so I got into the official end of it."

A relentless forechecker, an excellent face-off man with an ability to lead through inspiration rather than exhortation, Kennedy took part in five Stanley Cup championships. He was named an all-star three times, awarded the Hart Trophy in 1955 and inducted into the Hockey Hall of Fame 11 years later. Never considered a good skater, he admits, "I had to work hard at my skating. I relied heavily on my wings and I always had good fast wingmen with me. Whenever anyone was chasing me, I don't remember anyone ever catching me. Whether it was out of fear, I don't know."

After retiring from hockey, Kennedy worked with a building materials firm in Toronto before turning to raising horses. Before joining the ORC, he was a sales representative with a transport company.

Kennedy reflects: "I have no regrets for having chosen a career as a professional hockey player. I was a terrible disappointment to my mother. She wanted me to go on to university. I was slated to go on to the University of Western Ontario in London. There are times now when I get reminiscing and looking back over my life. I don't say I should have changed things or wished I had changed things, but I often feel I would have been much better off, I think, if I had gone on to university and then after university, taken up a hockey career. I really believe that."

Dave Keon

Toronto Maple Leafs

(b. 1940, Noranda, Que.)
Games played 1296
Goals 396
Assists 590
Total points 986
Penalties in Minutes 117

Dave Keon

By 1960 the Toronto Maple Leafs were true contenders. They were well enough stocked with hockey talent that a rookie cracking the lineup was a minor miracle. "The Leafs had just come off being beat in the finals two years in a row. They had a pretty good team. They didn't really expect anybody coming out of junior to make the team. They may have thought of someone from Rochester [Toronto's AHL affiliate]," remembers Dave Keon.

A diminutive centre from Noranda, Quebec who had completed his junior service with St. Mike's, Keon surprised more than a few experts with a training camp performance that won him a regular berth with the Leafs. "I came in just at the start of their reign and stayed there through it all," he says, alluding to the four Stanley Cups won by Toronto in seven years in the 1960s. "From my standpoint I was fortunate. There was an awful lot of guys who played an awful lot of years and never played on a championship team."

Keon was the epitome of the offensive two-way hockey player, a fact acknowledged by the awards he was given: the Calder Trophy, 1961; the Lady Byng Trophy, 1962 and 1963; the Conn Smythe Trophy, 1967; league all-star, 1962 and 1971. "We played both ends of the rink," he comments, describing the Leafs' "not overly offensive" style in their glory years.

A disagreement with Leaf management found him going to Minnesota of the WHA in 1975. He prefers to describe it only as "a philosophical difference of opinion with the people who run the Leafs." The move, he says, "was one of the best things to happen to me. I got a new outlook on playing and a new outlook on the game. I went to a different city. I met new people and found out there were other places on the continent besides Toronto."

Keon finished his professional career with the Hartford Whalers. He was with the team when it was accepted into the NHL's fold in 1979. In the spring of 1982 he announced his retirement. "You just know it's time [to retire]," he says. "Looking back, maybe it was time the year before that. It was fun playing hockey all the time. There was a certain discipline to it. There's a certain way of life. Then you have to retool yourself to what 99 per cent of the population does. It takes a little while. It was time to leave the game. If it wasn't time, I'm sure I would miss it. I have no regrets."

"I had planned not to work the first year out," Keon says. He then managed a restaurant for some friends in Hartford. Two years ago he moved to Palm Beach Gardens, Florida where he is now involved in real estate.

Harry Lumley

Toronto Maple Leafs

(b. 1926, Owen Sound, Ont.)
Games played 804
Minutes 48,107
Goals against 2210
Shutouts 71
Average 2.76

His ruddy complexion as a youngster earned him the nickname "Apple Cheeks". The moniker, like a physical feature, followed Harry Lumley through life from his days as an amateur in his native Owen Sound, Ontario to the time he turned professional and developed into one of the steadiest goaltenders in NHL history.

Lumley broke in with Detroit in 1943-44 and stayed for 16 seasons backstopping the Red Wings, Chicago, Toronto and Boston. After facing some of the deadliest shooters the game has known, he posted a lifetime 2.76 goals against average and had 71 shutouts in 804 regular season games. A member of one Stanley Cup team in 1949-50, the winner of the Vezina Trophy in 1953-54 and a two time all-star, critics years after he retired wondered aloud why he hadn't been enshrined in the Hockey Hall of Fame. In 1980 he received that honour too.

Low-keyed, self-effacing, Lumley, now living in Owen Sound, explains his longevity in the league in this way. "I just don't know . . . I did start kind of young." He agrees that "some ability" had something to do with it. "You never feared a shooter," he says naming the greats: Richard, Howe, Bathgate, the Bentleys. "You had respect for them."

Being on the firing line game in and game out has made many a goaltender a nervous and emotional wreck. For that reason, he says, they are a different breed. "I think you have to get built up a little more so I think they're a little different."

Lumley retired after the 1959-60 season, "old in terms of years served", reflexes not what they once were. His final fling in the net was with a senior team, the Collingwood Shipbuilders. He operated an automotive firm known as Dominion Motors until a couple of years ago when he sold it. More recently he has been working for the local sheriff's office.

Frank Mahovlich
Toronto Maple Leafs

(b. 1938, Timmins, Ont.)
Games played 1181
Goals 533
Assists 570
Total points 1103
Penalties in Minutes 1056

Today Frank Mahovlich operates a travel agency that he purchased in 1967 in preparation for a retirement he thought was imminent. He had been with the Maple Leafs for ten seasons and had established himself as one of the league's superstars. He had experienced the sport's highs — the Calder Trophy in 1958, six all-star nominations, 48 goals in one season, four Stanley Cups — and its lows. He was a shy, sensitive person attempting to cope with the pressures and expectations of being a superstar under the constant scrutiny of the public.

Mahovlich was sure his career would soon end. "I got into the travel business because I didn't think I would last," he says. "Not enjoying it, I was thinking of ways to get out." His well-publicized troubles in Toronto had taken their toll. "I would've gone just another year or two if things kept going the way they were." He adds, "It was like working for someone and not enjoying it."

The media had a role in making life unpleasant for Mahovlich. "The papers here, they wrote a lot of things that I don't think had any reality to them," he says. "We had three or four newspapers. Everybody had to have a story. Each paper had three or four reporters. And so a lot of people would read things and, really, there was nothing to them." In other cities where he played, Detroit and Montreal, he had no problem with the media because they had more than just an NHL team to supply them with copy.

Mahovlich admits that he takes exception to some of the things written about him in Toronto though he does not want to be specific. "A lot of things that were written about me and Punch Imlach and what have you . . . The thing is written. The damage is done. There's nothing that can be done about it. The more attention you give to it the worse it gets."

In 1968 "the Big M" was traded to Detroit and his rebirth as a player began. "It opened new doors and I started to enjoy the game and I ended up playing another ten years," Mahovlich comments. Three years later he was acquired by Montreal and he played some of his most effective hockey in the Canadiens' livery. After leaving Toronto he made the all-star squad three more times, shared in another Stanley Cup with Montreal and skated for Team Canada in 1972.

Mahovlich signed on with the Toronto Toros of the WHA in 1974. Four years later, as a member of the Birmingham Bulls, he suffered a severe knee injury requiring surgery. He says it slowed him down tremendously. At that point he decided to make the move he had seriously contemplated a decade before and now operates his travel agency in Toronto.

Rudolph Migay

Toronto Maple Leafs

Rudy Migay

(b. 1928, Fort William, Ont.)
Games played 418
Goals 59
Assists 92
Total points 151
Penalties in Minutes 293

For eight seasons beginning in 1952, Rudy Migay skated with the Toronto Maple Leafs. Primarily a defensive player, he was also used along with Ron Stewart to kill penalties. After spending his initial three seasons in professional hockey in the minor leagues, elevation to the parent club was a welcome relief for the Thunder Bay, Ontario native. "When I came up it was a big deal," he comments. "The pay was better . . . everything was better."

Migay's goal was to try to stay in the NHL for ten full seasons. Club management handed him a different fate. In 1961 he was demoted to the minors. "I thought I might have a chance at coming back. I was hoping for a trade," he says. A trade never materialized and he played well in the minors until his retirement in 1965.

Migay operated a fuel oil business in his hometown for a couple of years before returning to the game as a coach, first in the American Hockey League and then in the Central Hockey League. Seven years later he accepted a scouting position with the Pittsburgh Penguins and more recently he has been the head scout for the Buffalo Sabres.

Scouting with the travelling it entails keeps Migay very occupied. "I don't have time to keep up with the paper work," he laughs. He assesses aspiring hockey stars across the continent by judging their vitals — size, skating ability, hockey sense, puckhandling, attitude, intensity and toughness.

Migay lives with his wife and four children on a five-acre piece of property in Thunder Bay. The place, he says, provides enough work to keep him busy all summer long when scouting slows down.

Jim Morrison

Toronto Maple Leafs

(b. 1931, Montreal, Que.)
Games played 704
Goals 40
Assists 160
Total points 200
Penalties in Minutes 542

Jim Morrison

Jim Morrison developed into an offensive-minded defenceman while playing junior hockey in Verdun, Quebec. That style was natural considering he was a converted centre. When Toronto acquired him from Boston in 1952, midway through his rookie season, he had to adopt the strict defensive ways of the Leafs. Looking back he says, "I shouldn't have changed my style of play to become so defensive. I should've kept to an offensive game even as a defenceman. The Leafs were a very defensive-oriented type of system. They just didn't want their defencemen carrying the puck deep."

Morrison played with the Leafs through a rebuilding era until 1958, just when the club was beginning its resurgence to Stanley Cup contention. He found himself with the Bruins once again and, two seasons later, went to Detroit. All the trading was discouraging enough to make him consider retiring. He spent the better part of a decade in the AHL and in 1969 found himself back in the NHL with Pittsburgh. Two years later he retired.

Morrison stayed in the game as a minor league coach with Baltimore. He held the job until 1974 when the franchise folded. Then, for eight years, he was coach of the Kingston Canadians of the Ontario Major Junior Hockey League. "It was an excellent experience," he says about his time in junior hockey. "I liked it very much. There are a lot of frustrations and problems involved with the everyday operation and learning to develop with the kids, but I think in the end, when you see someone go on and do well, you are rewarded by that."

Morrison left junior hockey to scout for the Boston Bruins. "I had my run in Kingston and the opportunity arose with Boston," he says. "I wanted to get back to the pro level of the game and it was a good avenue." A scout's work takes him not only throughout North America but also to Europe which the NHL is turning to as an important source of hockey talent. Morrison spent three weeks there this spring eyeing possible recruits. European players spend more time when they are younger developing the fundamentals, making them desirable commodities in the NHL. The younger draft age has made scouting a more exacting science. He explains, "There used to be standout players who were easy to pick out and now you have to do a little more research." In addition to scouting, he also acts as a representative for Delta Pipes in Toronto.

Gus Mortson

Toronto Maple Leafs

(b. 1925, New Liskeard, Ont.)
Games played 797
Goals 46
Assists 152
Total points 198
Penalties in Minutes 1380

When Conn Smythe embarked on a youth movement to shake up his Maple Leafs in the autumn of 1946, one of the rookie hopefuls who came to Toronto was defenceman Gus Mortson. He was paired with another neophyte professional, Jim Thomson, and the two became the "Gold Dust Twins". This blue-line tandem became an integral part of the resurgent Toronto team that went on to win four Stanley Cups.

The Leafs' teams of the middle and late 1940s were hard-charging, rough and ready squads. Combining his excellent skating with a relish for body contact, Mortson was the prototypical Leafs' player. "I used to carry the puck pretty good," he relates, understating the case somewhat. "I never scored that many goals [46 in 797 games]. I led the league in penalties in about three different seasons [It was four different seasons, a career total of 1,380 minutes.]." Punctuating the recollection with a chuckle, he adds, "I don't know if that means anything."

Mortson and his defensive cohorts perfected the tactic of playing the man rather than the puck. They bowled over, blocked, grabbed and otherwise impeded opposing forwards to effectively thwart scoring opportunities. "When you played hockey in our time, it wasn't so much how many goals you scored, it was how few you let be scored against you while you were on the ice," he maintains. "Thomson and I, we kept track of all the goals against because that was your only arguing point when you had to go see Smythe for a contract. All the years we played in Toronto, we had less than a one goal against average."

Mortson's career reached its pinnacle when he was voted to the first all-star team in 1950. Two years the Smythian tide of change swept over the Maple Leafs again and this time Mortson was carried out of Toronto to Chicago where he spent six seasons. His last season in the NHL was 1958-59 with Detroit.

During his summers in Toronto, Mortson began working for a food broker. "When I left hockey in 1960 I went into my own food brokerage business," he states. He sold that business in 1969 to become a stock broker. For the last eight years he has been a sales representative for a mining supply firm in Timmins, not far from his hometown of Kirkland Lake. "One of the benefits of playing hockey," he observes, "was that when I went into sales it opened a lot of doors for me. People knew my name. It certainly did help."

When Mortson decided to retire from the NHL he turned down an offer to continue playing in Providence, a minor league club. Today he wonders about the past. "If I had gone back to play hockey, I think I would have moved my family to the States. That's one thing I've always looked at and I've often wondered about whether maybe today I could still be in hockey if I had taken the offer in Providence." You can take the boy out of hockey but you can't take hockey out of the boy.

Bob Nevin
Toronto Maple Leafs

(b. 1938, South Porcupine, Ont.)
Games played 1128
Goals 307
Assists 419
Total points 726
Penalties in Minutes 211

Bob Nevin

Having won a Memorial Cup in junior hockey and two Stanley Cups as a professional, Bob Nevin added to his titles in 1984 by helping the Metro Toronto Old-Timers win the World Old-Timers' championship at a tournament held in Nice, France. He agrees that while it might not have been as significant as the others, the latest achievement was certainly a lot more fun.

Nevin, a former right wing with Toronto, New York, Minnesota, Los Angeles and Edmonton of the WHA, retired from professional hockey in 1977. Since then he has been living off income he deferred from his playing days. "So I'm basically taking it easy," he says. In addition to hockey, he plays golf and tennis to keep trim.

Nevin practically grew up in the Maple Leaf-sponsored minor hockey organization in Toronto. "I think I was the first in the organization to go right from a peewee-sponsored team called Shopsy's, all the way up to the Maple Leafs," he comments. He caught on with the Leafs in 1960 and established himself as a versatile, all-around forward who killed penalties and played on the power play. He was part of two successful Stanley Cup drives in Toronto.

In 1964 Nevin was traded to New York. Although he was initially disappointed, it "turned out to be the greatest thing that happened". He became the club's captain and contributed to its rise out of the doldrums. Later, in the post-expansion era, he went to Minnesota and Los Angeles. "As long as I was still enjoying playing, that was what I wanted to do," he points out. "Once it was over, it was over. I wanted to play as long as I felt I could still contribute."

A broken collarbone took Nevin out of the Edmonton Oiler lineup partway through the 1976-77 season and led him to retire. He joined his former linemate Bob Pulford, then coaching the Los Angeles Kings, as an assistant. He might have stayed on if Pulford had not left the organization the following year. "I said to hell with it. I had played 17 years in the NHL. I knew eventually it was going to come."

Bob Pulford
Toronto Maple Leafs

Bob Pulford

(b. 1936, Newton Robinson, Ont.)
Games played 1079
Goals 281
Assists 362
Total points 643
Penalties in Minutes 792

One of the most consistent Toronto forwards in the 1950s and 1960s was Bob Pulford. He developed in the Toronto minor hockey ranks, playing with the Memorial Cup-winning Toronto Marlboros before graduating to the Maple Leafs in 1956.

Pulford became a fine two-way centre with the club. He did everything well and shared in four Stanley Cups with the Leafs. In 1972 he was traded to Los Angeles where, as the captain, he continued to perform effectively until his retirement in 1972.

The Kings' captain became coach, bringing his defensive philosophy to the club and making it into a contender. He moved to

Chicago in 1977. In 1982 he relinquished the coaching reigns to Orval Tessier but stayed as general manager. When the club did not respond to Tessier, he resumed the coaching duties. In 1985, he guided the team to the Stanley Cup semi-finals.

Marc Reaume

Toronto Maple Leafs

(b. 1934, La Salle, Que.)
Games played 344
Goals 8
Assists 43
Total points 51
Penalties in Minutes 273

Marc Reaume

The end of Marc Reaume's professional hockey career came about suddenly and tragically. Late in the 1971 season, he was sent by the Vancouver Canucks to Rochester of the AHL. En route to Rochester, on Highway 3 near Hamilton, his car left the road and smashed into a tree. To this day he cannot remember exactly what happened.

"I had a broken leg, broken wrist, my head hit the top of the car and put me out for three or four days but not one cut," Reaume says, tallying the damage. "I woke up in the hospital and said 'who hit me'," something he had uttered in the past after having been knocked out by crushing checks on the ice. His time as defenceman in the big leagues, which had begun in 1954, ended. He was left to contend with a double trauma: retirement from the game and recuperation from the extensive injuries.

Reaume originally played for Toronto when the club was rebuilding in the mid-1950s. He was traded to Detroit for Red Kelly, a move he thought would work well for him. There he ran into a rash of debilitating injuries. "I think they lost faith in me as a steady with their team so I was moved out to the minor leagues," he says. He performed well in the farm system prompting the self-appraisal of being a "class A minor league player and a fringe National Hockey League player." He confesses, "I lacked confidence in the NHL. I was in awe of the players and the whole situation and I didn't play as well."

Reaume turned down offers to coach in the AHL because he did not feel he was prepared to assume the job. He left the game and worked at a number of jobs until ten years ago when he started at the General Motors transmission plant in Windsor, Ontario. Living in nearby LaSalle, he says he no longer has any connection to hockey other than watching his sons indulge in the game. Golf and raquetball are now his great passions.

Eddie Shack

Toronto Maple Leafs

(b. 1937, Sudbury, Ont.)
Games played 1047
Goals 239
Assists 226
Total points 465
Penalties in Minutes 1437

Eddie Shack

He stands alone at the blueline, his only companions a mess of gloves and sticks thrown on the ice in a fit of mock disgust by his old-timer teammates when it was announced he was one of the stars of the game. They deserted him, preferring to line up with the opposition. He revels in a kind of splendid isolation in which he has captured an audience of thousands. His eyes twinkle. Suddenly he skates off, wheeling, gathering speed and launching himself into a rough-hewn pirouette and then another — an athletic, vaudevillian feat accomplished as only Eddie "The Entertainer" Shack can.

Shack participates in many charitable old-timer hockey games in a year, but this particular one was a little more special because it was held in his hometown, Sudbury, Ontario. He left the city as a teenager to pursue a career in junior hockey in Guelph for a team sponsored by New York. A qualified butcher by that time, hockey gave him a chance to realize other ambitions. "I wanted to get out of Sudbury and travel," he says.

When the Rangers brought Shack up from their Providence farm club in 1958, they had great expectations that he would provide some of the offensive pep the Rangers needed at the time. Shack didn't meet those expectations. At the same time he wasn't too impressed with the Rangers' organization. He states, quite simply, "It was bullshit."

In 1960, Shack was traded to Toronto where he found new life as a hockey player and where "The Entertainer" was born. His headlong charges up the right wing, his large nose cutting the air in front of him, became renowned. They even inspired a recording "Clear the Track, Here Comes Shack". "I was lucky that I bounced back, that I could get back into hockey," he says. "I was fortunate that I came to Toronto. I changed my ways into being an entertainer." His best season with the Leafs was 1965-66 when he scored 26 goals and 17 assists.

Nearly every aspect of his career from the time Shack came to Toronto was liberally brushed with a coat of his sense of humour. He once scored a Stanley Cup winning goal, one of four championships in which he shared. Following the game he pointed out that the puck had gone in off his rump and that he had just wanted to get the hell out of the way. Whenever he was chosen a game star, he would skate out and wow the crowd with the pirouette that became his trademark.

Shack rounded out his 17 years in the NHL with stops in Boston, Los Angeles, Buffalo, Pittsburgh and, finally, for a second time, Toronto. He retired in 1974. "I had enough of it," he says. "I just wanted to say pass on it."

The erstwhile butcher, who admits to being illiterate, turned his attentions to a myriad of businesses. While there may have been more talented players in the NHL, there is no one who has exploited his marketability better than Shack. He has appeared on television commercials hawking garbage bags, automobile tires and lent his famous schnoz to promote soft drinks. Part of the publicity associated with the last campaign involved the big beak getting insured for a million dollars.

Shack shares the ownership of a golf course north of Toronto. He also runs a hockey school three times a year. Add to this a Christmas tree farm, endorsements and appearances and it is evident the man does have a nose for value.

Still a fan favourite, Shack makes about 50 appearances a year. He says, "I meet a hell of a lot of nice people and when you do that, that's what it's all about."

Tod Sloan

Toronto Maple Leafs

(b. 1927, Vinton, Que.)
Games played 745
Goals 220
Assists 262
Total points 482
Penalties in Minutes 781

The most often repeated quotation about former Maple Leaf and Black Hawk centre Tod Sloan is one attributed to Toronto owner Conn Smythe. "Tod is his own boss," he said. "He does what he likes with the puck. It took us a few years to discover that the best way to handle him is to leave him alone."

Born in Vinton, Quebec, Sloan was raised in the Sudbury area where he developed his hockey talents on the open air rinks. His first taste of NHL action came with Toronto in 1947-48 when he played a single game. It wasn't until his third visit to the Maple Leafs' training camp that he made the roster. He relied on quick, shifty moves to move the puck past defenders into scoring position.

One of Sloan's most important goals came at 19:23 of the third period of a Stanley Cup final game against Montreal in 1951. His marker tied the game and sent the teams into overtime, setting the stage for the late Bill Barilko's Cup-winning heroics. Sloan was named to the all-star team in 1956 after a season in which he scored 37 goals and 29 assists, his best year in the NHL. The smallish forward was perhaps best known for his toughness and resilience, his ability to rebound from checks and blows that would have felled bigger men.

Sloan joined with other players throughout the league in 1957 in trying to form a players' association. Others were punished for their roles in that attempt to organize and he was no exception. The Leafs sold him to Chicago. He and the other banished players, along with the good, young players being groomed in Chicago's farm system, contributed to a Black Hawk resurgence. In 1961, he was part of the team's Stanley Cup winning effort.

Sloan retired from professional hockey in 1961 because the fun had left the game. He was reinstated as an amateur and played with the Galt Terriers in the world championship tournament in 1962.

Sloan now lives in Jackson's Point, north of Toronto, where he runs a taxi business. Some teammates say that his hockey experiences, particularly the attempt to organize the players' association and its aftermath, have left him bitter about the game. True to Smythe's words, he prefers to be left alone today (at least by hockey writers).

Sid Smith

Toronto Maple Leafs

(b. 1925, Toronto, Ont.)
Games played 601
Goals 186
Assists 183
Total points 369
Penalties in Minutes 94

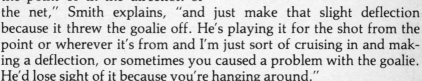

"Master of the tip-in" would be
an appropriate title for Sid
Smith, the Maple Leaf left winger
who made a career out of deflec-
tions through the 1950s. "It became my trademark, in a way,"
he agrees almost modestly.

"The thing was to keep an
eye on the puck coming in from
the point or in the direction of
the net," Smith explains, "and just make that slight deflection
because it threw the goalie off. He's playing it for the shot from the
point or wherever it's from and I'm just sort of cruising in and making a deflection, or sometimes you caused a problem with the goalie.
He'd lose sight of it because you're hanging around."

A player had to keep on moving through the area in front of the
net. "If you stood still you were going to get knocked on your
keester," Smith continues. In those years slapshots were unusual so a
player rarely had to worry about being struck by a wicked shot. "If it
was today, you'd really have to be careful or you're liable to get killed. That slapshot is just treacherous." The tip-in he remembers the
best was one against the Rangers. It glanced off his rear end rather
than his stick.

Smith grew up in Toronto but was overlooked until he started
playing junior B hockey. Even then the Leafs never expressed their
interest to him. "I never knew I was even on the list or anything," he
says. "I figured that was just about it as far as making the NHL goes.
I thought I was like a dead dog. I'll just play wherever I can and do
whatever I can do."

After playing a couple of seasons of senior hockey in Quebec, Smith was signed by Toronto and put on its Pittsburgh farm club roster in 1946. He moved back and forth between the big league and the farm team until 1948-49, a season in which he set new scoring records in the AHL. Called up by Toronto for the play-offs he added some needed fire to the offence and helped clinch the Cup. He replaced Vic Lynn in the lineup and played on a line with Ted Kennedy. His claim to fame, he remarks, came on April 10, 1949 in the second game of the Stanley Cup finals. He scored all of Toronto's goals in a 3-1 victory over Detroit in Detroit. It was their second victory in a four-game sweep.

In 1957, Toronto was considering trading Smith to Detroit which was then in need of a left winger after Ted Lindsay's departure. Instead, he accepted a two-year contract as a playing coach with the Whitby Dunlops, a senior club preparing for the world hockey championships. "I'm kind of sorry in one way and glad in another because we played for a world championship and we won it. On the other hand I would have liked to continue on with my career and score a few more goals. But winning the world championship against the Russians compensated for everything."

The change to international hockey for an ex-NHL player was drastic. Games were still played on outdoor rinks. He remembers having to play in snow and hail. Officials called strict penalties, especially those that involved body contact, much to the despair of the Canadians. "We could hardly make a move," he recalls. They did not call the stick infractions, like spearing and slashing, that were an art among European teams. "We had more injuries from sticks playing against those European teams than we did in our own league in Canada," he says.

Canada overcame a 1-0 disadvantage at the end of the first period to defeat the Soviets. Smith ranks the thrill of a world championship as "very, very close" to that of winning a Stanley Cup. He tends to lean in the direction of the NHL championship "because it's every hockey player's dream."

The Dunlops, with Smith, won the Allan Cup the following season. By then Punch Imlach, a teammate of Smith's in Quebec, wanted him to make a comeback with the Leafs. He felt he had a couple of good seasons left in him and thought he could help Toronto as it was rebuilding. The plan was squelched when the league refused to reinstate him. The end had come. The move out of professional sport was not easy, he confirms. Knowing he could have continued playing made it very difficult. He became a spectator who criticized under his breath the play he witnessed at the Gardens. "After you realize you're finished, you just sit up there and enjoy the game."

Smith went into the graphics business after hockey, a field in which he is still involved. With the love for the game still strong in his veins, in 1960, he formed an NHL old-timers' hockey club in Toronto. They played for fun and charity. He put in a quarter century with the old boys before finally hanging up his skates in 1985.

Allan Stanley
Toronto Maple Leafs

(b. 1926, Timmins, Ont.)
Games played 1244
Goals 100
Assists 333
Total points 433
Penalties in Minutes 792

Allan Stanley

The big left hand forms an imaginary ledger. The right hand, holding a smoldering cigarillo, becomes a pointer descending down an unseen list. "I could list the 20 worst things that I've had happen to me in hockey and they wouldn't match what I've experienced in business," comments Hall of Famer Allan Stanley, on making the transition from defenceman to entrepreneur.

Throughout his two-decade career in the NHL, Stanley did indeed see the best of times and the worst of times. After his introduction to the NHL with the New York Rangers in 1948, there was some doubt about whether the rangy rearguard from Timmins, Ontario would last long in professional company. The "Gallery Gods", as the boisterous bunch in Madison Square Gardens were called, singled him out for special verbal abuse, mocking his skating style and laid-back approach, calling him "Sonya" and "Snowshoes". Being heckled in an opposing rink can be inspirational at times, Stanley says, but in your own building it's unbearable. "It was tough to play," he admits. "To get them off my back the coach would bench me at home and play me on the road."

Stanley was eventually traded to Chicago, Boston and, finally, came to Toronto in 1958 at a time when experts reckoned his best years were behind him. Instead, in tandem with Tim Horton, he became an important defensive cog on the Maple Leaf club that won the Stanley Cup four times. According to longtime Toronto netminder Johnny Bower, no one played the angles better than "Snowshoes". He excelled in steering opposing forwards to the outside where the only shots they could take were low percentage ones.

When he was taken by the Philadelphia Flyers in the 1967 expansion draft, Stanley began contemplating retirement. He purchased a resort called the Bee Hive at Fenelon Falls near Peterborough, Ontario. He and his wife operate the resort which features a dining lounge and a golf course. Recently he has subdivided some of his resort property on a lake for retirement lots. "Nowadays business comes first. I'm dedicated 1,000 per cent to my business."

What hockey has taught him that he applies to enterprise, he says, is "how to work with people; you learn very quickly that you can't do it alone." Just as dedication and sacrifice were part of hockey, so they are part of the business world, he adds. Having had no formal training, he had to learn how to run the resort from the ground up, an on-the-job learning experience that was not without its rude awakenings.

Stanley and his ex-teammate Bobby Baun have been attempting to establish an organization for retired NHL players known as the Professional Hockey Alumni. Its primary objective, he explains "is to get our hockey family back together again" by locating members of that fraternity. Eventually he hopes it will address itself to helping with youth-oriented charities.

Ron Stewart

Toronto Maple Leafs

(b. 1932, Calgary, Alta.)
Games played 1353
Goals 276
Assists 253
Total points 529
Penalties in Minutes 560

Ron Stewart

"In all honesty, my association with Jack Kent Cooke and the Los Angeles Kings puts me right off," admits Ron Stewart when detailing his final involvement with NHL hockey. Having secured a promise from owner Cooke that he would not interfere, Stewart accepted the job as coach of the Los Angeles Kings for the 1977-78 season. When he got some of the meddling he was assured he wouldn't get, he left the Kings.

Stewart retired from playing in 1973, 21 years after his first NHL game with Toronto. He found himself on the right flank of a line with Sid Smith and Teeder Kennedy. "I was never a prolific goal scorer. I was a defensive type of hockey player," he adds. He joined the Maple Leafs as they were beginning a long rebuilding process. "In the first, second and third years we never made the play-offs," he recalls. "We got quite successful when Imlach came in and then we started to win some Stanley Cups."

In 1965, Stewart's tenure with the Leafs ended when he was traded to Boston. After expansion he moved to St. Louis, the New York Rangers, Vancouver and the New York Islanders. "I was almost 41 years old," he comments about his decision to quit playing. "And it was time, I would say. Expansion had a lot to do with keeping a lot of us there, but there comes a time when you have to finally decide that it's just about the end."

Stewart says the Islanders had promised him a job in the

organization when he came to the club, but "they screwed up on that". He then joined the Los Angeles organization and was coach of its farm club in Portland. Springfield of the AHL was his next coaching assignment. Despite "quite a bit of turmoil" involving Cooke and Shore, the team was able to win the league championship.

From Springfield he went to the Rangers as coach for part of the 1975-76 campaign. After John Ferguson was hired as coach and general manager, he stayed on for another year and a half as director of player personnel. He was then offered the Kings' coaching job by general manager George McGuire and Cooke. He originally refused the job, after weighing the offer. When Cooke called him again at his home in Calgary, he accepted. He would alter that decision if he could. "I guess my heart overruled my head and I figured there was a chance again in L.A."

Stewart returned to Calgary and got involved in some business enterprises that were "semi-successful". He then found himself back in hockey as manager of a local tier two team. Later he managed a tier one junior club, the Wranglers. "The rest is history and not for publication," he comments on his exit from that organization two years ago. Now in the automobile business, he declares himself to be semi-retired. "I spend a lot of time in my motor home with my wife, doing a lot of travelling, enjoying life."

James Thomson

Toronto Maple Leafs

(b. 1927, Winnipeg, Man.)
Games played 787
Goals 19
Assists 215
Total points 234
Penalties in Minutes 920

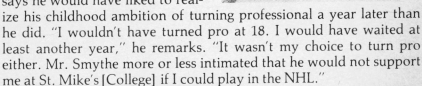

A player's hockey life in the six-team league was controlled from cradle to grave by the club owners. It is a fact evident in the careers of all players in that time but perhaps it is most graphically illustrated by former Toronto Maple Leaf Jim Thomson.

Looking back, Thomson says he would have liked to realize his childhood ambition of turning professional a year later than he did. "I wouldn't have turned pro at 18. I would have waited at least another year," he remarks. "It wasn't my choice to turn pro either. Mr. Smythe more or less intimated that he would not support me at St. Mike's [College] if I could play in the NHL."

With two years of junior eligibility left, the young defenceman joined the Leafs. For a time he was part of the constant parade of players who moved between the farm club in Pittsburgh and Toronto. Then, in 1946, he was paired with Gus Mortson, and an effective defensive tandem was born — the Gold Dust Twins.

"I was not too much of a goal scorer," Thomson confesses. "I guess keeping the other team from scoring was our main objective. Gus and I, when we were playing together and the teams were even, our goals against was usually less than a goal a game." In 12 seasons with Toronto he played on four Stanley Cup champions.

In 1957, Thomson became one of the activists in the league hoping to establish a players' association. "The things we were going to do were so minor compared to the things they're doing now," he comments. "Back then we just wanted some concessions." When the proponents of the association went public, Thomson was castigated publicly by Smythe for his role in the affair. The Leafs' boss felt that it was Thomson's role as team captain to report such transgressions to management. "It never would have gone as far as it did if the owners had known what was going on — and they didn't," Thomson says.

Smythe called Thomson a "Quisling and a traitor". Thomson, in turn, resigned, vowing never again to play for the Leafs. Next season he was part of a bevy of other association supporters shipped to Chicago. An unsubstantiated story claims that Smythe was at a race track with Chicago owner Bruce Norris where the Black Hawk boss had a horse running. Smythe offered him Thomson for the horse.

After playing in every game for Chicago in the 1958 season Thomson was sent back to Toronto. "Like I said last year," he recalls repeating, "I said I would never play for the Leafs again." He spurned an offer to become a playing coach for the Leafs' farm affiliate in Rochester. Leaving, he adds, was "easy in a way. O.K., so I played and I was 31. It was time to pack it in." His actions resulted in his name being added to a suspension list where it stayed for four years.

Thomson returned to operate a fuel business in Toronto, something he had done throughout his days as a player and something he continues to do today. At one time he played old-timers' hockey, but doesn't any longer.

Smythe, the hockey magnate who had so much control over his players, is remembered today by Thomson as "a tough guy, but most of the time he was fair." As for the modern-day version of the players' association, he says, "I don't follow hockey that much, but certainly the players' association has a lot of clout. Personally I don't see how some of these teams are surviving with salaries of the players and the crowds they get."

Harry Watson

Toronto Maple Leafs

(b. 1923, Saskatoon, Sask.)
Games played 805
Goals 236
Assists 207
Total points 443
Penalties in Minutes 150

There seems to be a consensus among veterans of the six-team era when they remember Harry Watson, a left winger who broke in with the New York Americans in 1941 and went on to a career that lasted until 1958. Watson, they agree, was a force to be reckoned with when agitated.

Attending a recent old-timers' banquet, the large and genial man sported a disarming smile as he traded tales of daring with other members of hockey's brotherhood. "I guess I was always classified as a lazy hockey player," explains the owner of five Stanley Cup championship rings. "I guess because I tried to play my position. I didn't try to play centre and right wing because I was a left winger. I tried to do my job. They also classed Gordie Howe as a lazy hockey player. I always wished that I was as lazy as he was because he was one exceptional hockey player."

The end of Watson's career came one day when he received a telephone call from Chicago general manager Tommy Ivan who asked him if he would like to be a playing coach in Calgary or Buffalo, two minor league affiliates. "Why are you telling me this?" he recalls asking. The Hawks had acquired Ron Murphy and Ted Lindsay and all the left wing positions were filled.

"I never really planned for retirement," he says, musing on that fateful day that every athlete must meet. "I always thought that I could play forever. I just had the feeling that hockey was my game . . .

and I loved to play, though I had a couple of opportunities to go into business with other people or business jobs and I decided that I would rather play for a couple more years. I thought they had a pretty good pension plan going in the NHL. I wanted to play the full ten years to get a full pension. But now, after all those years, looking back, the pension isn't that good."

Watson coached in the minor leagues for awhile before moving to Markham, Ontario in 1960 where he opened a bowling alley. Over the years he has mostly worked in sales, he says. Now, at the age of 62, his main pastime is "practising for retirement". He echoes the sentiments of others who have led the charmed existence of a professional hockey player: "It was a great life." He now works for a swimming pool concern.

Index

Lunde, Leonard	135	Raleigh, Don (Bones)	265
MacDonald, Parker	137	Ratelle, Jean	267
MacGregor, Bruce	138	Reaume, Marc	315
Mackell, Fleming	32	Regan, Lawrence	46
MacNeil, Al	78	Reibel, Earl (Dutch)	148
Mahovlich, Frank	306	Richard, Henri	205
Maki, Chico	80	Richard, Maurice	207
Marshall, Don	190	Roberts, Jim	210
Martin, Frank *	81	Rollins, Al	93
Martin, Pit *	34	Rousseau, Bobby	212
McDonald, Ab	83	St. Laurent, Dollard	213
McIntyre, John *	84	Sandford, Edward	48
McKenney, Don	35	Sawchuk, Terry	151
McKenzie, John	37	Schinkel, Ken	269
McNeill, William	140	Shack, Eddie	317
Meger, Paul	192	Skov, Glen	149
Mickoski, Nick	258	Sloan, Tod	319
Migay, Rudolph	308	Smith, Floyd	152
Mikita, Stan	85	Smith, Sid	321
Mohns, Doug	39	Spencer, Irv (Spinner) *	271
Moore, Dick	194	Stanfield, Fred	95
Morrison, Jim	309	Stanley, Allan	323
Mortson, Gus	311	Stapleton, Pat *	97
Mosdell, Ken	196	Stasiuk, Vic	50
Murphy, Ron	87	Stewart, Ron	325
Neilson, Jim	260	Sullivan, Red	272
Nesterenko, Eric	89	Talbot, Jean-Guy	215
Nevin, Bob	313	Thomson, James	327
Oliver, Murray	41	Toppazzini, Gerry	52
Olmstead, Bert	198	Tremblay, Gilles	217
Pavelich, Martin	142	Tremblay, J.C.	218
Peirson, John	43	Turner, Bob	220
Pilote, Pierre	91	Ullman, Norm	154
Plante, Jacques	200	Vasko, Elmer (Moose)	99
Popein, Larry	262	Watson, Harry	329
Prentice, Dean	264	Westfall, Ed	54
Pronovost, André	202	Wharram, Ken	100
Pronovost, Marcel	144	Williams, Tom	56
Provost, Claude	204	Wilson, Johnny	156
Prystai, Metro	146	Woit, Benedict	158
Pulford, Bob	314	Worsley, Lorne (Gump)	274
Quackenbush, Bill	45		

*Photographs of these players in the appropriate uniforms were not available. Instead, they are shown in the uniforms of other teams for whom they played.